DIRECTORY
OF
PSYCHOLOGICAL TESTS
IN THE
SPORT AND EXERCISE
SCIENCES

Edited by

__Andrew C. Ostrow, Ph.D.__
West Virginia University

Fitness Information Technology, Inc.
Morgantown, West Virginia

Library of Congress Catalog Card Number: 90-84378

ISBN 0-9627926-0-8

Cover Design: Alvan Allison
  Copy Editor: Pamela Schade
  Printed by: BookCrafters

Printed in the United States of America
10 9 8 7 6 5 4 3 2

Fitness Information Technology, Inc.
Box 4425, University Avenue
Morgantown, West Virginia 26505
(304) 599-FIT2
(304) 599-3482

To G. Lawrence Rarick,

Professor Emeritus

University of California, Berkeley--

my mentor, friend, and colleague

TABLE OF CONTENTS

TABLE OF CONTENTS (CONT'D)

3. ANXIETY

TABLE OF CONTENTS (CONT'D)

TABLE OF CONTENTS (CONT'D)

TABLE OF CONTENTS (CONT'D)

TABLE OF CONTENTS (CONT'D)

TABLE OF CONTENTS (CONT'D)

TABLE OF CONTENTS (CONT'D)

TABLE OF CONTENTS (CONT'D)

Preface

It has been a quarter of a century since the first International Congress of Sport Psychology was held in Rome, Italy. This historic conference brought together professionals from numerous countries who disseminated and shared research on the psychological aspects of sport and related physical activity. Many view this historic event as the inauguration of sport psychology as an academic discipline.

During these last twenty-five years, there has been a transition from the use of global personality inventories by sport psychology researchers to the creation of psychological tests situationally specific to the sport or exercise environment. This transition occurred, in part, because of a shift in theoretical focus by researchers from personality trait theory to the adoption of an interactionist perspective. Also, as researchers moved from developing a laboratory-based discipline to an interest in applied assessments and interventions, the development of sport- and exercise-specific psychological tests increased exponentially.

As sport- and exercise-specific psychological tests become more widely used in research investigations and applied services, it is important that students, teachers, researchers, clinicians, and other professionals have quick access to information on these tests. I felt that a directory was needed that provided interested individuals with information on the contents, psychometric properties, and availability of sport- and exercise-specific psychological tests. To this end, I have attempted to locate and overview all tests that have been reported in the international, scientific literature over the past twenty-five years since the first International Congress of Sport Psychology was held. When I began to search the literature, I was uncertain as to how many of these tests I would uncover. To my surprise, I have located over 200 sport- or exercise-specific psychological tests that have been reported in the refereed literature. In this directory, I report on 175 tests that meet the criteria that I will describe later.

Oscar Buros, founder and editor of the widely acclaimed Mental Measurements Yearbook series, was cited (Conoley & Kramer, 1989) regarding the benefits of a comprehensive directory of psychological tests. I believe his observations relative to the value of such a directory are reflected in the Directory of Psychological Tests in the Sport and Exercise Sciences:

1. To impel psychological test authors and publishers to promote higher standards for test construction and validation.

2. To make test users more aware of the strengths and limitations of psychological tests.

3. To stimulate comprehensive reviews of psychological tests.

4. To make consumers and the public more aware of appropriate test selection and use.

Almost all of the psychological tests reported in this directory were developed and are being used for research purposes, rather than for diagnostication or evaluation. Some of the tests are undergoing continued development. The majority of tests are not commercially published; rather, test users need to contact the author and/or source publisher to obtain a copy of the latest version of the test.

In the introduction to the book, I present information on why a directory is needed and how the directory was developed. I cite trends about the tests found in the directory, and make recommendations with the intent of promoting further psychometric test development in the field. The reader is then presented with information on how to use the directory. Following this discussion, information on the purposes, scope, construction, reliability, validity, and availability of each of the 175 tests is presented concisely.

The test summaries are organized by constructs such as aggression, anxiety, imagery, and motivation. The back of the directory contains subject, test author, test title, and test acronym indices to help the reader quickly locate a psychological test(s) of interest. In addition, the recently developed "Code of Fair Testing Practices in Education," prepared by the Joint Committee on Testing Practices, is reprinted. The Code presents standards for educational test developers and users in terms of developing /selecting tests, interpreting test scores, striving for fairness, and informing test takers.

The directory does not attempt to review or evaluate the sport- and exercise-specific psychological tests presented. It is my intent to edit a future edition of the directory that will provide reviews by distinguished test authors of the tests cited in the directory. I have encouraged test authors whose work is cited in this directory to keep me apprised of revisions to their test. In addition, new test authors (or authors of tests I have excluded inadvertently from the directory) are encouraged to forward to me copies of refereed publications that describe their sport- or exercise-specific psychological tests

Although I researched and wrote a preliminary summary for each of the 175 tests described in the directory, the content and quality of the book resides primarily with each of the several hundred test authors who devoted countless hours to developing and validating these sport- or exercise-specific psychological tests. I am particularly grateful to those test authors who updated the initial test summaries I sent them, and/or who provided me with additional references related to their tests.

I am also grateful to Dr. Joan Duda, Purdue University, Dr. Diane Gill and Dr. Daniel Gould, University of North Carolina, Greensboro, Dr. Robert Schutz, University of British Columbia, Dr. Ronald Smith, University of Washington, and Dr. Robin Vealey, Miami University, for their helpful comments in reviewing the proposed format of the book. As well, I would like to thank Dr. Timothy Lee, McMaster University, and Dr. Leonard Wankel, University of Alberta for their assistance in procuring a number of the proceedings of the annual conferences of the Canadian Society for Psychomotor Learning and Sport Psychology. A special thanks to Carol Straight, my typist, to Pam Schade who worked diligently as copyeditor, and to Alvan Allison and Gerri Angoli of AMPS Automation, Inc. for their assistance in preparing the camera-ready version of the manuscript. I am also grateful to my wife Lynne and daughters Jennifer and Olivia, whose patience, encourgagement, and love made the task of serving as editor of this directory more tolerable and even enjoyable.

INTRODUCTION

A. Why a Directory is Needed

While I was completing my master's thesis on "The Aggressive Tendencies of Male Intercollegiate Tennis Team Players" at the University of Maryland, I attended the second International Congress of Sport Psychology held in Washington, D. C. in 1968. My thesis employed the Thematic Apperception Test (TAT) and the Edwards Personal Preference Schedule (EPPS) to examine the extent to which college tennis players of varying abilities differed on the need to aggress. Attending the congress afforded me the opportunity to learn how leading professionals in the psychology of sport were building the discipline by employing psychological tests.

Part of my thesis centered on modifying an innovative word counting procedure to conduct a content analysis of subjects' written responses to selected TAT pictures. I was also interested in examining the extent to which subjects' aggression scores on the TAT (a projective technique) correlated with their scores on the need aggression subscale of the EPPS (an "objective" measure), since both tests had been constructed to assess Henry A. Murray's Personology Theory. At the time, projective techniques were represented in the sport psychology literature, but their validities in the sport setting were relatively unknown.

For the most part, the papers presented at the congress focused on the use of global personality inventories (such as the California Psychological Inventory) to achieve a better understanding of the personality characteristics of college athletes. This followed the tradition at the time of borrowing standardized personality inventories from the field of psychology in an effort to uncover unique personality traits of athletes. However, there were several presentations related to sport psychometrics (or the application of psychological assessment theory and techniques to sport) that I can still recall more than twenty years later.

For example, Brent Rushall astonished the audience by suggesting that he had found that the Cattell 16 PF was virtually useless in trying to uncover psychological characteristics associated with elite athletic performance. This important presentation made some professionals uncomfortable, since they had grown accustomed to conveniently using existing personality inventories without questionning their theoretical relevance to the sport setting.

Also at the congress, Gerald Kenyon highlighted some of his research using a sport-specific attitudinal inventory he had developed called the Attitude Toward Physical Activity Inventory (ATPA). This inventory was

1

constructed to test a conceptual model characterizing the perceived instrumental (satisfaction) value individuals held for physical activity that Kenyon had described in an article in the Research Quarterly a year earlier.

The ATPA subsequently had a significant influence on attitudinal research conducted in the field over the next decade. Furthermore, it led to the construction of additional field-specific attitudinal instruments such as the Children's Attitudes Toward Physical Activity Inventory. Most importantly, it set the stage for others to reject sport psychology's traditional dependence upon global personality inventories and, instead, encouraged the development of psychological tests that were theoretically alligned to and more predictive of behavior in sport.

Unrest concerning sport psychological assessment issues continued throughout the 1970's. Martens (1973) noted that despite the more than 200 studies that had been conducted in sport personology at the time, there was no information about the accurate prediction of behavior in sport. Martens indicated that this problem stemmed from conceptual, methodological, and interpretative problems in the sport personality research. For example, Martens noted that sport psychology researchers frequently ignored the theoretical basis of the psychological tests. This practice resulted in the selection of tests that were incompatible with the purposes of the investigation. While Martens advocated the systematic development of psychological tests more germane to the sport environment, he cautioned professionals about purchasing sport-oriented tests that had not been carefully validated.

By the mid-1970's, several leaders in sport psychology advocated abandoning the strict reliance on personality trait theory and its inventory mode of assessment in favor of an interactionist perspective toward understanding sport behavior. It was felt that psychological measures needed to consider how the characteristics of the individual were mediated within the sport environment to elicit a behavioral response.

Orlick (1974) succinctly described the beliefs at the time:

> In order for the field of Sports Psychology to make significant strides forward it is essential that we (sport psychologists) begin to construct our own measurement instruments which are designed specifically to deal with our own problem. We must begin to examine a variety of situational and environmental factors which are operational in and around a sporting context . . . . Only by creating measurement tools and utilizing measurement techniques which are specific to problems in sports and physical activity will we be enabled to advance into a new era of Sports Psychology (p. 13).

Perhaps one of the best examples of this position was the subsequent development of the Sport Competition Anxiety Test (SCAT) by Martens and his colleagues. Martens formulated a conceptual framework for the understanding of the competitive process. Within this framework, competitive trait anxiety was viewed as a characteristic of the individual that mediated perceptions of potentially stressful situations occuring within the competitive sport context. The SCAT was developed to assess individual differences in the tendency to perceive competitive situations as threatening and/or to respond to these situations with elevated state anxiety.

Martens and his colleagues presented at professional conferences a series of research studies describing the construction and validation of the SCAT. Furthermore, they presented the test, and information related to construction procedures, reliability, validity, and normative data in a landmark psychometric publication titled the Sport Competition Anxiety Test Manual (1977). Following guidelines established by the American Psychological Association, the SCAT was thus available for rigorous scientific scrutiny. As a consequence, several thousand research studies have been conducted in which the SCAT has been used and evaluated.

Research by Kenyon, Martens, and others led to a gradual increase in the development of sport-specific psychological tests. A majority of these tests were developed as part of theses and dissertations, and, unfortunately, rarely appeared in the scientific literature.

During the 1980's, the use of sport-specific psychological tests became more prominent. As several journals specific to sport psychology emerged in North America, such as the Journal of Sport Psychology (later called the Journal of Sport & Exercise Psychology), the Journal of Sport Behavior, the Sport Psychologist, and the Journal of Applied Sport Psychology, an increasing number of reports centered on the development and validation of sport-specific psychological tests. Furthermore, as the field broadened to encompass the concerns of exercise psychology, psychological tests targeted toward understanding the exercise environment emerged.

A review of the historical transition of sport- and exercise-specific psychological tests in the scientific literature reveals an increasing concern about the need for accurate reporting and rigorous psychometric development. No longer is it acceptable to merely report that a psychological test was piloted for use in the investigation. Manuscript reviewers are requiring information about the theoretical basis behind the test's construction, about subject reliability and test validity, and about the potential limitations and restrictions of the psychological test. This trend will certainly have a positive impact on developing a knowledge base in sport psychology.

In addition, the appropriate use of psychological tests has become even more important as the field of sport psychology has broadened to encompass professional user services in the form of educational and clinical psychological interventions. Sport- and exercise-specific psychological tests are being employed by professionals to evaluate the efficacy of psychological interventions, as well as provide diagnostic feedback to the client. In some instances, these tests are being used inappropriately as diagnostic instruments when the research is lacking or nonsupportive. In an excellent reference book written by Robert Nideffer on the Ethics and Practice of Applied Sport Psychology (1981), the author addresses the importance of employing valid tests in diagnostic evaluation, of being properly trained in the use of these psychological tests, of being able to recognize the strengths and limitations of each test employed, and in being properly trained to provide client feedback.

As sport- and exercise-specific psychological tests become more widely used, it is important that students, teachers, researchers, and practitioners have quick access to information about the nature and availability of these tests. Anshel (1987) noted the following:

> It would be extremely useful if sport psychologists could turn to a comprehensive list of inventories as an initial step in ascertaining the availability of research tools in order to assess the theoretical bases in the sport literature and examine the efficacy of implementing particular procedures in applied sport psychology. Further, the availability of such a list would allow researchers to determine future needs in the area of inventory measurement and to undertake long-term commitments toward creating new tools for better understanding, explaining, and predicting sport behavior (p. 331).

Anshel (1987) subsequently listed 30-40 psychological tests (some of which were not sport-specific) that have been frequently employed by researchers in the field.

Given the increased popularity of using sport- and exercise-specific psychological tests in research investigations and applied services, I believed that a directory was needed that provided quick access to information on the content, psychometric properties, and availability of these tests. At the outset, I was uncertain as to how many of these psychological tests I would uncover in the scientific literature. To my surprise, I located over 200 sport- or exercise-specific psychological tests that have been reported in the refereed international scientific literature over a 25-year period. In this directory, I report on 175 of these tests that meet the criteria that I will describe shortly.

Oscar Buros, initial founder and editor of the widely acclaimed Mental Measurements Yearbook series, had cited (Conoley & Kramer, 1989) what he believed were the benefits of a comprehensive directory of psychological tests. I believe these benefits espoused by Buros are reflected in the following four purposes for the Directory of Psychological Tests in the Sport and Exercise Sciences:

1. Impel psychological test authors and publishers to promote higher standards for test construction and validation.

2. Make test users more aware of the strengths and limitations of

psychological tests.

   3. Stimulate comprehensive reviews of psychological tests.

   4. Make the consumer and public more aware of appropriate test selection and utilization.

   In using a directory of this nature, the reader should be cautioned that self-report paper-and-pencil psychological tests, while extremely prominent in the psychology and sport psychology literature, are not the only means of assessment available. In fact, the standardized test is often only one of a battery of assessment approaches taken. For example, judges' ratings, psychophysiological assessment, structured or semi-structured interviews, coaches' obervational ratings, and other approaches are viable alternatives to be used in conjunction with the standardized test. However, given the prominence of sport- and exercise-specific psychological tests reported in the literature, it was believed that a directory of these tests would serve as a useful reference source.

   Almost all of the psychological tests* reported in the directory were developed and are being used for research purposes, rather than for diagnostication or evaluation. Many of the tests are undergoing continued development. The majority of tests are not commercially published. Consumers need to contact the author and/or source publisher to obtain a copy of the latest version of the test.

   The directory does not attempt to review or evaluate the psychological tests presented. A future edition of the directory will provide reviews of the tests cited in each chapter by distinguished test authors. I encourage test authors whose work is cited in this directory to keep me apprised of revisions to their test. In addition, new test authors (or authors of tests excluded inadvertently) are encouraged to forward to me copies of refereed publications that describe their sport- or exercise-specific psychological test.

B. How the Directory Was Developed

   I was not able to rely on computer-based literature searches to locate the tests reported in the directory. For the most part, I located the principal reference source describing each psychological test by meticulously scanning the methodology section of every published research investigation appearing in more than 35 journals and conference proceedings over a 25-year period. Needless to say, the reader may feel that there are more exciting ways to spend a sabbatical leave.

---

*Technically, these self-report instruments are better labeled questionnaires or inventories rather than tests. The term test is merely used to simplify the language used in the directory.

I delimited the literature search based on the following parameters:

1. Only reference sources that were refereed, that were written in the English language, and that appeared in the international scientific literature from 1965 to 1989 were evaluated.

2. The principal focus of psychological tests selected centered on the domains of sport, exercise, or related nonutilitarian physical activity. Tests related to areas such as sport pedagogy or leisure behavior were not considered.

3. Psychological tests were delimited to self-report paper-and-pencil tests that reported evidence of subject reliability and/or test validity. Tests not providing evidence for reliability or validity in the primary source evaluated were not included in the directory. (However, refer to the section on "Additional Sport-Specific or Exercise-Specific Psychological Tests" that appears at the end of the directory for information about additional tests that did not meet this criterion.)

4. Behavioral observation scales, surveys, psychophysiological tests, motor behavior tasks, and developmental and neuropsychological tests were excluded from the directory.

5. Tests frequently used by sport psychology researchers that were not initially conceived as sport- or exercise-specific, such as the Test of Attentional and Interpersonal Style or the Profile of Mood States, were excluded from the directory. Tests that merely represented slight modifications of these more global tests were also excluded.

Based on these criteria, I searched for sport- or exercise-specific psychological tests in the following reference sources:

Periodicals

Adapted Physical Activity Quarterly (1984*-1987)
Annals of Sports Medicine (1982*-1986; 1988)
Australian Journal of Sport Sciences (1981-1983)
British Journal of Sports Medicine (1979-1982; 1984-1987; 1989)
Canadian Journal of Sport Sciences (1976*-1989)
Exercise and Sport Sciences Reviews (1973*-1988)
Human Movement Science (1982*-1989)
International Journal of Physical Education (1980-1988)
International Journal of Sport Psychology (1970*-1989)
International Journal of Sports Medicine (1984-1987; 1989)
International Review of Sport Sociology (1966-1980)
Journal of Human Movement Studies (1975*-1988)
Journal of Motor Behavior (1969*-1988)
Journal of Sport & Exercise Psychology (1979*-1989)
Journal of Sport Behavior ((1978*-1989)

*Represents the first year of publication of the periodical.

Journal of Sports Medicine and Physical Fitness (1978; 1982-1989)
Journal of Sports Sciences (1984-1989)
Medicine and Science in Sport and Exercise (1975-1980; 1982-1989)
Motor Skills: Theory into Practice (1976*-1982)
Perceptual and Motor Skills (1965-1989)
Physical Educator (1965-1989)
Quest (1965-1989)
Research Quarterly for Exercise and Sport (1965-1989)
Scandinavian Journal of Sport Sciences (1980-1988)
Sociology of Sport Journal (1984*-1989)
Sport Psychologist (1987*-1989)
Sports Medicine (1984*-1989)
The Physician and Sportsmedicine (1979-1988)

Conference Proceedings

American Alliance for Health, Physical Education, Recreation, and Dance annual convention (1969; 1973-1974; 1980; 1984-1987)

Association for the Advancement of Applied Sport Psychology annual convention (1986*-1989)

British Proceedings of Sport Psychology (1975)

Canadian Society for Psychomotor Learning and Sport Psychology annual convention (1969*-1975; 1977-1979; 1982-1989)

National Association for Physical Education in Higher Education proceedings (1979-1985)

North American Society for the Psychology of Sport and Physical Activity annual convention (1973*; 1975; 1977-1984; 1988-1989.

North American Society for the Sociology of Sport annual convention (1981)

Proceedings of the International Symposium on Psychological Assessment in Sport (1975)

Proceedings of the World Congress of Sport Psychology (1969; 1973; 1989)

The limited holdings of the several university libraries I visited placed constraints on my ability to access every journal issue since 1965. However, I reviewed every issue of the more prominent journals in sport psychology (such as the Journal of Sport & Exercise Psychology and the International Journal of Sport Psychology) since their inception. In addition to these journals and conference proceedings, I also examined several edited books in sport psychology.

I developed the initial draft of each test summary in the directory. I forwarded the summary of the Sport Orientation Questionnaire (SOQ) to six

*Represents the first annual convention in which proceedings were published.

experts, who also are authors of tests in the directory. This sample summary had first been reviewed by Dianne Gill, the principal test author of the SOQ. The six experts were asked to critique the organizational format, content, and clarity of the synopsis of the SOQ. Their comments were, for the most part, favorable and extremely helpful in developing the other test summaries in the directory.

Each of the 175 test summaries that I had developed were then forwarded to the appropriate principal test author for his/her review. The test authors were asked to critique, update, and/or revise the summary of their test(s). It was indicated that if a response was not received by a designated date, it would be assumed that the test author was satisfied with the test summary I had developed.

A total of 105 test summaries (60.00%) were returned. The test authors typically did not make major revisions to the initial summaries. In several cases, test authors forwarded manuscripts that were recently accepted for publication that provided updated revisions to their test(s). The test authors were particularly helpful in providing additional psychometric references related to their tests. Ten test summaries (5.71%) were not evaluated by test authors because their current addresses were unknown.

C. Some Observations About the Tests Found in the Directory

1. Frequency of tests developed from 1965-1989. This book reports on the first known comprehensive project to identify existing sport- and exercise-specific psychological tests that have appeared in the scientific literature since the first World Congress in Sport Psychology was held in Rome, Italy more than 25 years ago. Figure 1 shows the trend in the frequency of when these psychological tests were developed from 1965-1989.

Figure 1
Frequency of Tests Reported from 1965 to 1989

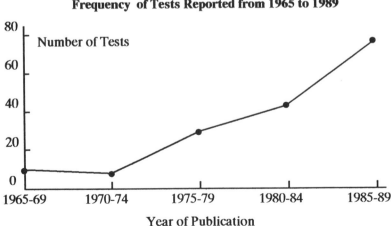

Year of Publication

As illustrated, the first marked increase in the publication of these tests occurred from 1975 to 1979. During this time period, the interactionist perspective became the more dominant theoretical focus of sport psychologists. Sport-specific tests representing this perspective, such as the Sport Competition Anxiety Test, became highly publicized. Also, a shift from laboratory research to research in applied settings occurred in North America.

Thus far, the most dramatic increase in the publication of sport- and exercise-specific psychological tests has occurred from 1985-1990. This trend is partially reflective of an increase in the number of new, sport psychology-related journals appearing on the market. This trend can also be attributed to the expansion of the discipline, particularly regarding research on exercise psychology, and on educational and clinical sport psychology interventions. This dramatic increase in the number of sport- and exercise-specific psychological tests being employed in research was the impetus for the development of this directory.

2. <u>Publication sources</u>. Figure 2 depicts the publication sources in which these psychological tests have appeared for the first time. As can be seen, a total of 40 new tests (22.86%) have been reported in the <u>Journal of Sport & Exercise Psychology</u>, while 22 new tests have appeared in the <u>Research Quarterly for Exercise and Sport</u>, 15 new tests have appeared in the proceedings of the North American Society for the Psychology of Sport and Physical Activity, and 9 new tests were reported in the <u>International Journal of Sport Psychology</u>. While the <u>Journal of Sport & Exercise Psychology</u> is a more recent publication than these other two journals, it appears to be the dominant journal for reporting data on new sport- or exercise-specific psychological tests.

Figure 2
Publication Sources of Tests

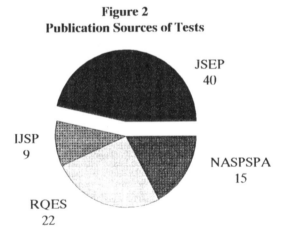

Only 19 (10.86%) of the test reports found in the directory are based on abstracts from conference proceedings. Several test authors forwarded manuscripts to me that had been accepted for publication, so that I did not have to rely solely on an abstract to report test information in the directory.

The majority (70%) of reports on these tests stemmed from refereed journals. Information on the remaining tests were found in either conference proceedings (20%), book chapters (6%), or were submitted as manuscripts in press (4%) by test authors (see Figure 3).

Figure 3
Publication Source Categories

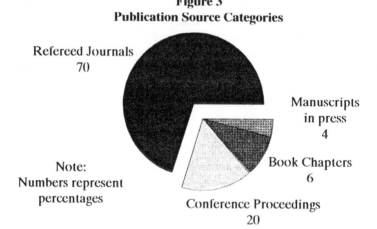

Refereed Journals
70

Manuscripts
in press
4

Note:
Numbers represent
percentages

Book Chapters
6

Conference Proceedings
20

3. <u>Content areas</u>. Figure 4 illustrates the five most popular content areas of the 175 sport- and exercise-specific psychological tests found in the directory. As illustrated, exercise or sport motivation (31 tests) was the most popular content area addressed.

Figure 4
Test Content Areas

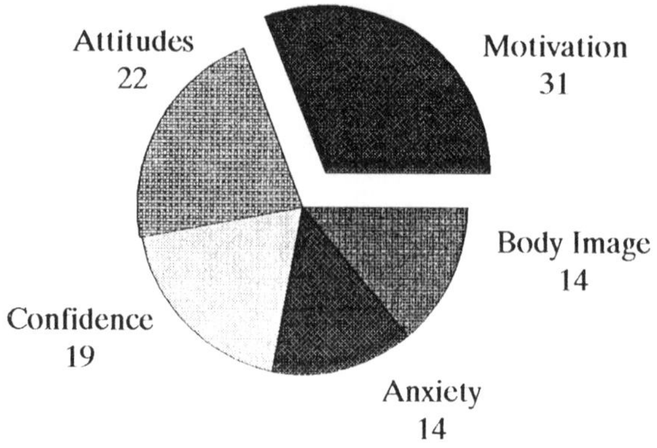

Attitudes
22

Motivation
31

Body Image
14

Confidence
19

Anxiety
14

Other popular content areas included subject attitudes toward exercise or sport (22 tests), subject movement or sport confidence (19 tests), and subject concerns about body image (14 tests) or sport-related anxiety (14 tests).

The vast majority of tests were not developed to assess psychological responses unique to one sport or other movement activity. The extent to which performance responses can better be predicted by psychological tests highly specific to a particular activity (such as the Competitive Golf Stress Inventory), versus the use of more general activity-specific tests (such as the Sport Competition Anxiety Test), remains to be verified. This is important to evaluate given the expenditures of time and cost that would be involved in attempting to develop psychological tests unique to every sport or movement activity known to exist.

4. Measurement scales. Figure 5 illustrates the frequency of the types of measurement scales used among the 175 tests. The most frequent measurement scale employed was a Likert scale or similar ordinal scale (68.58%), followed in popularity by the use of a semantic differential format (6.86%). Other (11.43%), less popular measurement scales used included Thurstone paired comparison scaling and the structured alternative format. There was no information on measurement scales available for approximately 12% of the tests found in the directory. Interestingly, among the tests indicating the use of a Likert scale, a 5-point scale was the more popular format reported (53.52%), followed by 7-point (18.31%) and 4-point formats (14.08%).

Figure 5
Types of Measurement Scales Employed

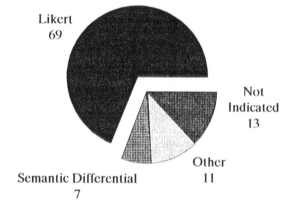

Note:
Numbers
represent
percentages

Likert
69

Not
Indicated
13

Other
11

Semantic Differential
7

5. Test construction procedures. It was indicated for only 58 tests (33.14%) that test items were derived based on a conceptual or theoretical framework. Test authors reported that for the construction of 50 tests (28.57%), items had been borrowed or modified from existing general or sport- or

exercise-specific psychological tests. This overlap in the development of test items may artificially inflate future attempts at establishing concurrent evidence of validity among these tests.

A systematic attempt at establishing content validity through expert or judges' evaluation was reported for only 42 tests (24.00%). Similarily, item refinement based on item analysis and/or exploratory factor analysis was reported for only 61 tests (34.86%). Reports on 43 tests (24.57%) made no mention of the construction procedures used to develop and refine test items.

6. Reliability. Reliability indicates the degree to which test scores are not contaminated by errors of measurement (Standards for Educational and Psychological Testing, 1985). Reliability estimates should be reported for each total score and subscore reported in a test. Estimates of internal consistency using the Cronbach alpha coefficient or an adjusted split-half procedure were reported for only 105 tests (60.00%) in the directory. For at least 5 tests, estimates of internal consistency were not appropriate to report given the extremely limited number of items (e.g., 3 items) comprising their subscales.

Test stability coefficients (test-retest reliability) were reported for only 91 tests (52.00%) found in the directory. The most common statistical procedure used to establish test stability was the use of a bivariate test statistic, such as the Pearson product-moment correlation coefficient. Only three tests reported that intraclass correlation was computed to estimate test stability. It was indicated for three tests that computations for test stability were not presented because the test was conceived as a state (rather than a trait) measure of personality.

Figure 6 illustrates the most frequent time intervals selected to estimate test stability.

Figure 6
Test-Retest Reliability Time Intervals

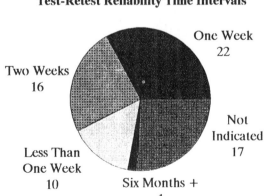

As indicated, the use of a one-week time interval was reported for 22 tests, a two-week time interval was used to establish test stability for 16 tests, and less than a one-week time interval was used to establish test stability among 10 tests. The use of a test-retest time interval beyond six months (i.e., nine months) was reported for only one test. Several test authors reported test stability coefficients across more than one time interval. There were no time intervals specified for 17 tests in which test stability coefficients were presented.

7. <u>Validity</u>. The most critical information regarding a test is its validity. Validity refers to ". . . the appropriateness, meaningfulness, and usefulness of the specific inferences made from test scores" (<u>Standards for Educational and Psychological Testing</u>, 1985, p. 9). Traditional categories used to describe test validity have included content-related validity (reported earlier in relation to test construction procedures), criterion-related validity (including predictive and concurrent evidence of validity), and construct validity.

Ideally, multiple sources of evidence spanning all three categories of validity should be addressed by test authors, if appropriate to the purposes of the test. However, these categories are not completely independent. For example, information on concurrent-related validity can be used to extrapolate information on the construct-related validity of a test (<u>Standards for Educational and Psychological Testing</u>, 1985).

Figure 7 illustrates the categories of validity addressed by test authors. A total of 107 tests (61.14%) indicated some evidence of construct-related validity, with the ability of a test to discriminate among groups in the hypothesized direction reported for 59 of these tests. Exploratory and/or confirmatory factor analytic procedures were used to establish construct-related validity in 42 tests. Experimental manipulation supported the construct-related validity of five tests.

Figure 7
Categories of Validity Examined

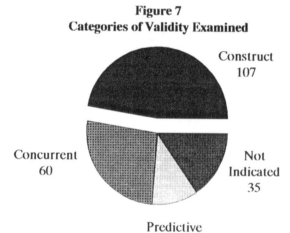

Concurrent evidence of validity was reported for 60 tests (34.29%) (Figure 7); of these 60 tests, 42 correlated subjects' responses to another related test (convergent evidence of validity). Judges' ratings or self-ratings were used as evidence of concurrent validity for nine tests.

Predictive evidence of validity was reported for 24 tests (13.71%), with performance used as a criterion in 18 of these tests. There are 35 tests (20.00%) presented in the directory for which no evidence of validity was reported.

8. <u>Norms</u>. Only 11 tests (6.29%) in the directory indicate the availability of norms, usually in the form of user norms (rather than national norms). Most test authors based descriptive/psychometric data on both male and female samples (100 tests), rather than just on male (20 tests) or female (14 tests) samples. (See Figure 8) Also, the majority of these samples were either college students (92 tests), high school students (46 tests), or junior high school students (26 tests). Descriptive and/or psychometric data based on older populations (i.e., 55 years or older), for example, were reported for only 4 tests. (Figure 8)

Figure 8
Test Sample Characteristics

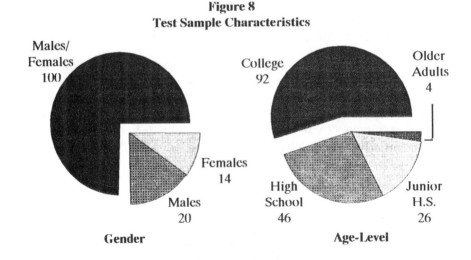

9. <u>Reference sources</u>. Reference sources helpful in further evaluating a test are presented at the end of each test description found in the directory. Up to five relevant references are listed. These reference sources were obtained from my review of 28 journals and the proceedings of nine professional associations over a twenty-five year period.

Figure 9 illustrates the distribution of the number of reference sources found per test. As indicated, no reference support was found for 82 tests (46.86%), and only one reference source was found for each of 42 tests (24.00%). I located extensive reference support (i.e., five or more references) for only 20 tests (11.43%) described in the directory.

Figure 9
Test Reference Support

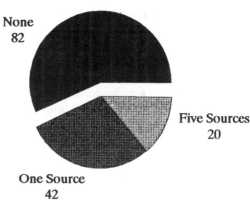

In many cases, however, these additional references were authored by the original test author rather than by other researchers who had adopted the test. This would seem to suggest a lack of replicative or continued research on the vast majority of sport- or exercise-specific psychological tests developed over the last twenty-five years.

D. Recommendations to Promote Psychometric Development in the Sport and Exercise Sciences.

Having spent almost two years locating and reviewing existing sport- and exercise-specific psychological tests published over a twenty-five year period, I have had the opportunity to ponder some of the directions needed to advance psychometric development in the sport and exercise sciences. Several recommendations follow that, while not technical in nature, I believe will, nevertheless, promote further advances in psychometric development in the field:

1. The need for continued test refinement. Almost all the test instruments found in the directory are research tools rather than diagnostic, evaluative, or prognostic instruments. Yet, less than ten percent of these research instruments show evidence of extensive reference support, indicat-

ing a lack of research on further developing and refining these instruments. Many of these tests appeared to have been developed as one-shot assessments.

It is encouraging that many researchers have abandoned their sole reliance on traditional psychometric instruments that are often conceptually incompatible with the intended purposes of an investigation. It is also encouraging that these researchers have invested creative energies in developing psychological instruments more germane to the situational demands of sport and exercise. Yet, there appears to be a lack of commitment on the part of many test authors to further refinement of psychological tests developed and used solely in a single research studies.

Test development is a long and arduous process. It requires numerous and extensive revisions of items across a number of samples. It takes several years before a test begins to show consistent evidence of validity and reliability across the intended population(s) upon which it is based.

Editors and publishers of research journals should encourage and promote continued psychological test development and refinement. It is encouraging that journal reviewers are now requiring more extensive information about the development and psychometric properties of the psychological tests used in research investigations. No longer is it merely acceptable to employ a test without providing documentation as to how items were constructed and refined, and to provide at least preliminary evidence of validity and reliability.

Perhaps special issues of appropriate journals should be dedicated to highlighting examples of promising psychological tests undergoing refinement that may be of special interest to readers. An issue of this nature would certainly underscore the important role tests play in building the disciplinary basis of sport psychology.

2. The need for test manuals. The lack of wide-spread dissemination and evaluation of tests can be attributable, in part, to a failure on the part of most test authors to develop a test manual. A test manual outlines evidence of reliability, validity, norms, guidelines for administration, precautions to test takers, and directions about the potentials uses and misuses of the test.

A good example of an early test manual in the field is the Sport Competition Anxiety Test Manual (Martens, 1977). This manual provided a conceptual framework for the investigation of the construct of competitive trait anxiety. It outlined the numerous considerations that were made in test item selection. The manual identified the procedures that were followed across various stages of test refinement. Chapters in the manual also provided evidence for test validity and reliability. Preliminary norms were presented. A copy of the Sport Competition Anxiety Test was made available in the manual, and was thus readily available for dissemination.

This manual contributed to the wide-spread use and evaluation of the Sport Competition Anxiety Test. In fact, several thousand unpublished and published reports on the Sport Competition Anxiety Test have appeared since the publication of the manual. The manual allowed for the public scrutiny and adoption of the Sport Competition Anxiety Test. As a consequence, this test has contributed substantially toward building a knowledge base on the role of anxiety in sport performance.

3. <u>The need for a central repository for tests and test data</u>. One of the problems facing researchers in sport and exercise psychology is a lack of knowledge regarding the availability of psychological tests germane to the field. While the more popular tests are recognized and employed, tests that are published in more obscure journals are rarely adopted and evaluated. For example, there are a number of tests in this directory that, while lacking broad-based research, show promise of making unique contributions to the field.

In addition to the problem of these tests appearing in journals that are not frequently read by researchers in sport and exercise psychology, it is often difficult to gain access to the actual test. If a test appears in a journal, permission is required from the copyright holder(s) to employ the test. The cost and time involved in gaining these permissions, while necessary, may deter researchers from adopting certain instruments.

When the actual test does not appear in the journal, it is frequently difficult to locate the principal test author. Also, the test author is sometimes reluctant to distribute a test for fear of its misuse, for concerns that other authors may dispute the preliminary evidence provided for the test, or because the test author realizes that frequently users borrow tests without providing to the test author the results of their follow-up data. In some cases, test users are reluctant to employ a test because of costly royalty payments associated with its adoption.

Some of these problems can be overcome by establishing a central repository for sport- and exercise-specific psychological tests. My suggestion is that an organization such as the International Society for Sport Psychology or the Association for the Advancement of Applied Sport Psychology partially fund an institution that would be willing to serve as a repository for new and existing psychological tests. A clearinghouse could be set up within a university setting, for example, that would become known as a center for psychometric testing and development in the field.

This clearinghouse (or center) would store copies of all (or selected) published psychological tests. It would disseminate these tests to interested researchers after securing appropriate permissions from test authors. The center would partially fund selected test authors to enable them to develop test manuals, computerized scoring sheets, and other test products. The center would arrange for royalty payments to authors where appropriate. The center could also arrange to store and access data researchers are required to provide as a condition for using a particular psychological test. In addition, the center could also provide on-site training sessions for test administrators and scorers. As well, the center could highlight and publicize test findings of interest to the general public.

In this way, test authors are kept abreast of the findings from research on their test, a situation sorely lacking at the present time. In addition, a center allows for the more accurate, systematic, and continuous evaluation of these psychological tests. I believe one or more clearinghouses of this nature would make a substantial contribution toward advancing test development in the field.

4. <u>Other recommendations</u>. There are other, perhaps more technical recommendations that could be made to advance psychological assessment in the field. For example, there is a need for test authors to pursue consensual validation of their test(s) (Nideffer, 1981). The use of several related psychological tests in a research investigation would provide collaborative evidence for the validity of a test under development.

In addition, researchers must question their traditional reliance on paper-and-pencil self-report instruments as the sole component of the assessment package. There is a need for a more ecclectic approach to psychological assessment in the sport and exercise sciences. The use by researchers of related neuropsychological instrumentation (e.g., electromyographic devices to examine muscular tension in movement), structured or semi-structured interviews, behavioral assessment scales, and other measures should be encouraged by journal reviewers.

The lack of instrumentation germane to special populations, such as the elderly, is also an important consideration. While the extent to which developmental age differences and/or cohort differences impact the validity of test items is not clear, there is a need for psychometricians to develop tests relevant to older populations. As indicated earlier, only four psychological tests in this directory sampled older adults in an effort to establish the psychometric properties of a test. There is some question as to whether test items developed for college students are appropriate for older groups. For example, a test author interested in assessing sport achievement orientation among older adults, may err in posing a Likert scaled item that asks a response to: "I would be willing to work considerably less in my occupation in order to train rigorously to excel in the Olympic games."

The use of psychological tests as diagnostic and evaluative tools is becoming more evident as professionals in sport psychology "take off their laboratory smocks" and provide sport-related client services. This raises several concerns. First, most psychological tests reported in the directory are not developed for, or are not sufficiently advanced psychometrically, to warrant their use as diagnostic tools. The danger here is that clients may receive inaccurate or false information about their psychological status in relation to athletic performance.

In addition, it is imperative that professionals using psychological testing as part of the intervention program clearly understand the strengths, limitations, and restrictions of the instruments employed. It is also essential that testors have adequate credentials, and be properly trained in the use, administration, and interpretation of test results. The process of providing correct, timely, and adequate feedback regarding test information to clients is a skill that requires extensive training.

E. Summary

In this introductory chapter, I tried to outline some of the events that have occurred over the last twenty-five years that have led to an acceleration in the development of psychological tests situationally specific to the sport and exercise environment. I have identified a number of factors that have led me to develop this first directory of sport- and exercise-specific psychological tests, and I have outlined the benefits to the reader of a directory of this nature. I also identified the procedures I followed in developing the directory. In addition, I outlined some of the more prominent findings one can elicit by systematically reviewing the information found in this directory. I reported on trends in terms of the number of tests developed from 1965-1989, the reference sources used to report these tests, the content/foci of the tests, and issues related to measurement scales adopted, construction procedures followed, validity, reliability, and normative data presented, and test reference support provided.

I concluded by offering a number of recommendations that may have some impact on advancing psychological assessment in the sport and exercise sciences. To this end, I have developed the Directory of Psychological Tests in the Sport and Exercise Sciences which, I am hopeful, the reader will view as a valuable reference source.

Andrew C. Ostrow, Ph.D
Editor

References

Anshel, M. H. (1987). Psychological inventories used in sport psychology research. The Sport Psychologist, 1, 331-349.

Conoley, J. C., & Kramer, J. J. (Eds.) (1989). The tenth mental measurements yearbook. Lincoln, NB: The University of Nebraska Press.

Martens, R. (1973, March). Sport personologists have problems--other sport personologists. Paper presented at the Midwest convention of the American Alliance for Health, Physical Education, and Recreation, Columbus, OH.

Martens, R. (1977). The Sport Competition Anxiety Test manual. Champaign, IL: Human Kinetics Publishers.

Nideffer, R. M. (1981). Ethics and practice of applied sport psychology. Ithaca, NY: Mouvement publications.

Orlick, T. D. (1974). An interview schedule designed to assess family sports environment. International Journal of Sport Psychology, 5, 13-27.

Standards for educational and psychological testing (1985). Washington, DC: American Psychological Association.

How to Use the Directory

The organization format is identical for each test described in the directory. Each test summary is intended to provide the reader with quick access to concise information about a test rather than to serve as a test review or critique. The test summaries do not contain all information required by the reader to administer, score, and interpret test results. Users are encouraged to contact test authors for additional information.

The format for each test summary is as follows:

Test Title: The test title and acronym appear exactly as cited in the source. Parentheses surrounding the acronym indicate that this is the acronym used by the test authors. Brackets surrounding the title or acronym signify that I assigned a title or acronym.

Test author(s): Test authors were listed originally as their names appeared in the source. Subsequently, these names were retained or modified based on correspondence with the principal author listed in the source.

Source: Cites the refereed publication or refereed professional presentation in which the most recent version of the test is described.

Purpose: Describes the general objective(s) and intent of the self-report assessment.

Description: Briefly describes the nature of subscales, presents examples of test items, and indicates the measurement scale used to evaluate test item responses.

Construction: Describes sequentially the procedures used to develop the test, prior to computing estimates of reliability and validity. Indicates how items were selected initially and subsequently modified. Also indicates the procedures followed during item analyses and in the establishment of content validity.

Reliability: Presents estimates of internal consistency and/or test stability based on data cited in the source.

Validity: Presents evidence for concurrent, predictive, and/or construct validity based on data cited in the source.

<u>Norms</u>: Indicates if tests norms are presented in the source. Otherwise, presents a description of the sample(s) upon which the descriptive and/or psychometric data were based.

<u>Availability</u>: Indicates the name, address, and office phone number of the principal author of the test. An asterisk indicates that the principal test author did not comment on the test summary developed by the editor.

<u>References</u>: Indicates up to five references that have utilized the test instrument. An asterisk indicates that the reference centered on further examination of the psychometric properties of the test instrument.

Chapter 1

ACHIEVEMENT ORIENTATION

Tests in this chapter assess the achievement orientations of sport participants in terms of competitiveness, the desire to win, striving for mastery (personal) goals versus competitive goals, and motives to approach/avoid success and to avoid failure.

(1)
ACHIEVEMENT MOTIVATION IN PHYSICAL EDUCATION TEST (AMPET)
Tamotsu Nishida

Source: Nishida, T. (1988). Reliability and factor structure of the Achievement Motivation in Physical Education Test. Journal of Sport & Exercise Psychology, 10, 418-430.

Purpose: To assess achievement motivation for learning in physical exercise, athletics, and sport.

Description: The AMPET contains seven 8-item subscales: Learning strategy (LS), overcoming obstacles (OO), diligence and seriousness (DS), competence of motor ability (CMA), value of learning (VL), anxiety about stress-causing situations (ASCS), and failure anxiety (FA). Subjects' responses to each item are assessed using a 5-point Likert scale. The AMPET also contains an 8-item lie scale to check response accuracy.

Construction: Original items of the AMPET were developed based on research and theories related to factors that constitute motivation/will to win in sport, and behavioral characteristics associated with individuals at various levels of achievement motivation. Item and factor analyses (see Nishida, 1987) reduced the original pool of items from 83 to 64. Principal component factor analysis supported seven principal factors essential for measuring achievement motivation for learning in physical education. These factors correspond to the subscales above.

Reliability: Alpha reliability coefficients for each subscale ranged from .80(FA) to .92 (CMA) among 3,220 Japanese elementary school children, from .82 (FA) to .94 (CMA) among 3,346 Japanese junior high school students, and from .84 (FA) to .95 (CMA and ASCS) among 3,489 Japanese high school students. Test-retest reliability coefficients across a five-week interval ranged from .71 (FA) to .85 (CMA) among these elementary school students ($n=$ 115), from .65 (VL) to .88 (CMA) among a junior high school student subsample ($n=120$), and from .68 (DS) to .80 (CMA) among the high school students ($n=137$). Acceptable internal consistency and test-retest reliability coefficients were also reported for two derived composite subscales: the tendency to achieve success and the tendency to avoid failure.

Validity: The construct validity of the AMPET was examined through factor analysis of these Japanese students' responses to the test. The analysis confirmed the seven factor structure for all samples combined. Similar factor structures emerged when factor analyses were conducted separately by grade level and by gender.

Norms: Psychometric data (including item descriptive statistics) were presented for the 10,055 Japanese students noted above. (See Nishida, 1989 for additional information on normative data).

Availability: Contact Tamotsu Nishida, Research Center of Health, Physical Fitness and Sports, Nagoya University, Furo-cho, Chikusa-ku, Nagoya 464-01, Japan. (Phone # 052-781-5111)

References

Nishida, T. (1987). A new test for achievement motivation for learning in physical education: Construction of a questionnaire and a preliminary study on typology of the motivation. Nagoya Journal of Health, Physical Fitness and Sports, 10, 47-60.

*Nishida, T. (1989). A study on standardization of the Achievement Motivation in Physical Education Test. Japanese Journal of Physical Education, 34, 45-62.

(2)
[APPROACH-AVOIDANCE MOTIVATIONS SCALE FOR SPORTS]
[AAMS]
Brent S. Rushall and Randy G. Fox

Source: Rushall, B. S., & Fox, R. G. (1980). An Approach-avoidance Motivations Scale for sports. Canadian Journal of Applied Sport Sciences, 5, 39-43.

Purpose: To assess an individual's motives to approach success and to avoid failure in competitive sports.

Description: The scale contains 23 items focusing on approach or avoidance orientations to competition, training, and the sporting experience. Subjects respond on a 4-point ordinal scale.

Construction: Gjesme and Nygard's general Achievement Motives Scale (30 items) was modified to be specific to sport situations. An additional six items were added which related to specific competition and training circumstances. An assessment of test-retest reliability across three days (n=29 physical education majors), as well as the establishment of content validity by 12 experts in the psychology of sport and in psychology, resulted in the retention of 28 items with at least 64 percent agreement.

Reliability: An additional evaluation of test-retest reliability (n=23 varsity team members) over a 4-day interval indicated at least 64 percent agreement for each of the 28 items.

Validity: Multiple regression analyses were conducted to examine the extent to which derived factor scores of the scale were predictive of improvement in swimming performance among athletes participating in the 1977 Canadian Winter Swimming Championships. Among 90 male elite swimmers, 4.39 percent of the variance in improved swimming performance was accounted for by four factors of the scale. For 86 female elite swimmers, three factors accounted for 9 percent of the variance in improved swimming performance.

Norms: Not cited. Psychometric data were reported for 176 male and female elite swimmers and 23 varsity athletes.

Availability*: Contact Brent S. Rushall, Department of Physical Education, San Diego State University, San Diego, CA 92182. (Phone # 619-594-4094)

Reference
Whitehead, J., & Edwards, S. (1984). A-state and achievement motivation in volleyball (abstract). Journal of Sports Sciences, 2, 202-203.

(3)
[ATHLETIC ACHIEVEMENT MOTIVATION TEST] [AAMT]
Luc M. Lefebvre

Source: Lefebvre L. (1978). Achievement motivation and causal attribution in male and female athletes. In U. Simri (Ed). Proceedings of the International Symposium on Psychological Assessment in Sport (pp. 163-170). Netanya, Israel: Wingate Institute for Physical Education and Sport.

Purpose: To assess the achievement motives of elite athletes.

Description: The test assesses four areas: intrinsic motivation, risk preference, positive fear of failure, and fear of success. Subjects respond to each item on a 7-point dimensional scale.

Construction: Items were constructed from the interview statements of 40 elite Belgian athletes, as well as from different achievement motivation questionnaires. A content analysis was performed yielding four sets of internally valid items.

Reliability: Split-half internal consistency (n=30) was reported as acceptable for each area, as well as for the entire test.

Validity: Not discussed.

Norms: Not presented. Psychometric data were reported for 30 elite Belgian athletes (15 males and 15 females) who were candidates for the 1976 Olympic games. Athletes represented track, swimming, and gymnastics.

Availability*: Unknown.

(4)
COMPETITIVE ORIENTATION INVENTORY (COI)
Robin S. Vealey

Source: Vealey, R. S. (1986). Conceptualization of sport-confidence and competitive orientation: Preliminary investigation and instrument development. Journal of Sport Psychology, 8, 221-246.

Purpose: To assess individual differences in the tendency to strive toward achieving a sport-related goal.

Description: The COI employs a matrix format of 16 cells. One dimension of the matrix (rows) represents different levels of performance in sport (e.g., very good, below average), while a second dimension establishes different outcomes (e.g., easy win, close loss). Subjects are asked to complete the matrix by assigning a number from 0 (very unsatisfying situation) to 10 (very satisfying situation) to each cell in the matrix. Two scores are derived--an outcome orientation score and a performance orientation score.*

Construction: A major consideration in the development of the COI was the need for a format in which the subject would be forced to weigh the values of wanting to win versus performing well. To this end, a matrix format was selected. A total of 99 high school students and 101 college students were administered the COI and the Marlowe-Crowne Social Desirability Scale in a noncompetitive situation. Subjects' responses to each cell were treated as a test item. Adequate variability between and within cells was found. No relationship was found between subjects' responses to the COI and the Marlowe-Crowne Social Desirability Scale. These findings were replicated with independent samples of high school ($n=$ 103) and college ($n=$ 96) athletes.

Reliability: Internal consistency coefficients were not computed, since the COI is not an additive scale. Test-retest reliability coefficients among a sample of high school ($n=109$) and college ($n=110$) athletes were .69 (1 day interval), .69 (1 week interval), and .69 (1 month interval) for the COI-performance score. For COI-outcome, test-retest reliability coefficients were .69 (1 day), .69 (1 week), and .63 (1 month).

Validity: Concurrent validity coefficients were reported between the responses of 199 high school and college athletes to the COI (performance

---

*Vealey (1988) indicated that the COI-outcome and COI-performance subscales are highly correlated, and recommended adoption of a COI composite score that has similar psychometric properties.

orientation) and their correponding responses to the physical self-presenta-
tion confidence subscale of the Physical Self-Efficacy Scale ($r=.17$). COI-
performance was inversely related to external locus of control ($r=-.29$), and
COI-outcome was positively correlated to external locus of control when
Rotter's Internal-External Control Scale was employed. COI-performance
and COI-outcome were not found to be related to subjects' responses to the
SCAT, CSAI-2, or the perceived physical ability subscale of the Physical Self-
Efficacy Scale.

Construct validity was established by demonstrating among elite
gymnasts ($n=48$) that both COI-performance and COI-outcome were correlated with subjects' pre- and post-competitive state sport-confidence levels.
COI responses were also found to influence athletes' attributional patterns
and COI-performance scores were related to their self-perceptions of performance.

Norms: Preliminary normative data were presented (Vealey, 1988) for 262
high school athletes, 156 athletes ages 12-14 years, 226 college athletes, and
48 elite gymnasts.

Availability: Contact Robin S. Vealey, Dept. of PHS, Phillips Hall, Miami
University, Oxford, OH 45056. (Phone # 513-529-2700)

References

Gill, D. L., & Dzewaltowski, D. A. (1988). Competitive orientations among
    intercollegiate athletes. Is winning the only thing? The Sport Psychologist,
    2, 212-221.
Kelley, B. C., Gill, D. L., & Hoffman, S. J. (1989). Competitive sport orienta-
    tion as a function of religious orientation, athletic experience, and gen-
    der (abstract). Psychology of motor behavior and sport (p. 124). Kent,
    OH: Proceedings of the North American Society for the Psychology of
    Sport and Physical Activity annual convention.
*Vealey, R. S. (1988). Sport-confidence and competitive orientation: An
    addendum on scoring procedures and gender differences. Journal of
    Sportt & Exercise Psychology, 10, 471-478.
Vealey, R. S. (1988). Achievement goals of adolescent figure skaters: Impact
    on self-confidence, anxiety, and performance. Journal of Adolescent
    Research, 3, 227-243.

(5)
[COMPETITIVENESS/COACHABILITY QUESTIONNAIRE] [CCQ]
Ardan O. Dunleavy

Source: Dunleavy, A. O. (1980). Competitiveness and coachability of male varsity swimmers as assessed by peer and coach ratings: A generalizability study with forecasting (abstract). Abstracts: American Alliance for Health, Physical Education, Recreation, and Dance (p. 68). Annual convention, Detroit, MI.

Purpose: To assess competitiveness and coachability among male college varsity swimmers.

Description: The CCQ contains 20 items; 10 items assess competitiveness and 10 items assess coachability.

Construction: Not discussed.

Reliability: Alpha internal consistency coefficients of .67 and .91 were reported for the competitiveness and coachability subscales, respectively (n=20).

Validity: Not discussed.

Norms: Not cited. Psychometric data were based on 20 male college varsity swimmers.

Availability*: Contact Arden O. Dunleavy, Department of Kinesiological Studies, Texas Christian University, Fort Worth, TX 76129.

(6)
ORIENTATIONS TOWARD WINNING SCALE (OTW)
Thomas R. Kidd and William F. Woodman

Source: Kidd, T. R., & Woodman, W. F. (1975). Sex and orientations toward winning in sport. Research Quarterly, 46, 476-483.

Purpose: To assess individual differences in the motive toward winning in sport.

Description: The OTW contains four items. Subjects respond to each item using a 5-point Likert scale.

Construction: The scale was derived from the factor analyses of the responses of 451 male and female college students to a larger questionnaire.

<u>Reliability</u>: An alpha internal consistency coefficient of .76 was reported ($\underline{n}$=451).

<u>Validity</u>: The OTW discriminated between men and women. As hypothesized, the men scored higher than the women on the OTW.

<u>Norms</u>: Not cited. Psychometric data were reported for 451 male and female college students representing one institution.

<u>Availability</u>*: Contact Thomas R. Kidd, School of HPER, University of Nebraska, Omaha, NE 68182-0216. (Phone # 402-554-2670)

References

Graham, R. H., & Carron, A. V. (1982). The impact of the national coaching certification program for hockey on coaching attitudes. In L. M. Wankel and R. B. Wilberg (Eds.), <u>Psychology of sport and motor behavior: Research and practice</u> (pp. 203-216). Proceeding of the Canadian Society for Psychomotor Learning and Sport Psychology, Edmonton, Alberta.

*Snyder, E. E., & Spretzer, E. (1979). Orientations toward sport: Intrinsic, Normative, and Extrinsic. <u>Journal of Sport Psychology</u>, <u>1</u>, 170-175.

(7)
SOCIAL-COGNITIVE SCALE OF MOTIVATION [SCSM]
Glyn C. Roberts and Gloria Balague

<u>Source</u>: Roberts, G. C., & Balague, G. (1989, August). <u>The development of a Social Cognitive Scale of Motivation</u>. Paper presented at the 7th World Congress in Sport Psychology, Singapore.

<u>Purpose</u>: To assess two major achievement goals that affect motivation in sport: Competitive goals and Mastery goals. Mastery goals enable individuals to focus upon improving ability and increasing mastery and skill in sport. Competitive goals lead people to focus on the adequacy of their abilities when compared to others.

<u>Description</u>: The SCSM contains 26 items and two subscales: Competitive goals and Mastery goals. Subjects are asked to indicate the extent to which they feel most successful when playing sport when, for example, they beat other people (Competitive goal) or when they reach a goal (Mastery goal). Subjects respond to each item using a 5-point Likert scale.

<u>Construction</u>: An intial pool of 48 items was developed, based on the work of major investigators in motivation and after a review of existing research questionnaires. A panel of experts evaluated the extent to which each item

was pertinent to mastery or competitive goals, leading to the retention of 29 items.

The 29-item questionnaire was administered to 137 undergraduate students ($\underline{n}$=66 females; $\underline{n}$=71 males) who participated in an introductory psychology course and who had been involved in sports. Principal components factor analysis followed by varimax rotation led to the retention of two factors (labeled Mastery motivation and Competitive motivation) that accounted for 48% of the variance.

Reliability: Cronbach alpha internal consistency coefficients ($\underline{n}$=137) were .92 (Mastery subscale) and .90 (Competitive subscale). Split-half reliability coefficients were .91 (Mastery) and .88 (Competitive).

Validity: Convergent validity was supported in that subjects' ($\underline{n}$=137) responses to the SCSM were moderately correlated ($\underline{r}$=.39) with their responses to Duda's (1989) Task and Ego Orientation in Sport Questionnaire. However, these subjects' responses to the SCSM were not correlated with Vealey's (1986) Competitive Orientation Inventory.

Norms: Not presented. Psychometric data were based on the responses of 137 male and female undergraduate students.

Availability: Contact Glyn Roberts, Department of Kinesiology, Louise Freer Hall, University of Illinois, 906 South Goodwin Ave., Urbana, IL 61801. (Phone # 217-333-6563)

(8)
SPORT ORIENTATION QUESTIONNAIRE (SOQ)
Diane L. Gill and Thomas E. Deeter

Source: Gill, D. L., & Deeter, T. E. (1988). Development of the Sport Orientation Questionnaire. Research Quarterly for Exercise and Sport, 59, 191-202.

Purpose: To assess the disposition to strive for success in competitive and noncompetitive sport activities.

Description: The SOQ contains 25 items incorporating three subscales: (1) competitiveness, (2) the desire to win in interpersonal competition in sport, and (3) the desire to reach personal goals in sport. Subjects respond to each item using a 5-point Likert format.

Construction: Items representing achievement orientation across sport and exercise activities were developed based on a literature review of achievement and sport competition, by consulting other sport psychologists, and by collecting open-ended responses from independent samples of sport participants during several exploratory projects. A total of 58 items were evaluated by 5 graduate students in sport psychology for content validity and item clarity. The reduced pool of 32 items was placed into inventory format, further evaluated for item clarity and lack of ambiguity among 10 subjects, and then all 32 items were administered to two independent samples of undergraduate students ($\underline{n}$=237; $\underline{n}$=218) and 266 high school students. Exploratory and confirmatory factor analyses supported a three-factor structure (see subscales labeled above), and led to the retention of 25 items.

Reliability: Across the three samples, alpha reliability coefficients averaged .94 (competitiveness), .86 (win), and .81 (goal). Test-retest reliability coefficients obtained among the second sample of university students ($\underline{n}$=218) across a 4-week interval were .89(competitiveness), .82 (win), and .73 (goal). Intraclass correlation coefficients were .94 (competitiveness), .90 (win), and .84 (goal).

Validity: Concurrent validity was demonstrated by showing that subjects' scores on the SOQ correlated with their scores on the Work and Family Orientation Questionnaire subscales. Construct validity was supported in that the competitiveness subscale differentiated students enrolled in competitive sport classes from students enrolled in noncompetitive classes. Competitive sport participants were also differentiated from nonparticipants. Win and goal orientation subscales appeared to be less discriminating variables.

Norms. Not reported. Psychometric data were cited for 455 undergraduate students and 266 high school students randomly selected from grades 9 through 12.

Availability: Contact Diane L. Gill, Exercise and Sport Science Department, University of North Carolina at Greensboro, Greensboro, NC 27412. (Phone # 919-334-3033)

References

*Deeter, T. E. (1989). Development of a model of achievement behavior for physical activity. Journal of Sport & Exercise Psychology, 11, 13-25.

*Gill, D. L. (1986). Competitiveness among females and males in physical activity classes. Sex Roles, 15, 233-247.

*Gill, D. L. (1988). Gender differences in competitive orientation and sport participation. International Journal of Sport Psychology, 19, 145-159.

Gill, D. L., & Dzewaltowski, D. A. (1988). Competitive orientations among intercollegiate athletes: Is winning the only thing? The Sport Psychologist, 2, 212-221.

*Gill, D. L., Dzewaltowski, D. A., & Deeter, T. E. (1988). The relationship of competitiveness and achievement orientation to participation in sport and nonsport activities. Journal of Sport & Exercise Psychology, 10, 139-150.

(9)
SPORTS ATTITUDES INVENTORY [SAI]
Joe D. Willis

Source: Willis, J. D. (1982). Three scales to measure competition-related motives in sport. Journal of Sport Psychology, 4, 338-353.

Purpose: To assess constructs related to sport competitiveness including the motives to approach success or avoid failure and the power motive.

Description: The SAI contains 40 items and three scales: Power motive (Pow), motive to achieve success (MAS), and motive to avoid failure (MAF). Subjects respond to each item using a 5-point Likert scale.

Construction: Based on a review of the theoretical and empirical literature on achievement motivation and power, an initial pool of 140 items was developed. A factor analysis of the responses of 256 high school athletes (in three sports), plus the evaluation of the content validity by three experts (1 professor and 2 graduate students in educational psychology) led to the retention of 40 items.

Reliability: Alpha reliability coefficients (n=764 male and 253 female athletes) reported were .76 (Pow), .78 (MAS), and .76 (MAF). Test-retest reliability coefficients across eight weeks, using an independent sample of 46 subjects, were .75 (Pow), .69 (MAS), and .71 (MAF).

Validity: Convergent validity was supported in that athletes' (n=158) scores on MAF correlated .65 with their responses to the Sport Competition Anxiety Test. Furthermore, subjects' (n=191) scores on MAS correlated .23 with their scores on the Mehrabian Need for Achievement Scale, and their scores on the Pow scale correlated .22 with the Dominance scale of the California Psychological Inventory.

Discriminant function analysis indicated that the SAI could discriminate between athletes (n=463) rated as either good or poor competitors by coaches with a 71 percent correct classification. Furthermore, the correlation coefficients of subjects' (n=132 high school students) scores on the three scales with their scores on the Crowne-Marlow Social Desirabilty Scale were not statistically significant.

Norms: Normative data were presented for 764 male and 253 female athletes representing 17 sports at 22 high schools or colleges. Data were presented by gender and sport group.

Availability: Contact Joe D. Willis, Department of Health, Physical Education, Recreation, and Dance, Georgia State University, Atlanta, GA 30303. (Phone # 404-651-2536)

References

*Bourgeois, A. E., Friend, J., & LeUnes, A. (1988). The identification of moderator variables that enhance the predictive utility of personality measures in sport research (abstract). Proceedings of the Association for the Advancement of Applied Sport Psychology annual convention, Nashua, NH.

*Willis, J. D., & Layne, B. H. (1988). A validation study of sport-related motives scales. Journal of Applied Research in Coaching and Athletics, 3, 299-307.

(10)
SPORTS COMPETITION TRAIT INVENTORY (SCTI)
Lou Fabian and Marilyn Ross

Source: Fabian, L., & Ross, M. (1984). The development of the Sport Competition Trait Inventory. Journal of Sport Behavior, 7, 13-27.

Purpose: To assess the trait of competitiveness as expressed in sport.

Description: The SCTI contains 17 items. Examples of items include: "I strive for supremacy in sports," and "I have a strong desire to be a success in sports." Subjects respond to each item using a 7-point Likert scale, with the anchoring hardly ever to almost always.

Construction: Based on a literature review of competitiveness, 86 items were developed. These items were reviewed by three colleagues which led to the retention of 76 items. These items were evaluated by six experts in the field of competition for content validity, resulting in the retention of 36 items. An item analysis of the responses of 104 high school students and 141 college students resulted in the final pool of 17 items.

Reliability: An alpha reliability coefficient of .96 was reported (n=389 high school and college students).

Validity: A discriminant function analysis resulted in a correct classification of 70.73% in differentiating varsity athletes from non-varsity athletes (n=389).

Also, the SCTI was successful in discriminating among swimmers of varying abilities. However, the correlation coefficient between the SCTI and the Sport Competition Anxiety Test was not statistically significant.

Norms: Not cited. Psychometric data were presented for 389 high school and college students.

Availability: Contact Lou Fabian, Department of Health, Physical Education, and Recreation, 149 Trees Hall, University of Pittsburgh, Pittsburgh, PA 15261. (Phone # 412-648-8276)

Reference
Fabian, L., Ross, M., & Hardwick, B. (1980). The human competitive process in intramurals and recreation. National Intramural-Recreational Sports Association Journal, 4(3), 46-50.

(11)
TASK AND EGO ORIENTATION IN SPORT QUESTIONNAIRE (TEOSQ)
Joan L. Duda and John G. Nicholls

Source: Duda, J. L. (1989). Relationship between task and ego orientation and the perceived purpose of sport among high school athletes. Journal of Sport & Exercise Psychology, 11, 318-335.

Purpose: To assess task versus ego orientation within a sport context. Task orientation refers to individuals whose perceived ability is self-referenced and based on personal improvement task mastery. Individuals high on ego orientation perceive their ability in reference to others; subjective success means being better relative to other individuals competing in that sport.

Description: Subjects are asked to think when they felt most successful in their sport, and to respond to 13 items indicative of task or ego orientation. For example, responding to the item "I feel most successful in sport when I work really hard" is indicative of Task orientation, while responding to the item "I feel most successful in sport when I'm the best" is indicative of Ego orientation. Responses are evaluated based on a 5-point Likert scale with the anchorings strongly agree to strongly disagree.

Construction: The TEOSQ is a modified, sport-specific version of an inventory developed by Nicholls (1989) and his colleagues to assess task and ego orientation in an academic classroom environment.

Reliability: Alpha internal consistency coefficients were .82 (Task orientation) and .89 (Ego orientation) among 123 female and male high school varsity basketball athletes. Among 198 high school varsity athletes participating in other sports, alpha coefficients of .62 and .85 were reported for the Task and Ego orientation subscales, respectively.

Validity: Principal component factor analyses ($\underline{n}$=321) followed by both orthogonal and oblique rotations indicated that task and ego orientations emerged as stable factors, supporting the construct validity of the TEOSQ. The concurrent validity of the TEOSQ was supported in that subjects' ($\underline{n}$=321) responses to the Task orientation subscale were correlated with their responses to a Purpose of Sport Questionnaire in terms of mastery/cooperation, active physical lifestyle, good citizen, and enhanced self-esteem. In contrast, their responses to the Ego orientation subscale were positively correlated with the competitiveness, high status career, enhance self-esteem, and social status/getting ahead subscales of the Purpose of Sport Questionnaire.

Norms: Not cited. Psychometric data were cited for 128 male and 193 female varsity interscholastic athlete participants representing six high schools in a midwestern community.

Availability: Contact Joan L. Duda, Department of PEHRS, Purdue University, Lambert 113, W. Lafayette, IN 47907. (Phone # 317-494-3172)

References
*Duda, J. L. (in press). Motivation in sport settings: A goal perspective analysis. In G. Roberts (Ed.), Motivation in sport and exercise. Champaign, IL: Human Kinetics Publishers.

*Duda, J. L., Olson, L. K., & Templin, T. J. (in press). The relationship of task and ego orientation to sportsmanship attitudes and the perceived legitmacy of injurious acts. Research Quarterly for Exercise and Sport.

Nicholls, J. G. (1989). The competitive ethos and democratic education. Cambridge, MA: Harvard University Press.

(12)
WILL TO WIN QUESTIONNAIRE [WW]
Vera Pęzer and Marvin Brown

Source: Pezer, V., & Brown, M. (1980). Will to win and athletic performance. International Journal of Sport Psychology, 11, 121-131.

Purpose: To measure the desire to defeat an opponent or to exceed some performance standard in sport.

Description: The questionnaire contains 14 items in which subjects respond in a true-false format.

Construction: A total of 34 items were selected from five personality tests. Items selected were reflective of the importance of winning, winning in relation to other reasons for competing, and personal feelings stemming from winning or losing. Fourteen additional items were created by the authors. Respondents ($\underline{n}$=254 undergraduate students) answered these 48 items using a true-false format. Based on item and factor analyses, and an evaluation of the social desirability of each item using an independent sample of 62 physical educationstudents, 25 items were retained. Additional item and factor analyses on data collected among another sample of 39 physical education undergraduate students and two samples of female curlers ($\underline{n}$=61; $\underline{n}$=68) led to a final 14-item version.

Reliability: A Kuder-Richardson-20 internal consistency coefficient of .66 was reported among 216 female curlers. A test-retest reliability coefficient of .87 was reported among a subsample of 47 female curlers across a 4-month interval.

Validity: A correlation coefficient of .78 was reported between female basketball players' ($\underline{n}$=10) WW scores and their coaches' assesment of their will to win. Using an additional sample of 10 female basketball players, a correlation coefficient of .72 was reported between their WW scores and their teammates' and their own evaluations of their will to win. Similarly, a correlation coefficient of .72 was reported between female curlers' ($\underline{n}$=24) WW scores and their teammmates' ratings of their will to win. Thus, there was evidence supporting the concurrent validity of the WW scale.

Norms: Not cited. Psychometric data were reported for 248 Canadian female curlers and 20 female basketball players.

Availability*: Contact Vera Pezer, Counselling Services, College of Arts and

Sciences, University of Saskatchewan, Saskatoon, Saskatchewan, Canada S7N 0W0.

References

Daino, A. (1985). Personality traits of adolescent tennis players. International Journal of Sport Psychology, 16, 120-125.

*Dorsey, B., Lawson, P., & Pezer, V. (1980). The relationship between women's basketball performance and will to win. Canadian Journal of Applied Sport Sciences, 5, 91-93.

*Hoffman, A. J. (1986). Competitive sport and the American athlete: How much is too much? International Journal of Sport Psychology, 17, 390-397.

*Woloschuk, W. (1986). Further evidence of a relationship between will to win and basketball performance. Perceptual and Motor Skills, 62, 253-254.

Chapter 2

AGGRESSION

Tests in this chapter assess the aggressive tendencies of sport participants in terms of instrumental and reactive aggression, physical and nonphysical aggression, and perceptions among players and spectators of the legitimacy of aggressive behavior.

(13)
AGGRESSIVE TENDENCIES IN BASKETBALL QUESTIONNAIRE
[ATBQ]
Joan L. Duda, Linda K. Olson, and Thomas J. Templin

Source: Duda, J. L., Olson, L. K., & Templin, T. J. (in press). The relationship of task and ego orientation to sportsmanship attitudes and the perceived legitimacy of injurious acts. Research Quarterly for Exercise and Sport.

Purpose: To assess an individual's agreement with and reasoning about aggressive behaviors in basketball.

Description: The ATBQ contains six written scenarios depicting aggressive acts in basketball with intended consequences that become increasingly more serious. These consequences (in order of severity) include nonphysical intimidation, physical intimidation, miss a few minutes, miss the rest of the game, miss the rest of the season, and permanently disable an opponent. The scenarios are presented in random order with the subject being asked to indicate for each scenario whether this is legitimate to do, and whether this is legitimate to do in order to win. Subjects respond using a 5-point Likert scale with the anchorings strongly disapprove to strongly approve.

Construction: The ATBQ is a basketball-specific version of Bredemeier's (1985) Continuum of Injurious Sport Acts. Four experts developed the scenarios as typical examples of each type of injurious act within the context of interscholastic basketball.

Reliability: Not reported.

Validity: Discriminant validity was supported in that male high school basketball players (n=56) perceived the depicted intentionally injurious acts to be more legitimate than female high school basketball players. This was true for each scenario except when the injured player would be permanently disabled.

Norms: Not cited. Psychometric data were reported for 56 male and 67 female interscholastic basketball players representing five high schools in a midwestern community.

Availability: Contact Joan L. Duda, Department of Physical Education, Health, and Recreation Studies, 113 Lambert Hall, Purdue University, West Lafayette, IN 47907. (Phone # 317-494-3172)

Reference

Bredemeier, B. (1985). Moral reasoning and the perceived legitimacy of intentionally injurious sport acts. Journal of Sport Psychology, 7, 110-124.

(14)
BREDEMEIER ATHLETIC AGGRESSION INVENTORY (BAAGI)
Brenda Bredemeier

Source: Bredemeier, B. (1975). The assessment of reactive and instrumental athletic aggression. In D. M. Landers (Ed.), Psychology of sport and motor behavior-II (pp. 71-83). State College, PA: Penn State HPER series.

Purpose: To assess reactive and instrumental athletic aggression.

Description: The BAAGI contains two 50-item scales measuring reactive and instrumental aggression, respectively. A reactive aggression response has as its primary goal the infliction of injury, whereas in instrumental aggression, the primary goal is the attainment of a particular reward. Subjects respond to each item using a 4-point Likert scale.

Construction: Item development was guided by the need for clarity, an emphasis on athletic rather than pathological aggression, adaptability to different sport areas, the need for an item to tap different intensities of the same act or emotion, and minimization of social desirability contamination. A pilot instrument of 149 items was administered to 104 male and female high school and college students, plus 6 judges evaluated content validity. Subsequent item refinement plus the addition of items from existing scales such as the Buss Durkee Hostility Scale led to construction of a questionnaire containing

200 items. These items were administered to 166 female athletes in conjuntion with the Buss Durkee Hostility Scale and the Crowne Marlowe Social Desirability Scale. Further item analyses led to the retention of 50 reactive and 50 instrumental items.

Reliability: Alpha reliability coefficients of .90 (reactive aggression) and .86 (instrumental aggression) were reported ($\underline{n}$=166).

Validity: Convergent validity was supported in that subjects' ($\underline{n}$=166) scores on the BAAGI were correlated with their responses to the Buss Durkee Hostility scale. However, there was also evidence of social desirability contamination in that these subjects' scores on the BAAGI correlated with their responses to the Crowne Marlowe Social Desirability Scale. Concurrent validity was also enhanced in that these subjects' responses on the BAAGI were correlated with their coaches' ratings of their aggressive behavior.

Norms: Not presented. Psychometric data were cited for 166 female athletes representing 6 sports at 11 state colleges, universities, or private schools.

Availability*: Contact Brenda Bredemeier, Department of Physical Education, 200 Hearst Gymnasium, University of California, Berkeley, CA 94720.

References

*Rice, T. S., Ostrow, A. C., Ramsburg, I. D., & Brooks, D. D. (1989). A reactive aggression measure for baseball: A pilot investigation (abstract). In Psycholology of motor behavior and sport. Kent, OH: Proceedings of the North American Society for the Psychology of Sport and Physical Activity annual convention.

*Wall, B. R., & Gruber, J. (1986). Relevancy of athletic aggression inventory for use in women's intercollegiate basketball: A pilot test. International Journal of Sport Psychology, 17, 23-33. (Developed 28-item short form of the BAAGI)

Worrell, G. L., & Harris, D. J. (1986). The relationship of perceived and observed aggression of ice hockey players. International Journal of Sport Psychology, 17, 34-40.

(15)
COLLIS SCALE OF ATHLETIC AGGRESSION [CSAG]
Martin L. Collis

Source: Collis, M. L. (October, 1972). The Collis Scale of Athletic Aggression. Proceedings of the Fourth Canadian Symposium on Psycho-Motor Learning and Sport Psychology (pp. 366-370). University of Waterloo, Waterloo, Ontario, Canada.

Purpose: To assess aggression as it relates to athletic success.

Description: The CSAG contains 50 items and measures two categories of aggression: legal aggression (25 items) and extra-legal aggression (25 items). Four response alternatives are presented for each item. Each alternative is weighted on a four-point scale, with a score of 4 on an item designating high aggression.

Construction: "The Scale has been constantly refined on the basis of item analysis of individual questions for their discriminatory characteristics...." (p. 368)

Reliability: Not presented.

Validity: Ice hockey players' (n=20) scores on extra-legal aggression correlated positively with the number of minutes of penalties they had been assessed during the previous season.

Norms: Not cited. Descriptive data were presented for 240 male athletes (ages 10 and under, 11-14, and 15-18 years) representing soccer, swimming, hockey, and gymnastics.

Availability*: Contact Martin L. Collis, Faculty of Education, University of Victoria, Victoria, British Columbia, Canada.

Reference
Reid, R. M., & Hay, D. (1979). Some behavioral characteristics of rugby and association footballers. International Journal of Sport Psychology, 10, 239-251.

(16)
RICE REACTIVE AGGRESSION MEASURE FOR BASEBALL
(RRAMB)
Timothy S. Rice, Andrew C. Ostrow, I. Dale Ramsburg,
and Dana D. Brooks

Source: Rice, T. S., Ostrow, A. C., Ramsburg, I. D., & Brooks, D. D.(1989). A reactive aggression measure for baseball: A pilot investigation (abstract). Kent, OH: Proceedings of the North American Society for the Psychology of Sport and Physical Activity Annual Convention.

Purpose: To assess the reactive aggression tendencies of baseball players.

Description: The RRAMB contains descriptions of four potentially reactive aggression evoking situations in baseball (e. g., a close play at second base). Each of the situations contain eight statements which require a seven-point Likert format response.

Construction: A panel of three experts evaluated the content validity of the four situations and 32 response alternatives of the RRAMB. These experts concurred that 3 of the 4 situations appeared to be measuring reactive aggression, but did not agree that the situation describing the conflict between a pitcher and batter was indicative of reactive aggression. Nevertheless, this situation was still included in this initial version of the RRAMB.*

Reliability: Alpha reliability coefficients for 58 high school baseball players ranged from .51 to .94 for each situation, with a value of .83 reported for the overall RRAMB score. Among 41 college varsity baseball players, alpha reliability coefficients ranged from .98 to .99 for each situation, with an overall RRAMB alpha reliability coefficient of .98.*

Validity: Concurrent validity was established by demonstrating that among these high school and college baseball players, the RRAMB correlated more highly with the reactive aggression subscale of the Bredemeier Athletic Aggression Inventory than the instrumental aggression subscale of this inventory. Furthermore, there was evidence that players' responses to the RRAMB were correlated with their assessments of other teams members in terms of reactive aggression, as well as with their own self-assessments on reactive aggression.

*Construction procedures and reliability coefficients cited are from a master's degree thesis by the first author, available at West Virginia University.

<u>Norms</u>: Not reported. Psychometric data were cited for 58 high school and 41 college varsity baseball players.

<u>Availability</u>: Contact Timothy S. Rice, Department of Sport and Exercise Studies, West Virginia University, Morgantown, WV 26506-6116. (Phone # 304-293-3295)

(17)
SCALE OF CHILDREN'S ACTION TENDENCIES (SCATS)
Brenda Jo Bredemeier

<u>Source</u>: Bredemeier, B. J., Weiss, M. R., Shields, D. L., & Cooper, B. A. B. (1987). The relationship between children's legitimacy judgments and their moral reasoning, aggression tendencies, and sport involvement. <u>Sociology of Sport Journal</u>, <u>4</u>, 48-60.

<u>Purpose</u>: To assess children's self-report aggression tendencies in a sport-specific context.

<u>Description</u>: The SCATS contains 10 stories within a sport or game context. Each of the ten stories is followed by three response alternatives-one aggressive, one assertive, and one submissive, which are presented in a paired-comparison format. Thus, the SCATS contains three pairs of choices per story. Scoring the SCATS involves summing the number of times aggression alternatives are selected. Aggression responses are subdivided into physical and nonphysical alternatives.

<u>Construction</u>: Not discussed.

<u>Reliability</u>: An internal consistency coefficient of .85 was reported.

<u>Validity</u>: Concurrent validity was supported in that there was a high, positive correlation coefficient between subjects' responses to the SCATS and their corresponding responses to the Children's Action Tendency Scale (CATS). A moderate correlation coefficient was reported between their scores on the SCATS and teachers' behavioral ratings.

<u>Norms</u>: Not cited.

<u>Availability*</u>: Contact Brenda Bredemeier, Department of Physical Education, 200 Hearst Gymnasium, University of California, Berkeley, CA 94720.

(18)
SPECTATOR MISBEHAVIOR ATTITUDINAL INQUIRY [SMAI]
Brian Cavanaugh and John Silva III

Source: Cavanaugh, B., & Silva, J. (1980). Spectator perceptions of fan misbe-havior: An attitudinal inquiry. In C. H. Nadeau, W. R. Halliwell, K. M. Newell, and G. C. Roberts (Eds.), Psychology of motor behavior and sport-1979 (pp. 189-198). Champaign, Il.: Human Kinetics Publishers.

Purpose: To assess spectator perceptions of factors that facilitate fan misbe-havior.

Description: The SMAI is a 14-factor, 28-item attitudinal questionnaire. Spectators respond to each item using a four-point Likert scale.

Construction: The factors derived for the questionnaire evolved from various theories of collective behavior. A total of 20 items were developed and then ranked by collegiate coaches, sport psychologists, sport sociologists, and former collegiate athletes in terms of each item's importance in facilitating spectator misbehavior. A total of 14 items were retained based on their consistently high rankings.

Reliability: An intraclass correlation coefficient ($\underline{n}=27$ undergraduate physi-cal education students) of .79 was reported across a five-day test-retest inter-val.

Validity: Construct validity was examined through factor analysis. Principal components and alpha factoring were applied to the responses to the SMAI by 241 spectators randomly selected from a total sample of 1,747 subjects. Items that loaded properly on factors across both methods were retained for the final questionnaire (Silva, personal communication, March 19, 1990).

Norms: Normative data were provided for 1,747 spectators attending one of three hockey games in either Buffalo, Rochester, or Brockport. A total of 1,006 males and 593 females particpated in the study. The gender of 148 spectators was not identified.

Availability: Contact John Silva, Department of Physical Education, CB #8700, Fetzer Gym, University of North Carolina, Chapel Hill, NC 27599-8700. (Phone # 919-962-0017)

(19)
SPORT AGGRESSION QUESTIONNAIRE (SAQ)
Mark Thompson

Source: Thompson, M. (1989). The development of a Sport Aggression Questionnaire for the study of justification of acts of aggression (abstract). Proceedings of the Association for the Advancement of Applied Sport Psychology (p. 104). Seattle, WA.

Purpose: To assess an individual's justification of acts of aggression occurring in specified sport situations.

Description: The SAQ focuses on five primary motivators of aggression in sport: injustice to self, injustice to teammate, frustration, aiding the team, and unprovoked aggression. An additional item on "no intent to harm" is included. Each sport situation identified is considered in relation to three possible outcomes signifying the severity of an injury due to the action.

Construction: Not discussed.

Reliability: A test-retest reliability coefficient (n=32 college males) of .84 was reported across a one-week interval.

Validity: Construct validity was supported in that male high school varsity basketball players (n=24) rated as high or low in aggression by their coaches were correspondingly high or low on aggression as measured by the SAQ. Players high on aggression as assessed by their coaches were more likely to justify actions of aggression in sport than were players rated as low on aggression.

Norms: Not presented. Psychometric data were based on the responses of 32 male college students and 24 male high school varsity basketball players.

Availability*: Unknown. Test items do not appear in the source.

Chapter 3

ANXIETY

Tests in this chapter assess anxiousness among sport partici-pants in terms of cognitive and somatic trait and state anxiety, worry cognitions, and concerns regarding concentration disruption, social evaluation, and fear of injury. Coping strategies for dealing with anxiety are also evaluated.

(20)
ATHLETIC WAYS OF COPING CHECKLIST (AWCC)
Peter R. E. Crocker

Source: Crocker, P. R. E. (1989). The development of a preliminary Athletic Ways of Coping Checklist (abstract). <u>Proceedings of the 20th annual conference of the Canadian Society for Psychomotor Learning and Sport Psychology</u> (p. 38). Victoria, British Columbia, Canada.

Purpose: To assess different coping strategies used by athletes in relation to a stressful sport situation.

Description: The AWCC contains eight coping scales: Active, Problem-Focused, Social Support, Positive Reappraisal, Wishful Thinking, Self-Control, Detachment, and Self-Blame. Athletes are asked to describe a recent stressful sport situation, and then indicate, using a 4-point Likert scale, the extent to which each coping strategy was used in that situation.

Construction: Numerous competitive athletes were interviewed and asked to recall coping strategies they used to manage athletic stress. Based on their responses, and on strategies reported in the sport literature, Lazarus and Folkman's (1985) Ways of Coping Checklist was modified to reflect a sport context. A 68-item AWCC was administered to 237 athletes representing 14 different sports. Principal axis factor analysis followed by varimax rotation led to the retention of eight factors accounting for 40% of the variance. A total of 38 items were retained based on this analysis.

Reliability: Cronbach alpha internal consistency coefficients ranged from .68

to .77 across the eight coping scales.

Validity: Crocker indicated that wishful thinking and self-blame were strong predictors of negative emotion. Also, active coping and positive reappraisal were moderate predictors of positive emotion (Crocker, personal communication, March 7, 1990).

Norms: Not presented. Psychometric data were based on the responses of 237 athletes from 14 sports.

Availability: Contact Peter R. E. Crocker, School of Physical Education, Lakehead University, 955 Oliver Road, Thunder Bay, Ontario, Canada P7B 5E1. (Phone # 807-343-8641)

Reference
*Crocker, P. R. E., & Bouffard, M. (1989). Ways of coping by athletes: Relationship to appraisal and emotion (abstract). Proceedings of the 20th Annual Conference of the Canadian Society for Psychomotor Learning and Sport Psychology (p. 41). Victoria, British Columbia, Canada.

(21)
[BASKETBALL] S-R SPORT INVENTORY OF ANXIOUSNESS
(S-RSIA)
A. C. Fisher, J. S. Horsfall, and H. H. Morris

Source: Fisher, A. C., Horsfall, J. S., & Morris, H. H. (1977). Sport personality assessment: A methodological re-examination. International Journal of Sport Psychology, 8, 92-102.

Purpose: To examine the relative contributions of the person and situation in accounting for anxiety responses in basketball.

Description: The S-RSIA contains 13 anxiety-eliciting situations in basketball. These situations focus on pre-game, game, and post-game conditions. Subjects respond to 13 response modes for each situation (such as "mouth gets dry") using a 5-point ordinal scale.

Construction: The 13 situations were reduced from a pool of 38 situations that had been developed by the investigators and a graduate sport psychology class. These basketball situations were felt to range from inocuous to potentially threatening. The modes of response were selected from Endler, Hunt, and Rosenstein's (1962) S-R Inventory of Anxiousness.

Reliability: The Cronbach alpha internal consistency coefficient ($n = 106$ male college basketball players) for the total inventory was .81. The alpha coefficients for the situational scales ranged from .61 to .76, and for the modes of response from .56 to .83.

Validity: Not discussed.

Norms: Not cited. Psychometric data were based on the responses of 106 college male junior varsity and varsity basketball athletes representing 9 teams in upstate New York.

Availability: Contact A. Craig Fisher, Exercise and Sport Sciences Department, Ithaca College, Ithaca, NY 14850. (Phone # 607-274-3112)

References
Endler, N. S., Hunt, J. M., & Rosenstein, A. J. (1962). An S-R Inventory of Anxiousness. Psychological Monographs, 76 (17, Whole No. 536).
Fisher, A. C., & Dixon, L. R. (1985). Psychological analysis of athletes' anxiety responses: An attempt at explanation (abstract). Proceedings of the annual conference of the Canadian Society of Psychomotor Learning and Sport Psychology (pp. 52-53). Montreal, Canada.
Fisher, A. C., & Zwart, E. F. (1981). Psychological analyses of athletes' anxiety responses (abstract). In G. C. Roberts and D. M. Landers (Eds.). Psychology of motor behavior and sport (p. 104). Champaign, IL: Human Kinetics Publishers.

(22)
COMPETITIVE GOLF STRESS INVENTORY (CGSI)
Peggy A. Richardson and Debra J. Norton

Source: Richardson, P. A., & Norton, D. J. (1983, February). A Competitive Golf Stress Inventory. Paper presented at the Texas Association for Health, Physical Education, Recreation, and Dance annual convention, Corpus Christi, TX.

Purpose: To assess factors that contribute specifically to athletes' heightened anxiety levels in intercollegiate golf competition.

Description: The CGSI contains 40 items that focus on situation, spectator, expectation, opponent, and attitudinal influences. Subjects are asked to respond on a 7-point Likert scale to items such as "I get tense when I am playing an important competitive round," or "I feel nervous when a crowd is watching my round."

Construction: Items for the CSGI were selected by analyzing and recording stress statements that appeared in newspapers and tournament reviews in Golf Magazine. A total of 75 items were evaluated by four LPGA Teaching Pros/ NCAA Division I coaches and one NCAA Division I golf coach for content validity, leading to the retention of 40 items.

Reliability: An uncorrected serial halves correlation coefficient of .93 was reported among 95 female college golfers.

Validity: Concurrent validity was supported in that subjects' ($\underline{n}$=95) responses to the CGSI correlated -.52 with their corresponding responses to the Sport Competition Anxiety Test. Furthermore, the CGSI discriminated between proficient and less proficient female intercollegiate golfers, where performance was defined as the average score over three 18-hole rounds.

Norms: Not cited. Descriptive and psychometric data were presented for 95 female intercollegiate golfers representing 15 golf teams from 9 states.

Availability: Contact Peggy A. Richardson, Department of Kinesiology, Health Promotion, and Recreation, Box 13857, University of North Texas, Denton, TX 76203-3857. (Phone # 817-565-3427)

Reference

*Adler, W., & Thode, R. (1989). Beyond the SCAT: A specific sport-specific measure of competitive stress in golf (abstract). Proceedings of the Association for the Advancement of Applied Sport Psychology annual convention (p. 23). Seattle, WA.

(23)

COMPETITIVE STATE ANXIETY INVENTORY-2 (CSAI-2)
Rainer Martens, Damon Burton, Robin S. Vealey, Linda A. Bump
and Daniel E. Smith

Source: Martens, R., Vealey, R. S., & Burton, D. (1990). Competitive anxiety in sport (pp. 117-213). Champaign, IL: Human Kinetic Publishers.

Purpose: To assess cognitive and somatic components of competitive state anxiety and self-confidence in relation to competitive sport performance.

Description: The CSAI-2 is a 27-item self-report test designed to measure three relatively independent competitive states: cognitive state anxiety, somatic state anxiety, and confidence. Each of these three states is assessed by subjects' responses to nine items using a 4-point Likert scale. An example of a cognitive A-state item is "I am concerned about losing." An example of a somatic A-state item is "I feel jittery." An example of a state self-confidence item is "I feel secure." Subjects total score on each subscale can range from a low of 9 to a high of 36.

The CSAI-2 was developed mainly as a research tool; its usefulness as a diagnostic instrument for clinical purposes has not been established.

Construction: Initially, the CSAI-2 was constructed to include fear of physical harm and generalized anxiety subscales, as well as cognitive and somatic A-state subscales. An initial pool of 102 items was developed from the first version of the CSAI-2 (called the CSAI), and by modifying items from existing general scales of somatic and cognitive A-state. An evaluation of these items for syntax, clarity, and face validity by three judges led to the retention of 79 items (Form A).

Form A was administered to 106 university football players prior to competition. It was also administered to 56 undergraduate physical education students who were asked to complete Form A based on a hypothetical competitive situation. On the bases of item analyses, item-to-subscale correlations, factor analyses, and discriminant analyses, 36 items (Form B) were retained comprising a 12-item somatic A-state subscale, a 12-item cognitive A-state subscale, a 10-item state self-confidence scale, and a 2-item fear-of-physical-harm subscale (which was subsequently eliminated based on further discrminant analysis).

Form C contained 6 additional self-confidence items, 6 new control items, and 12 internal-external locus of control items (hypothesized to be an important component of state self-confidence). Eight items were also deleted from Form B, resulting in a 52-item Form C containing four subscales. Form C was administered within one hour of competition to 80 male and female athletes who participated in collegiate swimming and track and field, high school wrestling, or road racing. Item analyses, item-to-subscale correlations, factor analyses, and discriminant analyses led to the deletion of the internal-external control subscale, and the retention of cognitive A-state, somatic A-state, and state self-confidence subscales, each containing nine items (Form D). (One item from the cognitive A-state subscale was changed).

It was found that both the cognitive and somatic A-state subscales were susceptible to social desirability contamination. The word "worry" was replaced by the word "concern" on all relevant items of the cognitive A-state subscale. This final version of the CSAI-2 was labeled Form E, and also included a set of anti-social desirabilty instructions.

Reliability: Cronbach alpha reliability coefficients (across three samples of athletes) ranged from .79 to .83 for the cognitive A-state scale, from .82 to .83 for the somatic A-state scale, and from .87 to .90 for the state self-confidence scale.

Validity: Concurrent validity was demonstrated by showing that the responses of these three independent samples of athletes to the CSAI-2 correlated in the hypothesized directions with their responses to the Sport Competition Anxiety Test, general state and trait anxiety scales, Rotter's Internal-External Locus of Control Scale, the Zuckerman Affect Adjective Checklist, and Alpert and Haber's Achievement Anxiety Test.

Research by Gould, Petlichkoff, Simmons, and Vevera (1987) supported the predictive validity of the somatic A-state and state self-confidence subscales (but not the cognitive A-state scale) in relation to pistol shooting performance. Furthermore, Burton (1988a) found support for the inverted U relationship between somatic A-state and swimming performance among 33 collegiate swimmers and 70 swimmers chosen to compete at the 1982 National Sports Festival. However, there was a negative linear relationship between cognitive A-state and swimming performance and a positive linear relationship between state self-confidence and swimming performance.

Generally, the results are equivocal regarding the state anxiety-performance relationship. A most critical factor affecting this relationship seems to be the method by which performance is assessed.

Norms: Normative data are cited in the Source for 593 male and female high school athletes, 378 male and female college athletes, and 263 male and female elite athletes. In addition, normative data are presented for the sports of basketball, cycling, golf, swimming, track and field, and wrestling.

Availability: Permission is granted by publishers of the Source, without written approval, for anyone to reproduce (but not publish) the CSAI-2 for research purposes. A copy of the CSAI-2 (Form E) is presented in the Source. The authors would like to receive reports of research findings resulting from the use of the CSAI-2.

References

*Barnes, M. W., Sime, W., Diensthbier, R., & Plake, B. (1986). A test of the construct validity of the CSAI-2 questionnaire on male elite collegiate swimmers. International Journal of Sport Psychology, 17, 364-374.

*Burton, D. (1988a). Do anxious swimmers swim slower? Reexamining the elusive anxiety-performance relationship. Journal of Sport & Exercise Psychology, 10, 45-61.

*Burton, D. (1988b). Competitive state anxiety: Use and interpretation of the Competitive State Anxiety Inventory-2 (abstract). In Psychology of motor behavior and sport (p. 33). Proceedings of the North American Society for the Psychology of Sport and Physical Activity annual convention, University of Tennessee, Knoxville.

*Gould, D., Petlichkoff, L., Simmons, J., & Vevera (1987). Relationship between Competitive State Anxiety Inventory-2 subscale scores and pistol shooting performance. Journal of Sport & Exercise Psychology, 9, 33-42.

*Gould, D., Petlichkoff, L., & Weinberg, R. S. (1984). Antecedents of temporal changes in, and relationships between CSAI-2 subcomponents. Journal of Sport Psychology, 6, 289-304.

(24)
[FEAR OF SOCIAL CONSEQUENCES SCALE] [FSCS]
K. Willimczik, S. Rethorst, and H. J. Riebel

Source: Willimczik, K., Rethorst, S., & Riebel, H. -J. (1986). Cognitions and emotions in sports games--a cross-cultural comparative analysis. International Journal of Physical Education, 23(1), 10-16.

Purpose: To assess the fear that others might give a negative judgment of one's performance in a sport context.

Description: The FSCS contains 10 items. For example, "It depresses me when I am criticized by my teammates." Subjects respond on a 7-point Likert scale.

Construction: Not discussed.

Reliability: Internal consistency coefficients of .73 (n=137 male and female German volleyball players) and .47 (n=150 male and female Indonesian volleyball players) were reported.

Validity: Not discussed.

Norms: Not cited. Psychometric data were based on the responses to the FSCS of 68 German male volleyball players, 69 German female volleyball players, 90 Indonesian male volleyball players, and 60 Indonesian female volleyball players.

Availability*: Contact K. Willimczik, Abteilung Sportwissenschaft, Universitat Bielefeld, Universitatsstr., D-4800 Bielefeld 1, Federal Republic of Germany.

(25)
MENTAL READINESS FORM (MRF)
Shane M. Murphy, Michael Greenspan, Douglas Jowdy, and
Vance Tammen

Source: Murphy, S. M., Greenspan, M., Jowdy, D., & Tammen, V. (1989). Development of a brief rating instrument of competitive anxiety: Comparisons with the Competitive State Anxiety Inventory-2 (abstract). Proceedings of the Association for the Advancement of Applied Sport Psychology (p. 82). Seattle, WA.

Purpose: To assess precompetitive state anxiety.

Description: The MRF is a three-item instrument employing a bipolar continuous scale assessment method. The MRF was developed so that the three ratings obtained would correspond to the cognitive anxiety, somatic anxiety, and self-confidence subscales of the Competitive State Anxiety Inventory-2 (CSAI-2). Subjects respond to thoughts, bodily feelings, and self-confidence before competition using calm-worried, tense-relaxed, and scared-confident bipolar adjective pairs, respectively.

Construction: The test authors were seeking to develop a self-report assessment of anxiety that would take athletes only seconds to complete prior to competing, and that would produce little distraction. They selected the three subscales of the CSAI-2 as a basis for the bipolar continous scale assessment.

Reliability: Not discussed.

Validity: Concurrent validity correlation coefficients between subjects' ($\underline{n}$=105 elite cyclists; $\underline{n}$=19 elite table tennis players; $\underline{n}$=15 elite junior figure skaters) responses to the MRF and the appropriate subscales of the CSAI-2 were .63 (cognitive anxiety/thoughts), .59 (somatic anxiety/bodily feelings), and .63 (self-confidence/self-confidence).

Norms: Not cited. Psychometric data were cited for 105 male and female senior and junior cyclists, 19 senior and junior table tennis players, and 15 junior figure skaters.

Availability: Contact Shane M. Murphy, Department of Sport Psychology, United States Olympic Committe, 1750 E. Boulder, Colorado Springs, CO 80909. (Phone # 719-632-5551)

(26)
PRECOMPETITIVE STRESS INVENTORY (PSI)
John M. Silva, Charles J. Hardy, R. K. Crace, and N. E. Slocum

Source: Silva, J. M., Hardy, C. J., Crace, R. K., & Slocum, N. E. (1987). Establishment of the psychometric properties of the Precompetitive Stress Inventory (Abstract). Research abstracts of the American Alliance for Health, Physical Education, Recreation, and Dance annual convention, Las Vegas, NV.

Purpose: To assess individual differences in the proneness toward experiencing precompetitive stress.

Description: The PSI is a 10-item questionnaire designed to assess sources of precompetitive stress. Subjects are asked to indicate the frequency with which certain stressors occur 24 hours pregame; they are also asked to rate the impact (positive, negative, or none) the stressors had on performance.

Construction: A panel of experts from sport psychology and clinical psychology were used to establish the content validity of the PSI.

Reliability: An alpha internal consistency coefficient of .98 was reported among 45 female and 78 male youth sport participants (ages 12-18).

Validity: A principal component factor analysis ($\underline{n}$=123) led to the emergence of 14 factors accounting for 75.82 percent of the variance; comparative factor analyses across two studies led to the retention of seven factors. These seven factors (and the corresponding accountable variance) were Group Motivation (21.13%), Self-confidence (15.56%), Performance Achievement (13.87%), Guilt/Fear of Misfortune (13.30%), Playing Time (12.97%), Material Rewards (11.68%), and Family Involvement (11.45%). Concurrent validity was supported in that subjects' ($\underline{n}$=123) scores on the PSI correlated with their responses to the Sport Competition Anxiety Test ($\underline{r}$=.56).

Norms: Not cited. Psychometric properties were reported for 123 youth sport participants, ages 12-18, with 1-13 years experience in youth sport.

Availability: Contact John M. Silva, Department of Physical Education, CB #8700, Fetzer Gym, University of North Carolina, Chapel Hill, NC 27599-8700. (Phone # 919-962-0017)

Reference

*Finch, L., Silva, J., & Hardy, C. (1988). An assessment of the factor validity of the Precompetitive Stress Inventory (abstract). Nashua, NH: Proceedings of the Association for the Advancement of Applied Sport Psychology.

(27)
PRE-RACE QUESTIONNAIRE (PRQ)
J. Graham Jones, Austin Swain, and Andrew Cale

Source: Jones, J. G., Swain, A., & Cale, A. (in press). Antecedents of multidimensional competitive state anxiety and self-confidence in elite intercollegiate middle-distance runners. The Sport Psychologist.

Purpose: To examine the antecedents of competitive state anxiety and self-confidence that exist prior to participating in a middle-distance running event.

Description: The PRQ contains 19 items that focus on situational variables perceived as contributing most to how runners feel during the period immediately preceding a race. (For example, "How important is it for you to do well in this race?") Subjects respond to each item using a 9-point ordinal scale.

Construction: The PRQ was developed using a series of structured interviews with middle-distance runners. Potential items were formulated from these interviews and administered to a group of middle-distance runners who assessed the suitability of the questions for such athletes. The 19 items that emerged from this review were evaluated in a pilot study of six middle-distance athletes prior to competition. Based on these athletes' feedback, adjustments were made to some items of the PRQ.

Reliability: Cronbach's alpha coefficients for the five factors (see validity section) ranged from .63 to .78 among 125 male middle-distance runners.

Validity: Principal component factor analysis using both varimax and oblique rotations supported the existence of five factors that were labeled Perceived Readiness, Attitude Toward Previous Performance, Position Goal, External Environment, and Coach Influence. These factors accounted for 63.10% of the variance in subjects' responses to the PRQ.

Stepwise multiple regression analyses indicated that subjects' ($n=125$) scores on the cognitive anxiety subscale of the Competitive State Anxiety Inventory-2 (administered one hour before a race) were predicted by the first three factors of the PRQ (identified above).

Norms: Not cited. Psychometric data were based on the responses of 125 male middle-distance runners (M age=22.18 years; SD=3.36). All subjects were elite intercollegiate runners.

Availability: Contact J. Graham Jones, Department of Physical Education and Sports Science, Loughborough University, Loughborough, Leicestershire, LE11 3TU, United Kingdom. (Phone # 0509-223287)

(28)
[SOURCES OF STRESS SCALE] [SSS]
Daniel Gould, Thelma Horn, and Janie Spreeman

Source: Gould, D., Horn, T., & Spreeman, J. (1983). Sources of stress in junior elite wrestlers. Journal of Sport Psychology, 5, 159-171.

Purpose: To assess perceived sources of competitive stress in wrestlers.

Description: Wrestlers respond to 33 items on a 7-point Likert scale in terms of how often a potential source of stress makes them nervous or worried.

Construction: Items were developed based on a previous review of the research literature on stress and athletics. The content validity of the items was established by two sport psychologists.

Reliability: A pilot research study produced a test-retest reliability coefficient of .74 for all items combined.

Validity: Principal component factor analysis of the responses of 458 elite wrestlers led to the identification of three factors: fear of failure-feelings of inadequacy, external control-guilt, and social evaluation. These factors accounted for 75%, 14%, and 11%, respectively, of the variance in the factorial model. Using multiple regression analyses, it was determined that subjects' scores on the Sport Competition Anxiety Test were predictive of the fear of failure-feelings of inadequacy factor.

Norms: Not reported. Psychometric data were cited for 458 elite wrestlers (ages 13-19) participating in the United States Wrestling Federation Junior National Championships.

Availability*: Contact Daniel Gould, Exercise and Sport Science Department, University of North Carolina, Greensboro, NC 27412. (Phone # 919-334-3037)

References

*Gould, D., & Weinberg, R. S. (1983). Sources of worry in successful and unsuccessful intercollegiate wrestlers (abstract). In Psychology of motor behavior and sport-1983 (p. 80). Proceedings of the North American Society for the Psychology of Sport and Physical Activity annual convention, Michigan State University, East Lansing, MI.

*Silva, J. M., & Hardy, C. J. (1984). Detecting and predicting perceptions of stress factors in senior elite wrestlers. Proceedings of the 1984 Olympic Congress (p. 104). Eugene, OR: College of Human Development and Performance Microform Publications.

(29)
SPORT ANXIETY INTERPRETATION MEASURE (SAD)
Dieter Hackfort

Source: Hackfort, D., & Schwenkmezger, P. (1989). Measuring anxiety in sports. Perspectives and problems. In D. Hackfort & C. D. Spielberger (Eds.), Anxiety in sports: An international perspective (pp. 55-74). New York: Hemisphere Publishing Corporation.

Purpose: To measure sport-specific trait anxiety among children across different sports.

Description: The SAD assesses fear of disgrace, fear of competition, fear of failure, fear of the unknown, and fear of injury using 22 items in the form of pictures. Response categories are also nonverbal (sketches of facial expressions portraying different degrees of anxiety).

Construction: Not discussed.

Reliability: Test-retest reliability coefficients ranged from .87 to .94.

Validity: Not discussed.

Norms: Not cited.

Availability*: Contact Dieter Hackfort, Institute for Sport, University of Heidelberg, Im Neuenheimer Feld 710, D-6900 Heidelberg, Federal Republic of Germany.

(30)
SPORT ANXIETY SCALE (SAS)
Ronald E. Smith, Frank L. Smoll, and Robert W. Schutz

Source: Smith, R. E., Smoll, F. L., and Schutz, R. W. (in press). Measurement and correlates of sport-specific cognitive and somatic trait anxiety: The Sport Anxiety Scale. Anxiety Research.

Purpose: To assess cognitive and somatic dimensions of competitive trait anxiety.

Description: The SAS is a 21-item questionnaire containing three subscales: Somatic Anxiety (9 items), Worry (7 items), and Concentration Disruption (5 items). Examples of items: "My body feels tight" (Somatic Anxiety), "I am concerned about choking under pressure" (Worry), and "My mind wanders during sport competition" (Concentration Disruption). Subjects respond to each item using a 4-point ordinal scale.

Construction: Some of the initial items of the SAS were developed from existing measures of cognitive and somatic anxiety. Pilot work led to the retention of 15 cognitive and 15 somatic items which were administered in questionnaire format to 250 male and 201 female high school athletes in basketball, wrestling, and gymnastics at 41 high schools; 123 college football players were also administered the questionnaire. Principal component factor analysis followed by varimax rotation led to the retention of three factors (somatic anxiety, worry, and concentration disruption) and 22 items which accounted for 48% of the variance in the high school samples, and 53% of the variance in the college football sample. Confirmatory factor analysis using the postseason data of 300 of these subjects supported a 22-item 3-factor model. However, cross-validiation with an independent sample (n=490) led to the elimination of one Concentration Disruption item.

Reliability: Cronbach alpha coefficients (n=490) were .88 (somatic), .82 (Worry), and .74 (Concentration Disruption). Test-retest reliability coefficients (n=64) over 7 days exceeded .85 across all scales.

Validity: Convergent validity was supported in that high school athletes' (n=837) responses to the SAS correlated with their responses to the Sport Competition Anxiety Test (particularly the Somatic scale), and to a lesser extent with their responses to Spielberger's State-Trait Anxiety Inventory. Predictive validity was evident in that football players' (n=47) scores on the SAS were predictive two weeks later of their pre-game Tension and Confusion subscale scores on a shortened version of the Profile of Mood States. In addition, football players (n=48) categorized as high or low on performance, based on coaches' gradings of game films over an entire season, differed on the Concentration Disruption scale.

Norms: Not presented. However, normative data were derived for 489 male and 348 female high school varsity athletes involved in one of six sports, and for 123 college football athletes competing at an NCAA Division I school.

Availability*: Contact Ronald E. Smith, Department of Psychology NI-25, University of Washington, Seattle, WA 98195. (Phone # 206-543-8817)

References

*Millhouse, J. I., Willis, J. D., & Layne, B. H. (1989). The clinical utility of three recent psychological instruments with advanced female gymnasts: A preliminary study (abstract). Proceedings of the Association for the Advancement of Applied Sport Psychology annual convention, Seattle, WA.

*Smith, R. E. (1989). Conceptual and statistical issues in research involving multidimensional anxiety scales. Journal of Sport & Exercise Psychology, 11, 452-457.

*Smith, R., Smoll, F., & Schutz, R. (1988). Reactions to competition: A sport-specific measure of cognitive and somatic trait anxiety (abstract). Proceedings of the Association for the Advancement of Applied Sport Psychology annual convention. Nashua, New Hampshire.

(31)
SPORT COMPETITION ANXIETY TEST (SCAT)
Rainer Martens, Dianne Gill, Tara Scanlan, and Julie Simon

Source: Martens, R., Vealey, R. S., & Burton, D. (1990). Competitive anxiety in sport (pp. 3-115). Champaign, IL: Human Kinetics Publishers, Inc.

Purpose: To assess individual differences in competitive trait anxiety, or the tendency to perceive competitive situations as threatening and/or to respond to these situations with elevated state anxiety.

Description: The SCAT contains 15 items. Subjects are asked to indicate how they generally feel when they compete in sports and games, and respond to each item using a three-point ordinal scale (hardly ever, sometimes, or often). Ten of the items assess individual differences in competitive trait anxiety proneness (e.g., "Before I compete I worry about not performing well"); five spurious items are also included to reduce possible response bias. Total scores on the SCAT range from 10 (low competitive trait anxiety) to 30 (high competitive trait anxiety).

The SCAT was developed as a research instrument, and its useful-ness as a diagnostic instrument for clinical evaluation has not been established. Both child (ages 10 thru 14) and adult versions of SCAT exist. Furthermore, SCAT has been translated into Spanish, French, German, Russian, Japanese, and Hungarian.

Construction: Psychometric development of the SCAT was guided by the theoretical conceptualization of competitive trait anxiety as a situation-specific form of anxiety proneness that mediates, in part, an individual's perceptions of and/or responses to threat within the competitive process. Several criteria guided the format of SCAT including the need for an objective rather than projective psychological test, the need to minimize response bias, the desirability of unambiguous administration procedures, a short completion time, and easy scoring procedures.

SCAT was initially constructed for use with children (ages 10 to 15). An initial pool of 75 items was developed by modifying items from existing general trait anxiety scales, and by adding additional sport-specific items. Based on item evaluations by six judges, a total of 21 items were retained (Version 1). The first version, consisting of 21 items retained from the original item pool plus 9 spurious items, was administered to 193 male junior high school students. Item analyses, correlation analyses between item responses and total SCAT scores, and discriminant analyses led to the retention of 14 items (Version 2). The second version, consisting of the 14 accepted items and 7 spurious items, was administered to two additional male junior high school samples ($\underline{N}=175$). Item analyses, triserial correlations, and discriminant analyses led to the retention of 10 items, which when combined with 5 spurious items, formed Version 3. The third version was administered to two samples: 106 male and female fifth and sixth graders, and 98 male and female junior high school students. Item analyses, triserial correlations, and discriminant analyses led to the final 15-item (including 5 spurious items) child form of SCAT.

An adult version of SCAT was developed by simply modifying the instructions, and by changing one word for one item. Item analyses, triserial correlations, and discriminant analyses, using a sample of 153 male and female university students, supported the item integrity of this adult version of SCAT.

Reliability: Test-retest reliability coefficients for the child form (SCAT-C) among four samples of boys and girls in grades 5, 6, 8, and 9 ranged from .57 to .93 (mean $\underline{r}=.77$) across four time intervals: 1 hour, 1 day, 1 week, and 1 month. ANOVA reliability coefficients, computed on the basis of the first test administrations among these four samples, were slightly higher (mean $\underline{r}=.81$) than the test-retest reliability coefficients reported. A higher ANOVA reliability coefficient ($\underline{r}=.85$) was obtained for the adult version of SCAT (SCAT-A) ($\underline{n}=153$).

Kuder-Richardson formula 20 (KR-20) internal consistency coefficients, computed for the four samples used to confirm the item integrity of

Version 3 of SCAT-C, and for two SCAT-A samples of 268 male and female undergraduate students, ranged from .95 to .97 for both forms of SCAT.

Validity: Content validity was evident during the initial item selection phase; six judges who were qualified researchers in sport psychology or motor learning, and who had either conducted or were knowledgeable about research on anxiety in sport, evaluated systematically the integrity of each item selected for Version 1 of SCAT-C. The convergent validity of SCAT was supported by showing that subject responses to SCAT were positively correlated to measures of sport-specific dispositions of fear of failure, ineffective attentional focus, and cognitive and somatic anxiety. Conversely, divergent validity was demonstrated by showing subject SCAT scores to be inversely related to sport-specific dispositions of need for power and self-confidence. Concurrent validity was also supported by the low, but statistically significant positive correlation coefficients with general measures of trait anxiety and external locus of control assessments, and negative correlation coefficients with internal locus of control and self-esteem measures. Generally, SCAT demonstrated stronger correlations with sport-specific measures than with general personality tests as hypothesized.

The predictive validity of SCAT was supported in that subject responses to SCAT related positively to future assessments of both general and competitive state anxiety. Subjects' SCAT scores correlated more highly with their competitive than noncompetitive A-state responses. A meta-analysis using the validity generalization model indicated that the average correlation coefficient between SCAT responses and competitive A-state was .61. Also, SCAT was a better predictor of athletes' A-state responses than were the coaches' ratings of their players.

However, the predictive validity of SCAT in relation to self-confidence and motor performance is equivocal. Furthermore, SCAT responses do not appear to be predictive of pre- and postcompetition performance expectancies.

Norms: Updated normative data on SCAT-C were provided for male and female youth sport participants ($\underline{n}$=1094), and on SCAT-A for male and female high school ($\underline{n}$=352) and college ($\underline{n}$=565) athletes. Also, normative data were provided on SCAT-A for baseball, basketball, football, soccer, swimming, tennis, volleyball, and wrestling participants.

Availability: Permission is granted by publishers of the Source, without written approval, for anyone to reproduce (but not publish) the SCAT for research purposes. SCAT can be found in the Source. The authors would like to receive reports of research findings resulting from use of the SCAT.

References

*Brand, H. J., Hanekom, J. D. M., & Scheepers, D. (1988). Internal consistency of the Sport Competition Anxiety Test. Perceptual and Motor Skills, 67, 441-442.

*Ostrow, A. C., & Ziegler, S. G. (1977). Psychometric properties of the Sport Competition Anxiety Test. In B. Kerr (Ed.), Human performance and behavior (pp. 139-142). Banff, Alberta: Proceedings of the 9th Canadian Psycho-motor Learning and Sport Psychology symposium.

*Rupnow, A., & Ludwig, D. A. (1981). Psychometric note on the reliability of the Sport Competition Anxiety Test. Research Quarterly for Exercise and Sport, 52, 35-37.

*Scanlan, T. K. (1978). Perceptions and responses of high- and low-competitive trait-anxious males to competition. Research Quarterly, 49, 520-527.

*Vealey, R. S. (1988). Competitive trait anxiety: Use and interpretation of the Sport Competition Anxiety Test (abstract). In Psychology of motor behavior and sport (p. 35). Proceedings of the North American Society for the Psychology of Sport and Physical Activity annual convention, Knoxville, TN.

(32)
SPORT PRESSURE CHECKLIST [SPC]
Brent S. Rushall and Cheyne A. Sherman

Source: Rushall, B. S., & Sherman, C. A. (1987). A definition and measurement of pressure in sport. The Journal of Applied Research in Coaching and Athletics, 2, 1-23.

Purpose: To assess elite athletes' perceptions of pressure prior to or during competition.

Description: The SPC contains 16 items and four subscales: Positive pressure, negative pressure, internal pressure, and external pressure. Items focus on areas such as coach expectations, audience effects, parental expectations, and the anticipated difficulty of the contest. Subjects respond to each item on a 7-point ordinal scale.

Construction: Items were derived based on a review of the stress and pressure research literature, an examination of stress and anxiety assessment tools, and interviews with 13 coaches. Item analyses ($\underline{n}=70$) and content analyses using 7 sport psychologists who had international coaching or competition experiences supported the retention of 16 items.

Reliability: Cronbach alpha internal consistency coefficients of .87 (internal subscale) and .82 (external subscale) were reported ($\underline{n}=70$). Test-retest reliability coefficients among 9 female and 9 male swimmers across one hour, one day, and two weeks ranged from .98 (Negative subscale-one day interval) to

.46 (Negative subscale-two-week interval).Test-retest reliability coefficients among 14 members of the Canadian Cross-country ski team across five different time intervals were all higher than .97. Similar encouraging results were reported among nine intercollegiate basketball players.

Validity: Content validity was established using 7 experts (above).

Norms: Not cited. Psychometric data were based on the responses of 70 elite athletes.

Availability*: Contact Brent S. Rushall, Department of Physical Education, San Diego State University, San Diego, CA. 92182-0171. (Phone # 619-594-4094)

Reference
Rushall, B. S. (1984). Pressure in olympic athletes-measurement and four case studies (abstract). Proceedings of the Canadian Society of Psychomotor Learning and Sport Psychology annual conference (p. 5). Kingston, Ontario, Canada.

(33)
WORRY COGNITION SCALE [WCS]
Maureen R. Weiss, Kimberley A. Klint, and Diane M. Wiese

Source: Weiss, M. R., Klint, K. A., & Wiese, D. M. (1989). Head over heels with success: The relationship between self-efficacy and performance in competitive youth gymnastics. Journal of Sport & Exercise Psychology, 11, 444-451.

Purpose: To assess worry cognitions about gymnastic performance and negative social evaluation among youth participants.

Description: The WCS contains two subscales: performance cognitions (9 items) and evaluation cognitions (8 items). However, given the correlation (.81) between subscales, a composite worry score is derived. Items specific to gymnastics include: "I worry about poor judging" and "I worry about doing better than another competitor." Subjects respond to each item on the WCS using a 5-point Likert scale.

Construction: The WCS was derived and adapted from previous sport-specific sources of stress and prematch cognition scales.

Reliability: Cronbach alpha reliability coefficients of .84 (performance cognition subscale) and .90 (evaluation cognition subscale) were reported.

Validity: Frequency of worry cognitions (in combination with self-efficacy, years of experience, and precompetitive anxiety) were predictive of the all-around gymnastic performance of 22 boys.

Norms: Not cited. Psychometric data were reported for 22 boys ranging in age from 7 to 18 years who were members of a competitive youth gymnastics club participating in the state gymnastics tournament.

Availability*: Contact Maureen R. Weiss, Department of Physical Education and Human Movement Studies, 131 Esslinger Hall, University of Oregon, Eugene, OR 97403. (Phone # 503-686-4108)

Chapter 4

ATTENTION

Three of the four instruments in this chapter are sport-specific versions of Nideffer's (1976) Test of Attention and Interpersonal Style. This instrument is based on a two-dimensional conceptual framework of attention containing broad/narrow and internal/external components. The instrument in this chapter developed by Etzel examines attention among elite rifle shooters from a multidimensional perspective.

(34)
BASEBALL TEST OF ATTENTIONAL AND INTERPERSONAL
STYLE (B-TAIS)
Richard R. Albrecht and Deborah L. Feltz

Source: Albrecht, R. R., & Feltz, D. L. (1987). Generality and specificity of attention related to competitive anxiety and sport performance. Journal of Sport Psychology, 9, 231-248.

Purpose: To assess attentional style as it relates to baseball/softball batting.

Description: The B-TAIS is a 59-item sport-specific version of Nideffer's (1976) Test of Attention and Interpersonal Style (TAIS). Six attentional subscales and the cognitive-information processing subscale from the TAIS were restructured to be specific to baseball/softball batting. The attentional subscales include: Broad external attention, External overload, Broad internal attention, Internal overload, Narrow attention, and Reduced attention.

Construction: All 59 items of the TAIS were converted to a baseball/softball batting-specific reference. As much of the TAIS context, grammatical structure, and wording were retained as was possible. Five experts who had used the TAIS in their research evaluated the revised items of the B-TAIS for content validity. Each item was also evaluated by an intercollegiate varsity baseball and softball coach.

Reliability: Cronbach's alpha internal consistency coefficients ($\underline{n}$=29) ranged from .50 (Reduced attention) to .85 (External overload). Test-retest reliability coefficients across a 2-week interval ranged from .72 (Internal overload) to .95 (Broad internal attention). None of the reliabilty coefficients statistically exceeded those computed for the TAIS.

Validity: Convergent validity was supported in that subjects' ($\underline{n}$=29) scores on the B-TAIS correlated .50 with their scores on the TAIS. Construct validity was supported in that subjects' scores on designated subscales of the B-TAIS correlated with their competitive trait anxiety scores. Also, subjects' scores on the B-TAIS were predictive of their seasonal batting performance scores.

Norms: Not cited. Psychometric data were based on the responses of 15 male varsity intercollegiate baseball players and 14 female varsity intercollegiate softball players attending Michigan State University.

Availability: Contact Deborah L. Feltz, Department of Physical Education, I. M. Sports Circle, Room 138, Michigan State University, East Lansing, MI 48824. (Phone # 517-355-4732)

Reference
Nideffer, R. M. (1976). Test of Attentional and Interpersonal Style. Journal of Personality and Social Psychology, 34, 397-404.

(35)
RIFLERY ATTENTION QUESTIONNAIRE (RAQ)
Edward F. Etzel, Jr.

Source: Etzel, E. F., Jr. (1979). Validation of a conceptual model characterizing attention among international rifle shooters. Journal of Sport Psychology, 1, 281-290.

Purpose: To assess the attentional style of elite rifle shooters.

Description: The RAQ is a 25-item self-report test containing five attention subscales: Capacity, Duration, Intensity, Flexibility, and Selectivity. Subjects respond to each item using a four-point Likert scale.

Construction: An original pool of 60 items was derived by the author using an intuitive-rational strategy plus a general item-developmental approach. All items were derived based on a hypothesized multi-dimensional conceptual model of attention in elite shooters. Two judges with background experience in both psychology and riflery assigned each item to the appropriate hypothesized subscale. Based on their review, 30 items were retained of which 25 items were included in the RAQ.

Reliability: Alpha reliability coefficients (n=71 elite rifle shooters) ranged from .10 (Capacity) to .82 (Selectivity).

Validity: The construct validity of the RAQ was partially supported through principal component factor analysis in which four of the five hypothesized attention factors emerged accounting for 85% of the variance in subjects' (n=71) responses to the RAQ. The predictive validity of the RAQ was partially supported. Elite shooters, classified as successful or unsuccessful based on 3-day smallbore shooting aggregate scores at the 1978 United States World Shooting Championship Team Tryouts, could not be distinguished based on their RAQ scores. However, multiple regression analysis supported the low but statistically significant relationship of these subjects' scores on Selectivity and Intensivity to their shooting performances.

Norms: Psychometric data were cited for 71 elite rifle shooters who represented 75% of the foremost male and female international rifle shooters in the United States.

Availability: Contact Edward F. Etzel, Department of Sport and Exercise Studies, 265 Coliseum, West Virginia University, Morgantown, WV 26506-6116. (Phone # 304-293-3295)

Reference
*Boutcher, S. H., & Crews, D. J. (1984). Multidimensional attentional measures of collegiate golfers (abstract). Proceedings of the 1984 Olympic Scientific Congress. Eugene, OR: College of Human Development and Performance Microform Publications.

(36)
TENNIS TEST OF ATTENTIONAL AND INTERPERSONAL STYLE (T-TAIS)
Stephen R. Van Schoyck and Anthony F. Grasha

Source: Van Schoyck, S. R., & Grasha, A. F. (1981). Attentional style variations and athletic ability: The advantages of a sports-specific test. Journal of Sport Psychology, 3, 149-165.

Purpose: To assess the attentional style of tennis players

Description: The T-TAIS is a 59-item sport-specific version of Nideffer's (1976) Test of Attention and Interpersonal Style (TAIS). Six attentional scales and one control scale from the TAIS were restructured to be tennis-specific. These scales include: Broad external attention, external overload, broad internal attention, internal overload, narrow attention, reduced attention, and information processing.

Construction: A rational approach to test construction was employed. Two item writers, one male and one female, with extensive backgrounds in tennis and psychology, converted the items from the TAIS to describe analogous situations in tennis. The writers independently listed their first association to tennis for each TAIS item, resulting in the retention of 39 common items. The remaining 20 items were included after extensive discussion and final agreement among the writers.

Reliability: Alpha reliability coefficients ($\underline{n}$=45 male tennis players; $\underline{n}$=45 female tennis players) ranged from .16 (Reduced attention) to .83 (Narrow attention; Internal overload). Test-retest reliabilty coefficients ($\underline{n}$=83 tennis players) across a mean test-retest interval of 29.2 days ($\underline{SD}$=17.1) ranged from .68 (Reduced attention) to .91 (External overload). All reliability coefficients were higher than those obtained for the TAIS among these subjects (except for the reduced attention scale).

Validity: Principal component factor analysis ($\underline{n}$=90) led to the retention of two primary factors accounting for 79.2% of the variance. Evaluation of these two factors led to the interpretation that bandwidth was multidimensional and not bipolar as suggested by Nideffer; the direction of attention dimension did not appear as a strong component of subjects' responses.

   The T-TAIS differentiated better among tennis skill levels ($\underline{n}$=90) than the TAIS. Furthermore, the T-TAIS better predicted match play tennis performance among advanced tennis players ($\underline{n}$=14 male intercollegiate tennis players) than did the TAIS.

Norms: Psychometric data were presented for 45 male and 45 female tennis players solicited from two local tennis clubs, public tennis facilities in Cincinnati, and the University of Cincinnati men's and women's tennis teams. ($\underline{M}$ age=29 years; $\underline{SD}$=9.8)

Availability*: Contact Stephen R. Van Schoyck, Behavioral Medicine Group, 340 E. Maple Ave., Suite 303, Langhorne, PA 19047. (Phone #215-752-7111).

Reference
Nideffer, R. M. (1976). Test of Attentional and Interpersonal Style. Journal of Personality and Social Psychology, 34, 397-404.

(37)
TEST OF SOCCER ATTENTIONAL STYLE (TSAS)
A. Craig Fisher and Adrian H. Taylor

Source: Fisher, A. C., & Taylor, A. H. (1980). Attentional style of soccer players (abstract). Reston, VA: Research abstracts-American Alliance for Health, Physical Education, Recreation, and Dance (p. 71). Annual convention, Detroit, MI.

Purpose: To assess assess attentional style as it relates specifically to soccer performance.

Description: The 72-item TSAS contains the six scales of Nideffer's (1976) TAIS, but is operationally defined to soccer. These scales include broad external focus, broad internal focus, overload external focus, overload internal focus, narrow effective focus, and underinclusive focus. Subjects respond to each item using a 5-point ordinal scale, with the anchorings never to always.

Construction; Not discussed.

Reliability: Alpha internal consistency coefficients ranged from .67 to .83 across the six subscales (n=104). Test-retest reliability coefficients ranged from .81 to .92.

Validity: The TSAS more effectively discriminated between high and low ability soccer players than did Nideffer's (1976) more general Test of Attentional and Interpersonal Style.

Norms: Not cited. Psychometric data were based on 104 college soccer athletes.

Availability: Contact A. Craig Fisher, Exercise and Sport Sciences Department, Ithaca College, Ithaca, New York 14850. (Phone # 607-274-3112)

References
Fisher, A. C. (1984). Specificity of attention in sport: The data speak clearly (abstract). Proceedings of the Canadian Society of Psychomotor Learning and Sport Psychology annual conference (p. 3). Kingston, Ontario, Canada.

Nideffer, R. M. (1976). Test of Attentional and Interpersonal Style. Journal of Personality and Social Psychology, 34, 397-404.

Wilson, V. E., & Parolini, J. (1984). Assessment and training of soccer players (abstract). Proceedings of the Canadian Society of Psychomotor Learning and Sport Psychology annual conference (p. 5). Kingston, Ontario, Canada.

Chapter 5

ATTITUDES TOWARD EXERCISE AND PHYSICAL ACTIVITY

Tests in this chapter assess attitudes of children, college students, physical education teachers, and other groups toward the values of participating in exercise and related physical activities. Attitudinal beliefs among nonexercisers are also evaluated.

(38)
ATTITUDE TOWARD PHYSICAL ACTIVITY INVENTORY (ATPA)
Gerald S. Kenyon

Source: Kenyon, G. S. (1968). Six scales for assessing attitude toward physical activity. Research Quarterly, 39, 566-574.

Purpose: To assess the perceived instrumental value held for physical activity.

Description: The ATPA assesses values held for physical activity participation in terms of physical activity as a social experience, as a catharsis, as a form of health and fitness, as the pursuit of vertigo, as an aesthetic experience, and as an ascetic experience. Both Likert and semantic differential versions of the ATPA are available.

Construction: The construct validities of two initial conceptual models characterizing the perceived instrumental (satisfaction) values held for physical activity were examined based on the factor analyses of the responses of independent samples (n=756 college students; n=100 college students; n=176 college students) to 73 Likert-type attitude statements. Partial support was found for the second conceptual model in terms of physical activity as a social experience, as a form of health and fitness, as the pursuit of vertigo, and as an aesthetic experience, but not as a recreational or competitive experience.

A third model, in which the subdomains of physical activity as an ascetic experience and as a catharsis were added, was examined based on the responses of 355 male and 215 female college students to 42 Likert-type items thought to be representative of each subdomain. Separate inventories for men and women were developed.

73

Reliability: Hoyt reliability (internal consistency) coefficients ranged from .70 (social experience) to .89 (pursuit of vertigo) among 215 female and 353 male college students.

Validity: The construct validity of the third model was supported through factor analyses. Five of the six scales discriminated between appropriate high and low preference groups in terms of values held for physical activity.

Norms: Not presented. Psychometric data cited were based on the responses of independent samples of 200-360 male and female college students.

Availability*: Contact Gerald Kenyon, Department of Sociology, University of Lethbridge, 4401 University Drive, Lethbridge, Alberta, Canada T1K3M4.

References

*Dotson, C. O., & Stanley, W. J. (1972). Values of physical activity perceived by male university students. Research Quarterly, 43, 148-156.

*Onifade, S. A. (1985). Relationship among attitude, physical activity behavior and physical activity belief of Nigerian students toward physical activity. International Journal of Sport Psychology, 16, 183-192, 1985.

*Singer, R., Eberspaecher, H., Rehs, H-J., & Boss Kl. (1978). Experience with a German version of the Kenyon-Scale (ATPA). In U. Simri (Ed.), Proceedings of the International Symposium on Psychological Assessment in Sport (pp. 171-180). Netanya, Israel: Wingate Institute for Physical Education and Sport.

*Smoll, F. L., Schutz, R. W., Wood, T. M., & Cunningham, J. K. (1979). Parent-child relationships regarding physical activity attitudes and behaviors. In G. C. Roberts and K. M. Newell (Eds.), Psychology of motor behavior and sport-1978 (pp. 131-143) Champaign, IL: Human Kinetics Publishers.

*Williams, L. R. T., & Coldicott, A. G. (1982). High school students: Their self-esteem, body esteem and attitudes toward physical activity. New Zealand Journal of Health, Physical Education, and Recreation, 15, 62-65.

(39)
[ATTITUDE TOWARD WARM-UPS SCALE] [AWS]
Judith L. Smith and Margaret F. Bozymowski

Source: Smith, J. L., & Bozymowski, M. F. (1965). Effect of attitude toward warm-ups on motor performance. Research Quarterly, 36, 78-85.

Purpose: To evaluate attitudes of college women toward the value of the warm-up prior to motor performance.

Description: The scale contains 34 items. Subjects respond using a 5-point Likert scale.

Construction: Responses to 42 statements pertaining to warm-ups in relation to performance, endurance, injury, fatigue, and efficiency while participating in sports were evaluated among 200 college women using the Flanagan Index of Discrimination. A total of 34 items were retained.

Reliability: A coefficient of equivalence of .94 was reported among 100 college women.

Validity: Discriminant validity was supported in that college women ($\underline{n}=86$) with more favorable attitudes toward warm-up performed better in an obstacle race than women with less favorable attitudes, when warm-ups were given prior to the race.

Norms: Not reported. Psychometric data reported were based on the responses of 186 college women.

Availability*: The scale is presented in the original Source.

(40)
[ATTITUDES TOWARD EXERCISE AND PHYSICAL ACTIVITY]
[AEPA]
Barry D. McPherson and M. S. Yuhasz

Source: McPherson, B. D., & Yuhasz, M. S. (1968). An inventory for assessing men's attitudes toward exercise and physical activity. Research Quarterly, 39, 218-220.

Purpose: To assess attitudes of individuals toward exercise and physical activity.

Description: The attitude inventory contains 50 items. Subjects respond using a 5-point Likert scale.

Construction: The investigators compiled a series of statements depicting common opinions, beliefs, attitudes, and fallacies about exercise and physical activity. Statements which appeared irrelevant or ambiguous were discarded.

Reliability: A split-half odd-even corrected internal consistency coefficient of .95 was obtained among 25 male physical education teachers. A test-retest reliability coefficient ($n=25$) of .92 was reported across a 7-day interval.

Validity: A t-test indicated that the inventory successfully discriminated between male physical education teachers ($n=25$) and a group of male teachers ($n=20$) identified by the physical education teachers as having unfavorable attitudes twoard exercise and physical activity.

Norms: Not cited.

Availability: See McPherson, B. D. (1965). The psychological effects of exercise for normal and post-cardiac males. Unpublished master's thesis, University of Western Ontario, London, Ontario, Canada. (Available through interlibrary loan.)

Reference
*McPherson, B. D., Paivio, A., Yuhasz, M. S., Rechnitzer, P. A., Pickard, H. A., & Lefcoe, N. M. (1967). Psychological effects of an exercise program for post-infarct and normal adult men. The Journal of Sports Medicine and Physical Fitness, 7, 95-102.

(41)
[ATTITUDES TOWARD JOGGING QUESTIONNAIRE] [AJQ]
Patricia K. Riddle

Source: Riddle, P. K. (1980). Attitudes, beliefs, behavioral intentions, and behaviors of women and men toward regular jogging. Research Quarterly for Exercise and Sport, 51, 663-674.

Purpose: To assess attitudes toward and beliefs about jogging.

Description: The questionnaire was based on Fishbein's Behavioral Intention Model. The questionnaire contained 68 items of which 19 items measured the beliefs an individual had about the consequences (advantages/disadvantages) of jogging, and 19 items assessed the evaluation of the consequences corresponding to those beliefs. Seven items measured beliefs about the expectations of those referents who might approve or disapprove of jogging regularly. In addition, 14 attitudinal items were included in the questionnaire. Subjects responded to each of the 68 items using 7-point bipolar adjective scales that employed the semantic differential technique.

Construction: The questionnaire was based on the responses of 40 subjects to a pilot study concerning beliefs about participation in regular jogging. The subject pool consisted of an equal number of female and male joggers and nonexercisers.

Reliability: Test-retest reliability coefficients ($n=63$) ranged from .72 to .87 across the four derived summary scores.

Validity: Discriminant validity was demonstrated in that joggers ($n=100$ males and 49 females) were more likely than nonexercisers ($n=98$ males and 49 females) to believe that regular jogging would have positive effects, and they evaluated being in good physical and mental condition more positively than nonexercisers. Nonexercisers thought jogging required too much discipline, took too much time, and made them too tired. Furthermore, there was a positive relationship ($r=.82$) between the intention to jog and jogging behavior.

Norms: Not cited. Psychometric data were reported for 296 males and females, 30 years or older, who were either joggers ($n=149$) or nonexercisers ($n=147$).

Availability*: Unknown. Test items are not available in the Source.

(42)
[ATTITUDINAL BELIEFS REGARDING EXERCISE QUESTIONNAIRE] [ABEQ]
Gaston Godin, Roy J. Shephard, and Angela Colantonio

Source: Godin, G., Shephard, R. J., & Colantonio, A. (1986). The cognitive profile of those who intend to exercise but do not. Public Health Reports, 101(5), 521-526.

Purpose: To examine among people who intend to but do not exercise their attitudinal beliefs about exercise, their evaluation of the associated consequences, and their normative beliefs and motivation to comply with these norms.

Description: The ABEQ contains 14 items focusing on one's exercise beliefs (B) and values (V) (e.g., "I think that participation in active sports or vigorous physical activities long enough to get sweaty at least twice a week in my leisure time during the next two months would help me look younger"). In addition, the ABEQ contains 5 items focusing on normative beliefs (NB) regarding exercise, and 5 items focusing on the motivation to comply (MC). Subjects respond to all items on a 7-point scale (-3 to +3).

Construction: The theoretical framework of the questionnaire was based on Fishbein-Ajzen's model of behavioral intentions.

Reliability: Internal consistency coefficients were reported as .71 (B), .74 (V), .67 (NB), and .72 (MC).

Validity: There were few differences on the ABEQ among individuals with positive intentions to exercise who eventually did exercise, versus individuals with positive intentions to exercise who did not then participate in exercise.

Norms: Not cited. Psychometric data were based on the responses of 163 male and female employees (M age = 39 years) obtained from a larger survey on corporate fitness.

Availability*: Contact Gaston Godin, School of Nursing, Laval University, Quebec, Canada G1K 7P4.

(43)
CHILDREN'S ATTITUDES TOWARD PHYSICAL ACTIVITY INVENTORY (CATPA)
Robert W. Schutz, Frank L. Smoll, and Terry M. Wood

Source: Schutz, R. W., Smoll, F. L., Carre, F. A., & Mosher, R. E. (1985). Inventories and norms for children's attitudes toward physical activity. Research Quarterly for Exercise and Sport, 56, 256-265.

Purpose: To assess among children the perceived instrumental value held for physical activity.

Description: The CATPA utilizes a semantic differential format. Attitudes children hold regarding physical activity participation are assessed within seven subdomains or scales: physical activity as an aesthetic experience, as the pursuit of vertigo, as an ascetic experience, as a form of health and fitness, as a means of social growth, as a catharsis, and as a means of continuing social relations. Children are asked to respond to five bipolar adjectives on a five-point scale for each of these seven domains. The health and fitness domain, while a unitary concept, is scored separately for Health & Fitness: Value and Health & Fitness: Enjoyment.

Construction: The original CAPTA (Simon & Smoll, 1974) was an adaption of Kenyon's (1968) semantic differential Attitudes toward Physical Activity (ATPA) inventory, and was prepared for use with elementary school children. The current revised version is viewed as psychometrically superior and less time-consuming to administer, and is appropriate for individuals from ages 12 to adulthood (Schutz, personal communication, March 28, 1990).

Reliability: Alpha reliability coefficients ($n=1038$ males and females-grade 7; $n=857$ males and females-grade 11) ranged from .76 (Health) to .91 (Aesthetic) for grade 7 subjects, and from .77 (Health) to .94 (aesthetic) for grade 11 subjects. Reliability coefficients did not statistically differ as a function of gender. Test stability coefficients (Schutz & Smoll, 1986) ranged from .80 to .87 across a 6-month test-retest interval among grade 10 and 11 students.

Validity: The construct validity of the seven hypothesized attitude domains was supported through principal component factor analyses among the grade 7 ($n=1038$) and grade 11 ($n=857$) subjects. However, among 127 boys and 137 girls in grades 4, 5, and 6, there was no evidence of a relationship between subject attitudes toward physical activity and motor skill (running, jumping, and throwing). Furthermore, the correlation coefficients between attitudes and self-reported levels of actual participation in physical activity, while statistically significiant, were low.

Norms: Psychometric data were reported for 1038 males and females in grade 7, and 857 males and females in grade 11 from the Canadian province of British Columbia. Stratified random sampling techniques were used to select these subjects from 67 schools in the province.

Availability: Contact Robert W. Schutz, Department of Sport Science, University of British Columbia, 6081 University Blvd., Vancouver, British Columbia, V6T 1W5 Canada. (Phone # 604-228-2767)

References

Kenyon, G. S. (1968). Six scales for assessing attitude toward physical activity. Research Quarterly, 39, 566-574.

*Martin, C. J., & Williams, L. R. T. (1985). A psychometric analysis of an instrument for assessing children's attitudes toward physical activity. Journal of Human Movement Sciences, 11, 89-104.

*Schutz, R. W., & Smoll, F. L. The (in)stability of attitudes toward physical activity during childhood and adolescence. In B. D. McPherson (Ed.), Sport and aging (pp. 187-197). Champaign, IL: Human Kinetics.

*Schutz, R. W., Smoll, F. L., & Wood, T. M. (1981). A psychometric analysis of an inventory for assessing children's attitudes toward physical activity. Journal of Sport Psychology, 4, 321-344.

*Simon, J. A., & Smoll, F. L. (1974). An instrument for assessing children's attitudes toward physical activity. Research Quarterly, 45, 407-415.

(44)
[PERCEPTIONS OF MOVEMENT ACTIVITIES QUESTIONNAIRE]
[PMAQ]
Linda L. Bain

Source: Bain, L. L. (1979). Perceived characteristics of selected movement activities. Research Quarterly, 50, 565-573.

Purpose: To assess individual differences in perceptions of the meaning of various physical activities.

Description: Subjects respond to one or more physical activities related to sport, dance or exercise using a semantic differential technique. The subject must differentiate between 21 bipolar adjectives using a 9-point ordinal scale.

Construction: In a pilot study, 67 college students rated 25 physical activities on 21 word pairs. These word pairs were derived from a literature review of conceptual models characterizing values or motives for participating in physical activity. A factor analysis of their responses led to the retention of four factors accounting for 38.7% of the variance. Only word pairs loading .40 or greater on one of these factors were retained.

Reliability: Not reported.

Validity: Alpha and incomplete principal components factor solutions led to the retention of 7 factors accounting for 37.19% of the variance.

Norms: Psychometric data were presented for 1,435 students enrolled in the physical education basic instructional program at a large urban university in the southwestern United States.

Availability: Contact Linda L. Bain, School of Communication and Professional Studies, California State University, 18111 Nordhoff St., Northridge, CA 91330. (Phone # 818-885-3001)

Chapter 6

ATTITUDES/VALUES TOWARD SPORT

Tests in this chapter assess the attitudes of sport participants towards the values of sport participation, professional versus play orientations expressed during sport participation, sportsmanship attitudes, and the values youth sport coaches hold regarding the potentional outcomes of competition for children.

(45)
[ATTITUDES TOWARD THE RECEIPT OF AN ATHLETIC SCHOLARSHIP QUESTIONNAIRE] [ARASQ]
Sharon A. Mathes, Shirley J. Wood, Charlene E. Christensen, and James E. Christensen

Source: Mathes, S. A., Wood, S. J., Christensen, C. E., & Christensen, J. E. (1979). An exploratory analysis of the attitudinal impact of awarding athletic scholarships to women. Research Quarterly, 50, 422-428.

Purpose: To assess the attitudes of female athletes toward receiving or not receiving an athletic scholarship.

Description: The questionnaire contains 86 items. Subjects respond to each item using a 5-point Likert scale.

Construction: The items were derived from a literature review on cognitive dissonance theory.

Reliability: Alpha reliability coefficients ($n=61$ female athletes) of .84, .77, and .80 were reported for three derived factors.

Validity: Factor analysis led to the retention of three factors that centered on (a) effect of scholarships on the sport, (b) athletes' attitudes toward their coaches, and (c) athletes' attitudes about team relationships and individual performances.

Norms: Not cited. Psychometric data were reported for 61 female athletes representing 10 teams at one midwestern university.

Availability*: Contact Sharon Mathes, Department of Physical Education and Leisure, Iowa State University, Ames, IA 50010. (Phone # 515-294-8766)

(46)
[ATTITUDES TOWARD THE REFEREE QUESTIONNAIRE] [ATRQ]
J. H. A. Van Rossum, C. R. Van der Togt, and H. A. Gootjes

Source: Van Rossum, J. H. A., Van der Togt, C. R., & Gootjes, H. A. (1984). The acceptance of referees' decisions in field hockey. International Journal of Sports Medicine, 5 (Supplement 1), 212-213.

Purpose: To examine the opinions held by referees and players regarding the practices of the referee in field hockey.

Description: The ATRQ contains 106 items. Cluster analysis identified 22 items (Cluster 1) focusing on "the degree to which the referee could be influenced" (p. 212), and 11 items (Cluster 2) focusing on "the influence of the referee" (p. 212) on the course of the game.

Construction: Not discussed.

Reliability: Kuder-Richardson (Formula 20) internal consistency coefficients were .75 and .69, for clusters 1 and 2, respectively.

Validity: Not cited.

Norms: Not presented. Psychometric data were based on the responses of 169 male and 47 female field hockey referees, and 154 male and 153 female field hockey players representing all levels of nationally organized field hockey competition in The Netherlands.

Availability*: Contact J. H. A. Van Rossum, Free University of Amsterdam, Interfaculty of Human Movement Science and Education, Department of Psychology, Amsterdam, The Netherlands.

(47)
COACHING OUTCOME SCALE (COS)
Rainer Martens and Daniel Gould

Source: Martens, R., & Gould, D. (1979). Why do adults volunteer to coach children's sports? In G. C. Roberts and K. M. Newell (Eds.), Psychology of motor behavior and sport-1978 (pp. 79-89). Champaign, Il.: Human Kinetics Publishers.

Purpose: To assess volunteer youth sport coaches' preferences for the outcomes of winning, having fun, and socialization for children involved in youth sport.

Description: The COS contains three items, with each item having three response alternatives (i.e., the three outcomes). Subjects are asked to indicate their most and least preferred alternatives for each item.

Construction: Based on a content analysis of the youth sport literature, and from interviews and observations of coaches, the three outcome categories were developed. The content validity of the COI was verified by 12 prominent sport psychologists with 100 percent confirmation that the alternatives for each item correctly assessed the intended outcomes.

Reliability: Test-retest reliability coefficients across a one-week interval were .89 (winning), .77 (fun), and .77 (socialization).

Validity: Not presented.

Norms: Not cited. Descriptive data were presented for 423 youth sport coaches representing eight sports in communities of three different sizes in Illinois and Missouri.

Availability: Contact Rainer Martens, Human Kinetics Publishers, Box 5076, Champaign, IL 61820. (Phone # 217-351-5076)

(48)
GAME ORIENTATION SCALE [GOS]
Annelies Knoppers

Source: Knoppers, A., Schuiteman, J., & Love, B. (1986). Winning is not the only thing. Sociology of Sport Journal, 3, 43-56.

Purpose: To assess professional and play orientations toward sport.

Description: The GOS contains two contrasting scenarios: participation in a recreational sport situation and participation in a competitive situation. Subjects are asked to rate each scenario in terms of how important they feel it is to win, to play fairly, to play well, and to have fun. Subjects respond to each area using a 5-point Likert scale.

Construction: The GOS is a modification of Webb's (1969) Professionalization Scale.

Reliability: Alpha internal consistency coefficients were .77 for the recreational sport situation and .82 for the competitive sport situation. Test-retest reliability coefficients were .56 and .60 for the recreational sport situation and the competitive sport situation, respectively.

Validity: Exploratory factor analysis indicated that both scenarios produced similar constructs varying only in the amount of explained variance.

Norms: Descriptive data were cited, categorized by race, gender, and athletic status for 910 high school students representing 9 schools in Missouri and 6 schools in Texas.

Availability: Contact Annelies Knoppers, Health and Physical Education Department, 131 IM Sports Circle, Michigan State University, East Lansing, MI 48824 (Phone # 517-355-4731)

References
*Knoppers, A., Zuidema, M., & Meyer, B. B. (1989). Playing to win or playing to play? Sociology of Sport Journal, 6, 70-76.
Webb, H. (1969). Professionalization of attitudes toward play among adolescents. In G. S. Kenyon (Ed.), Aspects of contemporary sport sociology (pp. 161-187). Chicago, IL: Athletic Institute.

(49)
ORIENTATIONS TOWARD PLAY SCALE [OTP]
Harry Webb

Source: Webb, H. (1969). Professionalization of attitudes toward play among adolescents. In G. S. Kenyon (Ed.), Aspects of contemporary sport sociology (pp. 161-187). Chicago, IL: Athletic Institute.

Purpose: To assess attitudes toward playing a game in terms of skill, fairness, and success.

Description: The OTP contains three items focusing on subject perceptions of skill, fairness, and success in sport. Subjects respond on a 3-point ordinal scale to whether they feel playing as well as you can, beating the other player or team, or playing the game fairly is most important.

Construction: Not discussed.

Reliability: Test-retest reliability coefficients were above .90 among 920 public and 354 parochial students.

Validity: Not discussed.

Norms: Descriptive and psychometric data were cited for 920 public and 354 parochial male and female students, stratified by grade level (grades 3,6,8,10,12), from Battle Creek, Michigan.

Availability*: OTP items can be found in the Source.

References
Albinson, J. G. (1974). Professionalized attitudes of volunteer coaches toward playing a game. International Review of Sport Sociology, 9(2), 77-87.

Hoffman, S. J., & Luxbacher, J. A. (1983). Competitive attitude and religious belief (abstract). In Psychology of motor behavior and sport (p. 120). Proceedings of the North American Society for the Psychology of Sport and Physical Activity annual convention, East Lansing, MI.

McElroy, M. (1983). Parents as significant others: Behavioral involvement and children's sport orientations (abstract). In Psychology of motor behavior and sport (p. 136). Proceedings of the North American Society for the Psychology of Sport and Physical Activity annual convention, East Lansing, MI.

*McElroy, M. A., & Kirkendall, D. R. (1980). Significant others and professionalized sport attitudes. Research Quarterly for Exercise and Sport, 51, 645-653.

*Snyder, E. E., & Spretzer, E. (1979). Orientations toward sport: Intrinsic, normative, and extrinsic. Journal of Sport Psychology, 1 170-175.

(50)
PURPOSES OF SPORT QUESTIONNAIRE [PSQ]
Joan L. Duda

Source: Duda, J. L. (1989). Relationship between task and ego orientation and the perceived purpose of sport among high school athletes. Journal of Sport & Exercise Psychology, 11, 318-335.

Purpose: To assess athletes' perceptions of the purposes of sport.

Description: Subjects read the stem "A very important thing sport should do," and then respond to 60 items (e.g., "make us loyal," or "make us mentally tough"). Subjects respond to each item using a 5-point Likert scale with the anchorings strongly disagree to strongly agree.

Construction: Items were developed by modifying relevant questions in the Purposes of Schooling Questionnaire (Nicholls, Patashnick, & Nolan, 1985), by reviewing the literature on the values and benefits of youth sport involvement, and through open-ended responses provided by high school students in a pilot investigation. Principal-components factor analyses (n=322) followed by both varimax and oblique rotations resulted in the retention of seven factors accounting for 81% of the variance. These factors were labeled Mastery/cooperation, Physically active lifestyle, Good citizen, Competitiveness, High status career, Enhance self-esteem, and Enhance social status.

Reliability: Cronbach alpha internal consistency coefficients (n=321) ranged from .75 to .83 across the seven factors.

Validity: Discriminant validity was supported in that male students believed competitiveness, social status, and high status career opportunities to be more important purposes of sport participation than did female students; conversely, female students perceived mastery/cooperation to be a more important purpose of sport than did males.

Norms: Not cited. Psychometric data were reported for 128 male and 193 female varsity interscholastic athletic participants from six high schools in a midwestern community. The students were in the 11th or 12th grades, and participated in sports such as basketball, track and field, tennis, and softball.

Availability: Contact Joan L. Duda, Department of PEHRS, 113 Lambert Hall, Purdue University, Lafayette, IN 47907. (Phone # 317-494-3172)

Reference

Nicholls, J., Patashnick, M., & Nolan, S. B. (1985). Adolescents' theories of education. Journal of Educational Psychology, 77, 683-692.

(51)
SPORT ATTITUDE QUESTIONNAIRE (SAQ)
Robert J. Smith, Donn W. Adams, and Elaine Cork

Source: Smith, R. J., Adams, D. W., & Cork, E. (1976). Socializing attitudes toward sport. The Journal of Sports Medicine and Physical Fitness, 16, 66-71.

Purpose: To evaluate and compare little league athletes with nonparticipants in terms of attitudes toward organization/authority, parental influence, aggression, the group experience, and other socializing factors.

Description: The SAQ contains 46 items. Subjects respond on a 7-point Likert scale.

Construction: Four researchers wrote a number of items pertinent to how they felt participants and nonparticipants would value differentially the little league experience. The items were modified to enhance their clarity and meaningfulness to preadolescents. A total of 86 items were administered to nine participants and eight nonparticipants of organized youth sport. Item analyses led to the retention of 15 items, the revision of 6 items, and the addition of 25 new items (based on 100 percent agreement among the four researcher-judges).

Reliability: Not discussed.

Validity: The SAQ discriminated between 52 male participants and 40 male nonparticipants, particularly in terms of items intuititvely labeled as "organization/authority." The nonparticipants consistently were opposed to adult-managed sport, and preferred friendly, informal games controlled by the players.

Norms: Not cited. Psychometric data were based on the responses of 52 male participants of organized youth sport leagues and 40 nonparticipants (M age= 10.75 years). These subjects resided in an American community, located in West Berlin, Germany.

Availability: Contact Robert J. Smith, Psychology Department, Hunterdon Development Center, Box 5220, Clinton, NJ 08809. (Phone # 201-735-4031)

(52)
[SPORTSMANSHIP ATTITUDE SCALES] [SAS]
Marion Lee Johnson

Source: Johnson, M. L. (1969). Construction of sportsmanship attitude scales. Research Quarterly, 40, 312-316.

Purpose: To assess sportsmanship attitudes of boys and girls in grades 7-9.

Description: Alternative forms A and B each contains 21 items.

Construction: The scale-discrimination technique was used to evaluate an initial set of 152 items descriptive of ethically critical sportsmanship behavior. These items were treated with the equal-appearing interval, summated rating, and scale analyses methods. Uni-dimensional scale rankings of the items were made by judges. Item analysis of half of the items judged least ambiguous were made among 208 junior high school boys and girls. Scale analysis led to the retention of 42 items, which were divided in half as alternative forms of the same test. A correlation coefficient ($n = 102$ 7-9 grade boys and girls) of .86 was reported among these equivalent forms.

Reliability: Not reported.

Validity: Correlation coefficients of .19 and .42 were reported when contrasting the composite scores of two groups of female junior high school students on the scale with their corresponding sportsmanship behavior as assessed by their instructors. However, correlation coefficients of -.01 and .16 were reported among male junior high school basketball players using the same criterion.

Norms: Not reported.

Availability*: Contact Marion Johnson, Health and Education Department, College of Education, Southeastern Louisana University, Box 670, Hammond, LA 70402. (Phone # 504-549-2129)

(53)
SPORTSMANSHIP ATTITUDES IN BASKETBALL QUESTIONNAIRE [SABQ]
Joan L. Duda, Linda K. Olson, and Thomas J. Templin

Source: Duda, J. L., Olson, L. K., & Templin, T. J. (in press). The relationship of task and ego orientation to sportsmanship attitudes and the perceived legitimacy of injurious acts. Research Quarterly for Exercise and Sport.

Purpose: To evaluate individuals' views regarding sportsmanship in basketball.

Description: The SABQ contains 22 items reflecting "unsportsmanlike" (e.g., faking an injury to stop the clock) and prosocial (e.g., helping a player up from the floor) behaviors. Subjects respond on a 5-point Likert scale with the anchorings strongly disapprove to strongly approve.

Construction: The SABQ is a basketball sport-specific version of Lakie's (1964) Competitive Attitude Scale. Four experts, with extensive experience in high school level basketball as players, coaches, and referees, developed the basketball-specific items. A principal component factor analysis with oblique rotation (n=56 male and n=67 female interscholastic basketball players) identified three factors accounting for 81.1% of the variance. These factors were labeled Unsportsmanlike Play/Cheating, Strategic Play, and Sportsmanship.

Reliability: Cronbach alpha internal consistency coefficients (n=123) were .80 (Unsportsmanlike Play/Cheating), .60 (Strategic Play), and .62 (Sportsmanship).

Validity: Discriminant validity was supported in that males scored higher than females on Unsportsmanlike Play/Cheating and Strategic Play, whereas females scored higher on Sportsmanship. Furthermore, canonical analysis revealed that a strong, negative emphasis on task orientation and a moderate, positive emphasis on ego orientation were correlated (r=.49) with an endorsement of unsportsmanlike play/cheating, thus supporting the concurrent validity of the SABQ.

Norms: Not available. Psychometric data were cited for 56 male and 67 female interscholastic basketball players representing five high schools in a midwestern community.

Availability: Contact Joan L. Duda, Department of Physical Education, Health, and Recreation Studies, 113 Lambert Hall, Purdue University, West Lafayette, IN 47907. (Phone # 317-494-3172)

Reference

Lakie, W. (1964). Expressed attitudes in various groups of athletes toward athletic competition. Research Quarterly, 35, 479-503.

(54)
SPORT SOCIALIZATION SUBSCALE (SSS)
Rainer Martens and Daniel Gould

Source: Martens, R., & Gould, D. (1979). Why do adults volunteer to coach children's sports? In G. C. Roberts and K. M. Newell (Eds.), Psychology of motor behavior and sport-1978 (pp. 79-89). Champaign, IL.: Human Kinetics Publishers.

Purpose: To examine the degree to which youth sport coaches emphasize the physical, psychological, and social outcomes of youth sport for children.

Description: The SSS contains three items, with each item having three response alternatives (i.e., the three outcomes). Subjects are asked to indicate their most and least preferred alternatives for each item.

Construction: Based on a content analysis of the youth sport literature, and from interviews and observations of coaches, socialization outcomes were derived. The content validity of the SSS was verified by 12 prominent sport psychologists with 100 percent confirmation that the alternatives for each item correctly assessed the intended outcomes.

Reliability: Test-retest reliability coefficients across a one-week interval were .70 (physical), .51 (psychological), and .76 (social).

Validity: Not presented.

Norms: Not cited. Descriptive data were presented for 423 youth sport coaches representing eight sports in communities of three different sizes in Illinois and Missouri.

Availability: Contact Rainer Martens, Human Kinetics Publishers, Box 5076, Champaign, IL 61820. (Phone # 217-351-5076)

(55)
SURVEY OF VALUES IN SPORT [SVS]
Dale D. Simmons and R. Vern Dickinson

Source: Simmons, D. D., & Dickinson, R. V. (1986). Measurement of values expression in sports and athletics. Perceptual and Motor Skills, 62, 651-658.

Purpose: To measure the role of personal values in sport.

Description: The SVS contains 14 sports-related values including Time-out, Energy release, Rewards, Being in a good place, Cooperation, Expressing feelings, Reaching personal limits, Group coordination, Winning, Physical pleasure, Being a good sport, Risk, Competition, and Maintaining good health. Respondents are asked to rank order the 14 values for a given sport, and then rate the importance of each value on a 14-point ordinal scale. A score for each value is derived by multiplying the rank times the rating.

Construction: Not discussed.

Reliability: Test-retest reliability coefficients (n=41 male and 54 female undergraduate students) ranged from .51 (Time-out) to .82 (Competition) over a two-week interval with an average coefficient of .65 reported across the 14 days.

Validity: A principal component factor analysis (n=95) of the SVS resulted in the retention of five factors accounting for 62.50% of the variance.

Norms: Not reported. Psychometric data were cited for 95 undergraduate students plus 21 female collegiate athletes representing two sports.

Availability*: Contact Dale D. Simmons, Department of Psychology, Oregon State University, Corvallis, OR 97331. (Phone # 503-754-2311)

Chapter 7

ATTRIBUTIONS

Tests in this chapter assess the explanations sport partici-pants give for their successes and failures in sport.

(56)
PERFORMANCE OUTCOME SURVEY (POS)
Larry M. Leith and Harry Prapavessis

Source: Leith, L. M., & Prapavessis, H. (1989). Attributions of causality and dimensionality associated with sport outcomes in objectively evaluated and subjectively evaluated sports. International Journal of Sport Psychology, 20, 224-234.

Purpose: To assess causal attributions athletes give to explain their sucesses and failures when competing in sport.

Description: The POS assesses the attributional dimensions of controllabil-ity, locus of control, and stability. Subjects are asked to recall vividly one successful and one unsuccessful athletic performance. They respond to three items per attributional dimension using a 7-point Likert scale.

Construction: The POS is a sport-specific version of Russell's (1982) Causal Dimensional Scale.

Reliability: Cronbach alpha internal consistency coefficients of .63 (control-lability), .74 (locus of control) and .83 (stability) were reported.

Validity: Not discussed.

Norms: Not cited. Psychometric data were based on the responses of 52 male and female athletes (ages 14 to 17 years) enrolled in an academic program for gifted athletes in a secondary school in Toronto, Canada.

Availability*: Contact Larry Leith, School of Physical and Health Education, University of Toronto, 320 Huron Street, Toronto, Canada M5S 1A1.

Reference

Russell, D. (1982). The Causal Dimension Scale: A measure of how individuals perceive causes. Journal of Personality and Social Psychology, 42, 1137-1145.

(57)
SOFTBALL OUTCOMES INVENTORY (SOI)
A. Craig Fisher and J. A. Soderlund

Source: Fisher, A. C., & Soderlund, J. A. (1985). Causal attributions to success and failure sport situations with self-confidence as a mediating factor (abstract). Proceedings of the Canadian Society of Psychomotor Learning and Sport Psychology annual convention (pp. 51-52). Montreal, Canada.

Purpose: To assess college female softball athletes' attributions for their success and failure in softball situations.

Description: The SOI presents athletes with 16 softball situations, each with varying degrees of success and failure. The athletes are asked to rate nine attributions (typical ability, task difficulty, effort expended, quality of opponents, ability expended, luck, typical effort, coaching, psychological state) on a scale of 1 to 5, indicating the degree to which each attribution accounted for each situation's outcome.

Construction: Not discussed.

Reliability: Not indicated.

Validity: Construct validity was supported in that ANOVA analyses indicated that individuals tend to attribute their successes to internal factors, while attributing their failures to external factors. However, individual differences scaling produced results that were not as conclusive. Furthermore, little relationship was found between subjects' responses to the SOI and their level of self-confidence.

Norms: Not presented. Psychometric data were based on the responses of 65 college female softball athletes.

Availability: Contact A. Craig Fisher, Department of Exercise and Sport Sciences, Ithaca College, Ithaca, NY 14850. (Phone # 607-274-3112)

(58)
SPORT ATTRIBUTIONAL STYLE SCALE (SASS)
Stephanie J. Hanrahan And J. Robert Grove

Source: Hanrahan, S. J, & Grove, J. R. (in press). Refinement of the Sport Attributional Style Scale. Journal of Sport Behavior.

Purpose: To assess attributional style in sport, based on subjective interpretatons of success and failure in sport.

Description: The SASS uses 7-point bipolar scales to measure the causal dimensions of stability, internality, controllability, globality, and intentionality. Separate attribution responses are required for eight positive and eight negative events. For each event, subjects are asked to vividly imagine themselves in the situation, to decide the single most likely cause of the event, and then they are asked to respond to questions about the cause and about the event. An example of a positive event presented is: "You perform well in a competition"; an example of a negative event is: "You are not selected for the starting team in an important competition." The positive and negative events are matched for content.

Construction: Not discussed.

Reliability: A mean alpha reliabilty coefficient (n=164 male and n=124 female college students) of .73 was reported, with alpha reliability coefficients at acceptable levels for all subscales (Hanrahan, 1888). Test-retest reliability coefficients (n=41) across a 5-week interval ranged from .54 to .63 for the positive events (mean reliability coefficient = .60), and from .46 to .80 for the negative events (mean reliability coefficient = .60).

Validity: Confirmatory factor analysis verified the hypothesized factor structure, supporting the construct validity of the SASS. Subjects'(n=288) scores on the SASS were also predictive of their scores on scales measuring achievement motivation and physical self-esteem (Hanrahan, 1988). Convergent validity was supported in that subjects' (n=55) responses to the SASS were correlated with their responses to the more global Attributional Style Questionnaire; these correlation coefficients ranged from .24 to .61 across dimensional subscales, with a mean coefficient of .42.

Norms: Not reported. Psychometric data were cited for 288 college students representing 40 different sports and all levels of participation, as well as 37 male and 59 female physical education undergraduate students.

Availability: Contact Stephanie J. Hanrahan, School of Physical Education, University of Otago, Box 56, Dunedin, New Zealand. (Phone # 024-798-991)

References

*Hanrahan, S. J. (1988). The development of a tool to measure attributional style in sport (abstract). In Psychology of motor behavior and sport (p. 13). Proceedings of the North American Society for the Psychology of Sport and Physical Activity annual convention, Knoxville, TN.

*Hanrahan, S. J., & Grove, J. R. (1989). Psychometric properties of a measure of sport-related attributional style. In Sport psychology and human performance (pp. 89-90). Proceedings of the 7th World Congress in Sport Psychology, Singapore.

*Hanrahan, S. J., & Grove, J. R. (1989). Intrinsic motivation and attributional style in sport: Does a relationship exist? In Sport psychology and human performance (pp. 89-90). Proceedings of the 7th World Congress in Sport Psychology, Singapore.

*Hanrahan, S. J., Grove, J. R., & Hattie, J. A. (1989). Development of a questionnaire measure of sport-related attributional style. International Journal of Sport Psychology, 20, 114-134.

(59)
WINGATE SPORT ACHIEVEMENT RESPONSIBILITY SCALE
(WSARS)
Gershon Tenenbaum, David Furst, and Gilad Weingarten

Source: Tenenbaum, G., Furst, D., & Weingarten, G. (1984). Attribution of causality in sport events: Validation of the Wingate Sport Achievement Responsibility Scale. Journal of Sport Psychology, 6, 430-439.

Purpose: To assess an athlete's enduring attitudes or expectations in attributing success and failure in sport.

Description: The WSARS includes two versions: one for team sport athletes and one for individual sport athletes. Each version is divided into successful (11 items) and unsuccessful (11 items) events. The items represent a wide range of negative and positive events in sport settings, such as interactions with coach, teammates, and audience, and perceived successful and unsuccessful athletic performance. Each item contains two alternatives: external or internal. For example, subjects are asked if "good results in sport are usually a result of luck or uncontrollable factors" or "the personal efforts invested by the participants." Athletes are asked to respond to each item on a 5-point ordinal scale, ranging from "0" (externality) to "5" (internality).

Construction: A total of 44 items (22 for successful and 22 for unsuccessful events) were developed from interactions with coaches, athletes, and sport psychologists, and the responses typically given for success and failure. Using the probabilistic Rasch model, and estimates of internal consistency, the pool of items was reduced to 22 items.

Reliability: Internal consistency coefficients, based on testing 107 adult athletes (69 participating in team sports and 39 in individual sports) from the Wingate School of Coaching in Israel, were reported as greater than .70 for each subscale (i.e., successful and unsuccessful events) for each test version (i.e., team sports versus individual sports).

Validity: Concurrent validity was supported in that low but statistically significant correlation coefficients were reported between subjects' ($\underline{n} = 107$) responses to the WSARS and the more general Rotter I-E scale.

Norms: Not reported. Psychometric data were reported for 107 adult athletes residing in Israel.

Availability: Contact Gershon Tenenbaum, Department of Research and Sport Medicine, Wingate Institute, Wingate Post, Netaya, Israel 42902. (Phone # 053 29400-7)

Reference

*Tenenbaum, G., & Furst, D. (1985). The relationship between sport achievement responsibility, atttribution and related situational variables. International Journal of Sport Psychology, 16, 254-269.

Chapter 8

BODY IMAGE

Tests in this chapter assess the attitudes of individuals toward their body appearance, structure, and movement. Tests assessing individual differences in body esteem and body satisfaction are also prominent.

(60)
BODY ATTITUDE SCALE (BAS)
Richard M. Kurtz

Source: Kurtz, R. M. (1969). Sex differences and variations in body attitudes. Journal of Consulting and Clinical Psychology, 33(5), 625-629.

Purpose: To assess an individual's general, overall global attitude or feeling about the outward form and appearance of his/her body.

Description: Three separate body attitudes (Evaluation, Potency, and Activity) are measured using a semantic differential technique. Subjects respond to 30 body concepts using nine bipolar 7-point adjective scales.

Construction: The BAS is a modification of Osgood's (Osgood et al., 1957) Semantic Differential.

Reliability: Not discussed.

Validity: The BAS discriminated among 89 male and 80 female undergraduate students. The females liked their bodies better than the males, and had a more clearly differentiated idea of what they liked and disliked about their bodies. The males viewed their bodies as more potent and more active than did the female students.

Norms: Not cited. Psychometric data were reported for 89 male and 89 female undergraduate Caucasians from predominantly middle-class backgrounds.

Availability: Contact Richard M. Kurtz, Department of Psychology, Box 1125,

Washington University, One Brookings Drive, St. Louis, MO 63130. (Phone # 314-889-6520)

References
*Collingwood, T. R., & Willett, L. (1971). The effect of physical training upon self-concept and body attitude. Journal of Clinical Psychology, 27,411-412.
*Kurtz, R. M. (1971). Body attitude and self-esteem (Summary). Proceedings of the 79th annual convention of the American Psychological Association, 6, 467-468.
*Kurtz, R., & Hirt, M. (1970). Body attitude and physical health. Journal of Clinical Psychology, 26, 149-151.
Osgood, C., Suci, G., & Tannenbaum, P. (1957). The measurement of meaning. Urbana, IL: University of Illinois Press.
*Van Denburg, E. J., & Kurtz, R. M. (1989). Changes in body attitude as a function of posthypnotic suggestions. The International Journal of Clinical and Experimental Hypnosis, 37, 15-30.

(61)
BODY CONSCIOUSNESS QUESTIONNAIRE [BCQ]
Lynn C. Miller, Richard Murphy, and Arnold H. Buss

Source: Miller, L. C., Murphy, R., & Buss, A. H. (1981). Consciousness of body: Private and public. Journal of Personality and Social Psychology, 41, 397-406.

Purpose: To assess individual differences in the awareness of internal body sensations and the external appearance of the body.

Description: The BCQ contains three subscales: Private Body Consciousness [PBC], Public Body Consciousness [PBCS], and Body Competence [BC]. The BCQ contains 15 items. For example, subjects are asked to respond to the item "I'm capable of moving quickly" (Body Competence). Subjects are asked to respond to each item on a 4-point ordinal scale with the anchorings extremely uncharacteristic to extremely characteristic.

Construction: Items were selected at face value that dealt with either the public or private aspects of the body. After pilot research, the final form was administered to 561 college men and 720 college women. Factor analysis of all subjects' responses revealed three factors (see subscales labeled above) accounting for 46% of the variance. These results were replicated among two new samples of 460 and 680 college students. Low intercorrelation coefficients ($\underline{n}=628$) were observed across the three defined factors.

Reliability: Test-retest reliability coefficients (n=130) over a 2-month interval were .69 [PBC], .73 [PBCS], and .83 [BC].

Validity: In terms of concurrent validity, the BCQ subscales generally evidenced low correlation coefficients (n=275 males, n=353 females) with the Self-Consciousness Inventory, but were not related to measures of social anxiety, hypochondriasis, or emotionality. Construct validity was evident, since college students who scored higher on the PBC subscale were more aware of the stimulating effects of caffeine than low scoring subjects.

Norms: Norms were presented for 568 college men and 731 college women on
each of the three subscales.

Availability: Contact Lynn C. Miller, GFS Hall, Communication Arts & Sciences, University of Southern California, Los Angeles, CA 91107 (Phone 213-743-5092)

Reference
*Skrinar, G. S., Bullen, B. A., McArthur, J. W., Check, J. M., & Vaughan, L. K. (1986). Effects of endurance training on body-consciousness in women. Perceptual and Motor Skills, 62, 483-490.

(62)
BODY ESTEEM SCALE [BES]
Stephen L. Franzoi and Stephanie A. Shields

Source: Franzoi, S. L., & Shields, S. A. (1984). The Body Esteem Scale: Multidimensional structure and sex differences in a college population. Journal of Personality Assessment, 49, 173-178.

Purpose: To examine individual differences in perceptions of body esteem.

Description: The BES contains 35 items focusing on such factors as perceived upper body strength and physical attractiveness in men, and perceived attractiveness and weight control in women. Subjects respond to each item using a 5-point Likert scale.

Construction: Principal component factor analyses of the responses of 366 female and 257 male undergraduate students to the Body Cathexis Scale led the authors to the conclusions that body esteem is multidimensional, and that there are gender differences in the factor structure of the Body Cathexis Scale. The BES was then constructed from 23 Body Cathexis Scale items, and 16 new items reflective of the derived factor structures within gender. A second principal component factor analysis was conducted with another sample of 483 undergraduate students ($\underline{n}$=301 females; $\underline{n}$=182 males). This analysis led to the re- tention of 35 items accounting for 39 percent (males) and 36 percent (females) of the variance in the 3-factor solution models derived.

Reliability: Alpha reliabilty coefficients of .81 (Attractiveness factor), .85 (Upper body strength factor), and .86 (General physical condition factor) were reported for 331 male undergraduate students. Similarly, alpha coefficients of .78 (Attractiveness), .87 (Weight concerns), and .82 (General physical condition) were reported for 633 female undergraduate students.

Validity: Convergent validity was demonstrated when correlating the responses of 44 male and 78 female undergraduate students to the BES with Rosenberg's Self-Esteem Scale. Discriminant validity was demonstrated in that anorexic women scored higher on the BES weight concern factor than non-anorexic women. Similarly, 39 male weightlifters scored higher on the factor of perceived upper body strength than 41 male nonweightlifters.

Norms: Presented for 331 males and 633 female undergraduate students for each of the three derived factors.

Availability*: Contact Stephen Franzoi, Department of Psychology, Marquette University, Milwaukee, WI 53233. (Phone # 414-224-1650)

(63)
BODY-ESTEEM SCALE [FOR CHILDREN] [BES-C]
Beverley Katz Mendelson and Donna Romano White

Source: Mendelson, B. K., & White, D. R. (1982). Relation between body-esteem and self-esteem of obese and normal children. Perceptual and Motor Skills, 54, 899-905.

Purpose: To assess children's affective evaluations of their bodies.

Description: The BES-C currently contains 20 items reflecting how children evaluate their appearance and body, and how they feel they are evaluated by others. Subjects respond yes or no to items such as "I wish I were thinner" and "Kids my own age like my looks."

Construction: Not discussed.

Reliability: A split half odd-even internal consistency coefficient of .85 was reported among 36 children ($\underline{n}$=15 males and $\underline{n}$=21 females), ages 7.5 to 12 years.

Validity: Concurrent validity was supported in that a correlation coefficient of .67 was obtain between these children's (n=36) scores on the BES-C and their corresponding scores on the Physical Appearance and Attributes component of the Piers-Harris Children's Self-concept Scale.

Norms: Not reported. Psychometric data were cited for 20 normal and 16 obese children residing in Montreal, Canada.

Availability: Contact Donna Romano White, Department of Psychology, Concordia University, 1455 De Maisonneuve Blvd. West, Montreal, Quebec, Canada H3G 1M8.

Reference
*Mendelson, B. K., & White, D. R. (1985). Development of self-body-esteem in overweight youngsters. Developmental Psychology, 21, 90-96.

(64)
BODY-IMAGE DISTORTION QUESTIONNAIRE [BIDQ]
Harriett M. Mable, Williams D. G. Balance, and Richard J. Galgan

Source: Mable, H. M., Balance, W. D. G., & Galgan, R. J. (1986). Body-image distortion and dissatisfaction in university students. Perceptual and Motor Skills, 63, 907-911.

Purpose: To assess subjects' perceptions of their body size.

Description: Subjects are asked to indicate the point which they thought represented their body size on a line ranging from "50% underweight" to "50% overweight," with the half-way point designated as "just right." Questions center on height, weight, and body build.

Construction: Not discussed.

Reliability: Test-retest reliability coefficients across a three-week interval were .83 (n=40 males), .89 (n=41 females), and .92 (the combined sample) (from Mable, Balance, & Galgan, 1988).

Validity: Concurrent validity was supported in that a correlation coefficient of .89 was obtained between subjects'(n=81) responses to the BIDQ and their actual body size (from Mable, Balance, and Galgan, 1988).

Norms: Not cited. Psychometric data were based on the responses of 40 male and 41 female undergraduate students.

Availability*: Contact Williams D. G. Balance, Department of Psychology, University of Windsor, 401 Sunset Ave., Windsor, Ontario, Canada N9B 3P4.

Reference
*Mable, H. M., Balance, W. D. G., & Galgan, R. J. (1988). Reliability and accuracy of self-report of a new body-image measure. Perceptual and Motor Skills, 66, 861-862.

(65)
BODY-IMAGE IDENTIFICATION TEST [BIIT]
Eleanor G. Gottesman and Willard E. Caldwell

Source: Gottesman, E. G., & Caldwell, W. E. (1966). The body-image identification test: A quantitative projective technique to study an aspect of body image. The Journal of Genetic Psychology, 108, 19-33.

Purpose: To measure feelings of masculinity-femininity as they relate to body image.

Description: The BIIT is a projective technique containing seven silhouette drawings of the human figure. Each subject is asked to choose which body and body part seem most like his or hers, and which body and body part he/she would prefer to have. The figures were scaled from 1 (most masculine) to 7 (most feminine).

Construction: In developing the figures, "the artist tried to incorporate some of the essential differentiating qualities between masculine and feminine attributes. . . ." (pp. 22-23).

Reliability: Not reported.

Validity: The BIIT discriminated among normal, disturbed, and slow learning subjects.

Norms: Not cited. Psychometric data were based on 21 female and 21 male slow learners (ages 13 to 17), 30 disturbed males (ages 8 to 11), and 31 normal males (ages 8 to 11).

Availability: Contact Willard E. Caldwell, Apt. #316, 1101 New Hampshire Ave., NW, Washington, DC 20037. (Phone # 202-223-0223, Ext. 316)

References
*Darden, E. (1972). Masculinity-femininity body rankings by males and females. The Journal of Psychology, 80, 205-212.

Darden, E. (1972). A comparison of body image and self-concept variables among various sport groups. Research Quarterly, 43, 7-15.

(66)
BODY-IMAGE QUESTIONNAIRE [BIQ]
Marilou Bruchon-Schweitzer

Source: Bruchon-Schweitzer, M. (1987). Dimensionality of the body-image. The Body-image questionnaire. Perceptual and Motor Skills, 65, 887-892.

Purpose: To assess perceptions, feelings, and attitudes induced by one's body, in terms of satisfaction, anxiety, accessibility, and sexual identity.

Description: The BIQ is a 19-item questionnaire in which subjects respond to bipolar adjective pairs using a 5-point Likert format.

Construction: A total of 65 male and 72 female high school students were interviewed and 300 words related to the body image were elicited. These words were grouped into 13 large categories containing antonyms and synonyms. Each category was illustrated by one or two items resulting in a 19-item questionnaire.

Reliability: The average test-retest reliability coefficient of the 19 items was .67 for a 10-day interval (n=89 male and female French students).

Validity: A principal factor analysis of the responses of 245 male and 374 female subjects (ages 10 to 40 years) to the French version of the BIQ (with communalities in the diagonals) yielded four axis (with 84.60% accountable variance). The first one was identified as Favourable Body Perceptions (with 29.21% accountable variance). Varimax rotations were carried out resulting in four meaningful factors. These factors were labeled Accessibility/closeness, Satisfaction/dissatisfaction, Activity/passivity, and Relaxation/tension.

Norms: Normative data were presented for 245 male and 374 female students, ages 10-40, residing in France.

Availability: Contact Marilou Bruchon-Schweitzer, Department of Psychology, U.F.R. des S.S.P., Universite de Bordeaux II, France.

(67)
BODY PARTS SATISFACTION SCALE (BPSS)
Ellen Berscheid, Elaine Waltser, and George Bohrnstedt

Source: Berscheid, E., Waltser, E., & Bohrnstedt, G. (1973). The happy American body: A survey report. Psychology Today, 7(6), 119-123, 126-131.

Purpose: To assess an individual's satisfaction with his or her body.

Description: The BPSS contains a list of 25 body parts and characteristics. Subjects rate their satisfaction/dissatisfaction with each body part and characteristic using a 6-point ordinal scale.

Construction: Not discussed.

Reliability: Not discussed.

Validity: Subjects' (n=2000) responses on the BPSS correlated positively with the Janis-Fiel-Eagley Self-Esteem Scale supporting convergent validity.

Norms: Presented for 1000 males and 1000 females categorized by three age groups--under 24, 25-44, and 45+ years.

Availability: Contact George Bohrnstedt, American Institutes for Research, Box 1113, 1791 Arastradero Road, Palo Alto, CA 94302. (Phone # 415-493-3550)

Reference
*Butters, J. W., & Cash, T. F. (1987). Cognitive-behavioral treatment of women's body-image dissatisfaction. Journal of Consulting and Clinical Psychology, 55, 889-897.

(68)
[BODY SATISFACTION SCALE] [BSS]
Gerald M. Rosen and Alan O. Ross

Source: Rosen, G. M., & Ross, A. O. (1968). Relationship of body image to self-concept. Journal of Consulting and Clinical Psychology, 32, 100.

Purpose: To evaluate a person's satisfaction with his/her physical appearance.

Description: The BSS contains a list of 24 body parts. Subjects are asked to indicate, using a 6-point Likert scale, how satisfied they are with the appearance of each body part, and how important that body part is to them.

Construction: Not discussed.

Reliability: Not cited.

Validity: Concurrent validity was supported in that the correlation coefficient between subjects' (n=82) responses to the BSS and the Gough Adjective Check List was .52, indicating a positive but low relationship between satisfaction with one's body image and satisfaction with one's self-concept.

Norms: Not cited. Psychometric data were based on the responses of 82 undergraduate students.

Availability: Contact Gerald M. Rosen, Cabrina Medical Tower, 901 Boren Ave., Suite 1910, Seattle, WA 98104. (Phone # 206-343-9474). Also can be obtained from ADI Auxilary Publications Project, No. 9756, Photoduplication Service, Library of Congress, Washington, DC 20540.

(69)
BODY-SELF RELATIONS QUESTIONNAIRE (BSRQ)
Thomas F. Cash and Barbara A. Winstead

Source: Cash, T. F., Winstead, B. A., & Janda, L. H. (1986). The great American shape-up. Psychology Today, 20(4), 30-34, 36-37.

Purpose: To assess feelings and attention paid toward one's appearance, health, and physical fitness, as well as how one rates the importance of various aspects of body image.

Description: The BSRQ is an attitudinal measure of body image that produces data on the attitudinal components of evaluation, attention/importance, and activity for the somatic domains of appearance, fitness, and health.

The BSRQ also provides a sexuality evaluation score. Subjects respond to 140 items using a 5-point Likert scale.

Construction: Not discussed.

Reliability: Cronbach alpha coefficients of .88 and .80 were reported for the Appearance Evaluation scale and the Body Areas Satisfaction scale, respectively (Cash, 1989).

Validity: The BSRQ discriminated among 1020 females and 980 males, in that female subjects evaluated themselves more negatively than the males across all body image areas.

Norms: Normative data were cited for 1020 females and 980 males ranging in age from less than 20 to 75 years.

Availability*: Contact Thomas Cash, Department of Psychology, Old Dominion University, Norfolk, VA 23529-0267. (Phone # 804-683-4213)

References

*Butters, J., W., & Cash, T. F. (1987). Cognitive-behavioral treatment of women's body-image dissatisfaction. Journal of Consulting and Clinical Psychology, 55, 889-897.

*Cash, T. F. (1989). Body-image affect: Gestalt versus summing the parts. Perceptual and Motor Skills, 69, 17-18.

*Cash, T. F., & Green, G. K. (1986). Body weight and body image among college women: Perception, cognition, and affect. Journal of Personality Assessment, 50, 290-301.

*Noles, S. W., Cash, T. F., & Winstead, B. A. (1985). Body image, physical attractiveness, and depression. Journal of Consulting and Clinical Psychology, 53, 88-94.

(70)
[MOVEMENT SATISFACTION SCALE] [MSS]
Barbara A. Nelson and Dorothy J. Allen

Source: Nelson, B. A., & Allen, D. A. (1970). Scale for the appraisal of movement satisfaction. Perceptual and Motor Skills, 31, 795-800.

Purpose: To assess an individual's satisfaction or dissatisfaction with his or her movement ability.

Description: The MSS contains 50 items focusing on time, force, flow, the quality of movement, and the use of space (e.g., "ability to walk with poise," "ability to produce sudden movement"). Subjects describe the strength of their feelings about each items on a 5-point scale, with responses ranging from strong negative feelings to strong positive feelings).

Construction: A total of 129 items were developed based on Laban's elements of movement. These items were evaluated by eight experts in psychology and in physical education in terms of item clarity, content relevance, and appropriateness for high school and college age groups. A total of 75 items were retained, which were then administered to 176 males and females, ages 18-21 years. Item analyses led to the retention of 50 items.

Reliability: An internal consistency coefficient (based on the Kuder-Richardson formula) of .95 was obtained among 359 men and 518 women.

Validity: The MSS discriminated between males (n=359) and females (n=518) in that males had greater satisfaction than females. Older subjects (18-21 years) responded with more dissatisfaction regarding movement ability than younger subjects (14-17 years).

Norms: Descriptive and psychometric data reported were based on the responses of 359 males and 518 females (ages 14-21 years) who were enrolled in either one of 3 high schools, 1 junior high school, or at Ohio State University.

Availability*: Order document NAPS-01152 from ASIS National Auxiliary Publication Service, c/o CCM Information Corporation, 909 Third Ave., 21st. floor, New York, NY 10022.

Reference
*Burton, E. C. (1976). Relationship between trait and state anxiety, m o v e - ment satisfaction, and participation in physical education activities. Research Quarterly, 47, 326-331.

(71)
MY BODY INDEX [MBI]
Carol Cutler Riddick and Robin Stanger Freitag

Source: Riddick, C. C., & Freitag, R. S. (1984). The impact of an aerobic fitness program on the body image of older women. Activities, Adaptation & Aging, 6(1), 59-70.

Purpose: To examine perceived body image among older women.

Description: The MBI contains 13 pairs of bi-polar adjectives. For each pair of adjectives, subjects indicate how they feel about their bodies by responding to a six-point semantic differential continuum.

Construction: Four academics in recreation (2 males and 2 females) were instructed to identify, for each pair of adjectives, the adjective which would more likely be construed as negative (in relation to body image) among women 50 years of age or older.

Reliability*: A Cronbach alpha reliability coefficient of .96 ($\underline{n}=26$) was reported.

Validity: Construct validity was supported in that females 50 years of age or older ($\underline{n}=6$) had higher MBI scores after participation in an eight-week aerobic fitness program than control subjects ($\underline{n}=8$).

Norms: Not cited. Psychometric data were reported for 14 females, 50 years of age or older, who were enrolled in an aerobic exercise program in Laurel, Maryland.

Availability: Contact Carol Cutler Riddick, Department of Physical Education and Recreation, Gallaudet University, 800 Florida Ave. NE, Washington, DC 20002-3625. (Phone # 202-651-5510)

*Personal correspondence by principal author on March 9, 1990.

(72)
PERCEIVED SOMATOTYPE SCALE (PS)
Larry A. Tucker

Source: Tucker, L. A. (1982). Relationship between perceived somatotype and body cathexis of college males. Psychological Reports, 50, 983-989.

Purpose: To assess males' perceptions of their actual versus ideal body build.

Description: The scale contains a lineup of seven male figures representing seven different somatotypes. Subjects select the figure most representative of their own body build. They are also asked to select their ideal body figure, that is, the body build they would like to have as their own.

Construction: Figures were drawn from photographs and sketches of Sheldon's (1954) classification of somatotypes.

Reliability: Test-retest reliability coefficients ($\underline{n}$=63 males) were reported as .96 (perceived body image) and .94 (ideal body image) across a two-week time interval.

Validity: Not discussed. The author* noted, however, that "indirect validation of the Perceived Somatotype Scale is supported by a number of studies in which PS scores were strongly related to body image, global self-concept, neuroticism, extraversion, and physical fitness levels."

Norms: Not cited. Psychometric data were reported for 63 male college students.

Availability: Contact Larry A. Tucker, 273 S. F. H., Brigham Young University, Provo, UT 84602. (Phone # 801-378-4927)

References
*Davis, L. L. (1985). Perceived somatotype, body-cathexis, and attitudes toward clothing among college females. Perceptual and Motor Skills, 61, 1199-1205.

Sheldon, W. H. (1954). Atlas of men. New York: Harper.

*Tucker, L. A. (1983). Self-concept: A function of self-perceived somatotype. The Journal of Psychology, 113, 123-133.

*Tucker, L. A. (1984). Physical attractiveness, somatotype, and the male personality: A dynamic interactional perspective. Journal of Clinical Psychology, 40, 1226-1234.

*Personal correspondence with author on March 6, 1990.

Tucker, L. A. (1985). Physical, psychological, social, and lifestyle differences among adolescents classified according to cigarette smoking intention status. Journal of School Health, 55, 127-131.

(73)
SOCIAL PHYSIQUE ANXIETY SCALE (SPAS)
Elizabeth A. Hart, Mark R. Leary, and W. Jack Rejeski

Source: Hart, E. A., Leary, M. R., & Rejeski, W. J. (1989). The measurement of social physique anxiety. Journal of Sport & Exercise Psychology, 11, 94-104.

Purpose: To assess the extent to which people become anxious when others observe or evaluate their physiques.

Description: The SPAS is a 12-item self-report scale focusing on anxiety arising as a result of others' evaluations of one's body. Subjects respond to each item using a 5-point Likert scale.

Construction: A pool of 30 self-report items that dealt with physique anxiety were reviewed by experts in body movement, psychology, or exercise science for item clarity, content validity, and appropriateness for both sexes. Based on their evaluation, the pool was reduced to 22 items. Factor analysis of 195 undergraduate students' (n=97 females; n=98 males) responses to the 22 items led to the retention of 11 items loading greater than .60 on a single unrotated factor. An additional item was added to the test. Similar factor loadings emerged when a principal component analysis was then applied to the responses of 46 females and 43 males on this 12-item test.

Reliability: An alpha reliability coefficient of .90 was reported (n=89). Eight-week test-retest reliability for this sample was .82.

Validity: Concurrent validity was demonstrated by showing that subjects' (93 women and 94 men) responses to the SPAS correlated with measures that relate to general concerns with others' evaluations. The SPAS also correlated with public self-consciousness and measures of body cathexis and body esteem. Discriminant validity was evident by lack of correlation with a social desirability measure, and by the failure of these subjects' scores on the SPAS to relate to a measure of private self-consciousness.

Further support for criterion-related validity was evident by demonstrating that women (n=56 undergraduate women) who scored high on the SPAS were heavier and had a higher percentage of body fat than low scorers on the SPAS. Furthermore, high scorers reported greater anxiety than low scorers during an actual evaluation of their physiques.

<u>Norms</u>: Not reported. Psychometric data were presented for 195 women and 137 men.

<u>Availability</u>: Contact W. Jack Rejeski, Department of Health and Sport Science, Box 7234, Wake Forest University, Winston-Salem, NC 27109. (Phone # 919-759-5837)

Chapter 9

COGNITIVE STRATEGIES

Tests in this chapter assess the cognitive skills athletes employ prior to and during sport competition. These strategies include self-talk, coping with anxiety, imagery, association/dissociation, and concentration.

(74)
COGNITIVE ACTIVITY DURING COMPETITION (CADC)
Eric J. Cooley

Source: Cooley, E. J. (1987). A process study of cognitions during competition (abstract). <u>Proceedings of the Association for the Advancement of Applied Sport Psychology annual convention</u> (p. 43). CA: Newport Beach.

Purpose: To examine the cognitive patterns relating to competitive sport performance.

Description: The CADC contains 58 items describing possible thoughts occurring immediately before (10 minutes) and during the event. For example, subjects are asked to respond to the item "I analyzed the appearance and behavior of my competition." Subjects respond to each item using a 5-point Likert Scale in which items are rated for frequency of occurrence.

Construction: Not discussed.

Reliability: Not reported.

Validity: Subjects' responses to the CADC were correlated with self-rated performance outcome. Good performance was associated with self-confidence, strategic thinking, positive self-talk, and lower levels of self-criticism.

Norms: Not cited. Psychometric data were reported for 32 male and 22 female intercollegiate track athletes.

Availability*: Contact Eric J. Cooley, Department of Psychology, Western Oregon State University, Monmouth, OR 97361.

Reference

Cooley, E. (1988). A process approach to cognitions during competition (abstract). Proceedings of the Association for the Advancement for Applied Sport Psychology annual conference, Nashua, NH.

(75)
DIVING QUESTIONNAIRE [DQ]
Pamela S. Highlen and Bonnie B. Bennett

Source: Highlen, P. S., & Bennett, B. B. (1983). Elite divers and wrestlers: A comparison between open- and closed-skilled athletes. Journal of Sport Psychology, 5, 390-409.

Purpose: To identify cognitive and behavioral strategies used by divers when preparing for and engaging in major competitive events.

Description: The DQ contains 5 subscales and a total of 65 items representing these subscales. The five subscales include: Thoughts, Coping with anxiety, Positive-negative thoughts, Attributions for better performance, and Imagery. Subjects respond to each item on a 11-point interval scale.

Construction: An initial pool of 110 items were placed into 14 factors if they appeared conceptually related. These items were derived from previous research on elite wrestlers and discussions with one college diving coach. The DQ was pilot tested with several collegiate divers. An item analysis led to the retention of 65 items.

Reliability: Alpha internal consistency coefficients (n=44 elite divers) were .82 (Thoughts), .78 (Coping with anxiety), .75 (Positive-negative thoughts), .68 (Attributions), and .64 (Imagery).

Validity: The DQ discriminated between eventual qualifiers (n=8) versus nonqualifiers (n=36) to Canada's diving team at the Pan American Games. The qualifiers scored higher on self-confidence, concentration, and the use of imagery.

Norms: Not reported. Psychometric data were cited for 44 elite Canadian divers.

Availability: Contact Pamela S. Highlen, 142 Townshend Hall, Department of Psychology, Ohio State University, 1885 Neil Ave. Mall, Columbus, OH 43210. (Phone # 614-422-5308)

(76)
PSYCHOLOGICAL PREPARATION IN WRESTING QUESTION-NAIRE [PPWQ]
Daniel Gould, Maureen Weiss, and Robert Weinberg

Source: Gould, D., Weiss, M., & Weinberg, R. (1981). Psychological characteristics of successful and nonsuccessful Big Ten wrestlers. Journal of Sport Psychology, 3, 69-81.

Purpose: To assess the cognitive and behavioral strategies employed by wrestlers as they prepare for or engage in competition.

Description: This 107 item questionnaire contains 15 demographic and background information items and 92 items requiring subjects to respond on a 11-point Likert scale. The latter items center on eight scales plus 13 individual items. These eight scales include: Kinds of thoughts, quantity of thoughts, imagery, best performance attributions, poor performance attributions, cope with anxiety, anxiety, and self-talk.

Construction: The majority of items used in the questionnaire were adopted from an inventory developed by Highlen and Bennett (1979). In addition, a smaller number of items assessing preperformance mental preparation techniques and self-efficacy were included in the questionnaire.

Reliability: Alpha reliabilty coefficients (49 collegiate wrestlers) ranged from .60 (Quantity of thoughts) to .83 (Anxiety).

Validity: Self-confidence, maximum potential, and use of attentional focusing were the most important variables discriminating successful from less successful wrestlers based on tournament placements and seasonal won-loss records.

Norms: Not reported. Psychometric data were cited for 49 wrestlers who participated in the Big Ten Conference Wrestling championships at Michigan State University.

Availability*: Contact Daniel Gould, Exercise and Sport Science Department, University of North Carolina, Greensboro, NC 27412. (Phone # 919-334-3037)

Reference
*Highlen, P. S., & Bennett, B. B. (1979). Psychological characteristics of successful and nonsuccessful elite wrestlers: An exploratory study. Journal of Sport Psychology, 1, 123-137

(77)
PSYCHOLOGICAL SKILLS INVENTORY FOR SPORTS (PSIS)
Michael J. Mahoney, Tyler J. Gabriel, and T. Scott Perkins

Source: Mahoney, M.J., Gabriel, T. J., & Perkins, T. S. (1987). Psychological skills and exceptional athletic performance. The Sport Psychologist, 1, 181-199.

Purpose: The PSIS is designed to assess psychological skills that are relevant to elite athletic performance.

Description: The PSIS (Form R-5) contains 45 items, and assesses anxiety, concentration, self-confidence, mental preparation, and team orientation. For example, athletes are asked to respond (on a 5-point Likert scale) to items such as : "I sometimes feel intense anxiety while I am actually performing " (anxiety scale).

Construction: The PSIS was rationally derived and constrained by the use of a true-false format. The test was then modified to a 5-point Likert format and nondifferentiating items have been replaced.

Reliability: Internal consistency coefficients of .72 (Spearman-Brown), .70 (Guttman-Rulon), and .64 (Cronbach alpha) were reported (Mahoney, 1989).

Validity: Construct validity was evidenced by support of the hypothesized discrimination of elite athletes from nonelite athletes on the 5 subscales using item analyses, stepwise discriminant and regression analyses, and factor and cluster analyses. The authors caution that the PSIS is a pilot instrument awaiting formal and extensive psychometric evaluation.

Norms: Not available. Psychometric data were reported for elite athletes (n=126), preelite athletes (n=141), and nonelite athletes (n=446) representing nationally a total of 23 sports. Average ages of the elite, preelite, and nonelite athletes sampled were 24.1, 18.6, and 19.8 years, respectively.

Availability: Contact Michael J. Mahoney, Counseling Psychology Department, Graduate School of Education, University of California, Santa Barbara, CA 93106. (Phone # 805-961-4083)

References
Bryant, F., Mahoney, M., & Meyers, A. (1989). Removing performance feedback to assess strength of psychological skills (abstract). Proceedings of the annual conference of the Association for the Advancement for Applied Sport Psychology (p. 33). Seattle, WA.

*Cox, R. H. (1989). A comparison of disabled and able-bodied athletes relative to psychological skills (abstract). <u>Psychology of motor behavior and sport</u> (p. 116). Proceedings of the North American Society for the Psychology of Sport and Physical Activity annual convention, Kent, OH.

*Greenspan, M., Murphy, S. M., Tammen, V., & Jowdy, D. (1989). Effects of athlete achievement level and test administration instructions on the Psychological Skills Inventory for Sport (PSIS) (abstract). <u>Proceedings of the annual conference of the Association for the Advancement for Applied Sport Psychology</u> (p. 55). Seattle, WA.

*Mahoney, M. J. (1989). Psychological predictions of elite and non-elite performance in Olympic weightlifting. <u>International Journal of Sport Psychology</u>, 20, 1-12.

*Millhouse, J. I., Willis, J. D., & Layne, B. H. (1989). The clinical utility of three recent psychological instruments with advanced female gymnasts: A preliminary study (abstract). <u>Proceedings of the annual conference of the Association for the Advancement for Applied Sport Psychology</u> (p. 79). Seattle, WA.

(78)
RUNNING STYLES QUESTIONNAIRE [RSQ]
John M. Silva and Mark Appelbaum

<u>Source</u>: Silva, J. M., & Appelbaum, M. (1983). Association-dissociation patterns of contestants at the 1980 United States Olympic Marathon Trials (abstract). In <u>Psychology of motor behavior and sport-1983</u> (p. 70). Proceedings of the North American Society for the Psychology of Sport and Physical Activity annual convention, Michigan State University, East Lansing.

<u>Purpose</u>: To assess association-dissociation cognitive strategies employed by elite long-distance runners.

<u>Description</u>: The RSQ contains 12 multiple choice items and 6 open-ended type questions.

<u>Construction</u>: A panel of experts from collegiate track and field programs, sport psychology, and psychology were used to establish the content validity of the RSQ (Silva, Personal communication, March 19, 1990).

<u>Reliability</u>: An intraclass correlation coefficient of .73 was obtained among 43 males (who were enrolled in either a long distance running class or who were members of a collegiate cross country team) across a one-week interval.

<u>Validity</u>: Subjects ($\underline{n}$=32) less or more successful at the 1980 United States Olympic Marathon Trials could successfully be differentiated on the basis of

their responses to the RSQ.

<u>Norms</u>: Not cited. Psychometric data were reported for 32 male participants in the Olympic marathon trials and for 43 male undergraduate students.

<u>Availability</u>: Contact John M. Silva, Department of Physical Education, CB #8700, Fetzer Gym, University of North Carolina, Chapel Hill, NC 27599-8700. (Phone # 919-962-0017)

(79)
SELF-STATEMENT QUESTIONNAIRE (SSQ)
Gerry Larsson and I. Anderzen

<u>Source</u>: Larsson, G., & Anderzen, I. (1987). Appraisal, coping, catecholamine excretion and psychomotor performance during calm and stressful conditions. <u>Scandinavian Journal of Sports Sciences</u>, <u>9</u>, 47-51.

<u>Purpose</u>: To assess competition specific cognitive coping.

<u>Description</u>: The SSQ contains 36 items. Subjects are asked to indicate (on a 3-point ordinal scale) the extent to which they use positive self-talk (18 items) or negative self-talk (18 items) during competition. An example of a positive self-talk item is "You can handle the pressure, just take one shot at a time." An example of a negative self-talk item is "I'll probably make a mistake right at the beginning."

<u>Construction</u>: Not discussed.

<u>Reliability</u>: Not presented.

<u>Validity</u>: The construct validity of the SSQ was supported in that 14 Swedish elite male golfers reduced the amount of negative self-talk (when compared to a control group of 14 Swedish elite male golfers) after being exposed to a stress innoculation training program (Larsson, Cook, & Starrin, 1988).

<u>Norms</u>: Not presented. Psychometric data were based on the responses of 28 Swedish elite male golfers, ages 16-17 years.

<u>Availability</u>*: Contact Gerry Larsson, College of Health Professions at Varmland, Sweden.

Reference

Larsson, G., Cook, C., & Starrin, B. (1988). A time and cost efficient stress innoculation training program for athletes: A study of junior golfers. Scandinavian Journal of Sports Sciences, 10, 23-28.

(80)
[SPORT COGNITIVE INTERFERENCE QUESTIONNAIRE] [SCIQ]
Peter Schwenkmezger and Lothar Laux

Source: Schwenkmezger, P., & Laux, L. (1986). Trait anxiety, worry, and emotionality in athletic competition. In C. D. Spielberger and R. Diaz-Guerrero (Eds.), Cross-cultural anxiety (Volume 3) (pp. 65-78). Washington, D. C.: Hemisphere Publishing Corporation.

Purpose: To assess task-irrelevant cognitions experienced by elite athletes in handball.

Description: The SCIQ contains ten items. Subjects respond to items such as "I thought about things unrelated to the game" or "I was concerned about previous mistakes" using a 5-point ordinal scale.

Construction: An initial set of 18 items were formed by modifying Sarason's (1978) Cognitive Interference Questionnaire. Experts (coaches and players) in handball were asked to evaluate which items were relevant to occurrences during handball competition, and were related to deteriorations in performance. Based on the experts' evaluations, 10 items were retained.

Reliability: Not reported.

Validity: Construct validity was supported in that elite female handball athletes (n=35) high on trait anxiety experienced an increase in task-irrelevant cognitions in handball competition versus handball practice, while low trait anxiety athletes experienced no change in task-irrelevant cognitions under these two conditions. Concurrent validity was partially supported in that there was some evidence of a relationship between subjects'(n= 42 male and female elite handball athletes) scores on the SCIQ and their corresponding scores on Spielberger's (1970) trait anxiety scale. Predictive validity was supported in that these subjects' post-competition scores on the SCIQ were related to two experts' evaluations of their game performance based on video-taped assessments.

Norms: Not cited. Psychometric data were reported for 35 elite female handball athletes (M age=22.5 years), two additional groups of 10 male and 10 female members of the German national handball team, and 22 male and female youth elite handball athletes also residing in the Federal Republic of Germany.

<u>Availability</u>: Contact Peter Schwenkmezger, Department of Psychology, University of Trier, P. B. 3825, D-5500 Trier, Federal Republic of Germany. (Phone # 0651-201-2889)

Reference

Sarason, I. G. (Ed.). (1978). The test anxiety scale: Concept and research. In C. D. Spielberger and I. G. Sarason (Eds.), <u>Stress and anxiety</u> (Volume 5). Washington, D. C.: Hemisphere Publishing Corporation.

Chapter 10

COHESION

Tests in this chapter assess attraction to the group, interpersonal interactions, group integration, and team unity across sport team members and coach.

(81)
GROUP ENVIRONMENT QUESTIONNAIRE (GEQ)
Albert V. Carron, W. Neil Widmeyer, and Laurence R. Brawley

Source: Carron, A. V., Widmeyer, W. N., and Brawley, L. R. (1985). The development of an instrument to assess cohesion in sport teams: The Group Environment Questionnaire. Journal of Sport Psychology, 7, 244-266.

Purpose: To assess the task and social aspects of an individual's perceptions of a sport group as a totality and the individual's attraction to the group, as they relate to the development and maintenance of group cohesion.

Description: The GEQ is an 18-item, four-scale measure of group cohesion. The four subscales are: Individual attractions to group-task (ATGT), individual attractions to group-social (ATGS), group integration-task (GIT), group integration-social (GIS). Subjects are asked to respond to each item using a 9-point Likert format.

Construction: The perceptions of independent samples of active sport group members and a review of the literature on cohesion formed the conceptual basis for item development. An initial item pool was generated by four investigators and a senior research assistant.
   Item-trimming was based on sub area representation, item clarity, lack of ambiguity, and other factors. Items were further evaluated by five experts in the area of group dynamics. The reduced 53 item pool was placed in questionnaire format and administered to 212 male and female athletes representing 20 intercollegiate and adult municipal association sport teams. Based on item analyses and estimates of internal consistency, the GEQ was reduced to 24 items.

This decision was supported by a replication study involving 247 athletes representing 26 different sport teams. Factor analyses of subjects' ($\underline{n}= 212$) responses and further item analyses ($\underline{n}=247$) led to the retention of an 18-item GEQ.

Reliability: For ATGT, ATGS, GIT, and GIS, alpha reliability coefficients ($\underline{n}=247$) were .75, .64, .70, and .76, respectively.

Validity: Content validity was demonstrated during the test construction process. Construct validity was demonstrated by factor analysis of subjects' ($\underline{n}=212$) responses to the 24-item GEQ in which the hypothesized four factors emerged. Carron noted that further research (see reference list) has supported the concurrent and predictive validity of the GEQ (Personal communication, March 14, 1990).

Norms: Psychometric data were reported for independent samples ($\underline{n}=212$; $\underline{n}=247$) of male and female athletes representing intercollegiate and municipal association sport teams.

Availability: Contact Albert V. Carron, Faculty of Physical Education, University of Western Ontario, London, Ontario, Canada N6A 3K7. (Phone # 519-679-2111-Ext. 5475)

References

*Brawley, L. R., Carron, A. V., & Widmeyer, W. N. (1987). Assessing the cohesion of teams: Validity of the Group Environment Questionnaire. Journal of Sport Psychology, 9, 275-294,

*Brawley, L. R., Carron, A. V., & Widmeyer, W. N. (1988). Exploring the relationship between cohesion and group resistance to disruption. Journal of Sport & Exercise Psychology, 10, 199-213.

*Carron, A. V., Widmeyer, W. N., & Brawley, L. R. (1988). Group cohesion and individual adherence to physical activity. Journal of Sport & Exercise Psychology, 10, 127-138.

*Frierman, S. H., & Weinberg, R. S. (1989). The relationship between cohesion and performance in competitive bowling teams (abstract). Psychology of motor behavior and sport (p. 138). Kent, OH: Proceedings of the North American Society for the Psychology of Sport and Physical Activity annual convention.

*Widmeyer, W. N., Brawley, L. R., & Carron, A. V. (1985). The measurement of cohesion in sport teams: The Group Environment Questionnaire. London, Ontario: Spodym Publishers.

(82)
HOWE SPORT BEHAVIOUR SCALE-I* [HSBS]
Bruce L. Howe and P. Zachary

Source: Howe, B. L., & Zachary, P. (1986). Revision and validation of the Howe Sport Behavior Scale (abstract). Proceedings of the Canadian Association of Sport Sciences annual convention, Ottawa, Canada.

Purpose: To examine achievement and affiliation orientations in sport.

Description: The questionnaire contains two subscales--Achievement and Affiliation, each containing 15 items. For example, subjects are asked to respond to the item "I am loyal to my team members (Affiliation). Subjects respond to each item using a 5-point ordinal scale.

Construction: Based on item analyses (n=426 high school and university students) of the original 25 item scale (Howe, 1976), a total of 15 items were retained.

Reliability: Internal consistency coefficients (n=426) were .78 (Achievement) and .68 (Affiliation). Test-retest reliability coefficients (n=74) over a one week period were .86 and .81 for achievement and affiliation, respectively. Over a 6-month period, test-retest reliability coefficients (n=31) were .80 (Achievement) and .82 (Affiliation).

Validity: The authors indicated that the discriminant validity of the HSBS-I was supported in that males scored lower on affiliation and higher on achievement than females.

Norms: Not cited. Psychometric data were cited for 426 university and high school students.

Availability: Contact Bruce L. Howe, School of Physical Education, Box 1700, University of Victoria, Victoria, British Columbia, Canada V8W 2Y2. (Phone # 604-721-8383)

Reference
Howe, B. L. (1976). Validating a new scale of personality traits important in sport performance. In J. Broekhoff (Ed.), Physical education, sports and the sciences (pp. 346-352). Eugene, OR: College of Health, Physical Education, and Recreation Microform Publications.

*Howe indicated that the HSBS has been revised considerably, and he is in the process of preparing the revised version for publication (Personal communication, March 7, 1990).

(83)
MEDFORD PLAYER-COACH INTERACTION INVENTORY [MPCII]
Pamela Medford and JoAnne Thorpe

Source: Thorpe, J., & Medford, P. (1986). An inventory for measuring player-coach interaction. Perceptual and Motor Skills, 63, 267-270.

Purpose: To assess positive interactions of the coach with his/her team.

Description: Subjects respond to 23 adjectives using a 7-point Likert scale. Two forms are available: a player's form and a coach's form.

Construction: The literature relevant to attitude inventories and inventories that dealt with interaction or interpersonal relations were reviewed. Following this review, adjectives and statements indicative of player-coach interactions were collected from five female coaches and two female former coaches. These adjectives were sorted by three judges (one linguist and two physical educators) into 20 synonyms in order to reduce redundancy by using a card-sorting technique. A total of 23 (out of 81) adjectives that seemed most indicative and easily understood were selected for the inventory.

Reliability: Test-retest reliability coefficients (n=55 female athletes) ranged from .50 to .83 over a one-week interval for each adjective; 60% of the adjectives were found reliable. A test-retest reliabilty coefficient, based on the total test score, was .87.

Validity: Content validity was examined by having players and coaches rate (using a 5-point scale) the predictive value for each adjective. Ratings were "high," indicating that the adjectives were appropriate predictors of player-coach interaction.

Norms: Not reported. Psychometric data were cited for 55 female collegiate athletes.

Availability: Contact JoAnne Thorpe, 119 Davies, Physical Education Department, Southern Illinois University, Carbondale, IL 62901-4310. (Phone # 618-536-2431)

(84)
MULTIDIMENSIONAL SPORT COHESION INSTRUMENT (MSCI)
David Yukelson, Robert Weinberg, and Allen Jackson

Source: Yukelson, D., Weinberg, R., & Jackson, A. (1984). A multi-dimensional group cohesion instrument for intercollegiate basketball teams. Journal of Sport Psychology, 6, 103-117.

Purpose: To assess group cohesion based on both task related and social related forces that presumably exist in intercollegiate basketball.

Description: The MSCI is a 22-item self report test. Factor analyses indicated that four factors are discernable (accounting for 62% of the variance): Attraction to the Group, Unity of Purpose, Quality of Teamwork, and Valued Roles. Subjects are asked to respond to each item (e.g., "How good do you think the teamwork is on your team?") using an 11-point ordinal scale.

Construction: Items for the MSCI were logically derived by: a) modifying items found in previous cohesion instruments, b) synthesizing information from theoretical work on cohesion, c) surveying research in the area of industrial and organizational psychology, and d) interviewing coaches or social scientists regarding their perceptions of group cohesion. An initial pool of 41 items (23 items were task-related items and 17 were social-related items), plus a 4-item lie scale were administered and evaluated among 95 male and 101 female intercollegiate basketball players representing 16 colleges throughout Texas, Michigan, and California. The results of alpha and canonical factor analyses led to the retention of four meaningful factors (see test description above) representing 22 items.

Reliability: Alpha reliability coefficients (n=196) were .93 (total test), .88 (Attraction to the Group), .86 (Unity of Purpose), .86 (Quality of Teamwork), and .79 (Valued Roles).

Validity: Construct validity was supported by the retention of the four hypothesized factors based on factor analyses.

Norms: Not reported. Psychometric data were cited for 196 male and female intercollegiate basketball players residing in three states.

Availability: Contact David Yukelson, Academic Support Center for Student Athletes, 328 Boucke Building, Pennsylvania State University, University Park, PA 16802. (Phone # 814-865-0407)

References

*Foster, C., & McClure, B. (1987). The effects of membership in a personal growth group on group cohesiveness within a women's gymnastics team (abstract). Proceedings of the annual conference of the Association for the Advancment for Applied Sport Psychology (p. 76). Newport Beach, CA.

*Yukelson, D., Weinberg, R., & Jackson, A. (1983). Group cohesion in sport: A multidimensional approach (abstract). Psychology of motor behavior and sport (p. 127). Preceedings of the annual conference of the North American Society for the Psychology of Sport and Physical Activity, East Lansing, MI.

(85)
[SPORTS COHESIVENESS QUESTIONNAIRE] [SCQ]
Rainer Martens and James A. Peterson

Source: Martens, R., & Peterson, J. A. (1971). Group cohesiveness as a determinant of success and member satisfaction in team performance. International Review of Sport Sociology, 6, 49-61.

Purpose: To assess various dimensions of group cohesiveness in sport.

Description: Seven questionnaire items focus on interpersonal attraction, contributions of members based on ability and enjoyment, influence(power) of each member, sense of belonging, value of membership, and perceptions of teamwork and how closely knit the sport group was. Subjects are asked to respond to each item using a 9-choice alternative between two polarities.

Construction: Item selection was based on a review of literature on the theoretical basis of cohesiveness and assessment alternatives.

Reliability: Not reported.

Validity: When comparing successful to unsuccessful college intramural basketball teams, only members' (n=1200 males) ratings of the cohesivenss of their team as a whole was a discriminating factor. However, the majority of cohesiveness items discriminated between satisfied and unsatisfied teams.

Norms: Psychometric data were cited for 1200 male undergraduate students participating on 144 intramural basketball teams at the University of Illinois.

Availability: Contact Rainer Martens, Human Kinetics Publishers, Box 5076, Champaign, IL 61825-5076. (Phone # 217-351-5076)

References

*Carron, A. V., & Ball, J. R. (1977). An analysis of the cause-effect character-istics of cohesiveness and participation motivation in intercollegiate hockey. International Review of Sport Sociology, 12(2), 49-60.

*Carron, A. V., & Chelladurai, P. (1981). The dynamics of group cohesion in sport. Journal of Sport Psychology, 3, 123-139.

Hacker, C. M., & Williams, J. M. (1981). Cohesion, satisfaction, and perform-ance in intercollegiate field hockey (abstract). In Psychology of motor behavior and sport-1981 (p. 99). Proceedings of the North American Society for the Psychology of Sport and Physical Activity annual conven-tion, Asilomar, CA.

*Peterson, J. A., & Martens, R. (1972). Success and residential affiliation as determinants of team cohesiveness. Research Quarterly, 43, 62-76.

*Widmeyer, W. N., & Martens, R. (1978). When cohesion predicts perform-ance outcome in sport. Research Quarterly, 49, 372-380.

(86)
TEAM CLIMATE QUESTIONNAIRE [TCQ]
Robert R. Grand and Albert V. Carron

Source: Grand, R. R. & Carron, A. V. (1982). Development of a Team Climate Questionnaire. In L. M. Wankel and R. B. Wilberg (Eds.). Psychology of sport and motor behavior: Research and practice   (pp.217-229). Proceedings of the annual conference of the Canadian Society for Psychomotor Learning and Sport Psychology, Edmonton, Alberta.

Purpose: To assess role clarity, role acceptance, perceived role performance, conformity, task cohesion, and social cohesion in sport groups.

Description: The TCQ consists of 60 items pertaining to the six constructs above. Each construct is assessed by 10 items; subjects respond to each item using a 7-point Likert scale. In addition, a single, direct cohesion measure was included bringing the total number of item on the TCQ to 61.

Construction: Operationalization of the six constructs involved modifying some items from a number of psychological inventories and scales including Jackson's Personality Inventory, the Sport Cohesiveness Questionnaire, and the Role Conflict and Ambiguity Scale. Other items were developed based on the objectives of the study.

A series of pilot studies followed in which item analyses and evalu-ations of internal consistency were made. Samples included 112 undergradu-ate students, 34 Canadian high school hockey players, and an additional 111 undergraduate students. The first pilot study involved an evaluation of 58 items, while the second pilot study involved a subanalysis of the most reliable

36 items. In the final stage of the pilot project, a revised version of the original questionnaire with 61 items was included for analyses, since it was found that the shorter version of the questionnaire was less reliable.

Reliability: Kuder-Richardson-20 internal consistency coefficients ($\underline{n}$=75) ranged from .76 to .91.

Validity: Not discussed.

Norms: Not cited. Psychometric data were reported for 75 hockey players participating on five selected university and junior hockey teams in Canada.

Availability: Contact Albert V. Carron, Faculty of Physical Education, University of Western Ontario, London, Ontario, Canada N6A 3K7. (Phone # 519-679-2111-Ext. 5475)

References
*Bolger, P., & Carron, A. V. (1984). The relationship of task and social cohesion to sex, starting status, participation level, and performance of high school and university basketball teams (abstract). Proceedings of the annual conference of the Canadian Society of Psychomotor Learning and Sport Psychology (p. 4). Kingston, Ontario, Canada.
*Brawley, L. R., Carron, A. V. & Widmeyer, W. N. (1987). Assessing the cohesion of teams: Validity of the Group Environment Questionnaire. Journal of Sport Psychology, 9, 275-294.
*Foster, C., & McClure, B. (1987). The effects of membership in a personal growth group on group cohesiveness within a women's gymnastic team (abstract). Proceedings of the annual conference of the Association for the Advancement for Applied Sport Psychology (p. 76). Newport Beach, CA.

(87)
TEAM COHESION QUESTIONNAIRE [TCQ]
Joseph J. Gruber and Gary R. Gray

Source: Gruber, J. J., & Gray, G. R. (1981). Factor patterns of variables influencing cohesiveness at various levels of basketball competition. Research Quarterly for Exercise and Sport, 52, 19-30.

Purpose: To provide a measure of interpersonal working relationships, success obtained by the sport group, and personal forces attracting individuals to the sport group.

Description: The cohesiveness questionnaire contains 13 items. Subjects are asked to respond to each item using a 9-point Likert scale.

Construction: Items were selected for inclusion in the questionnaire based on their frequency of use in previous investigations of sport cohesion, and their relevance to an hypthesized factor structure of sport cohesiveness.

Reliability: Intraclass correlation coefficients across a two-week interval, computed by analysis of variance procedures, ranged from .73 to .94 among 89 varsity junior high school basketball players, and from .80 to .98 among 34 varsity small college basketball players.

Validity: Factor analyses of the responses of 515 male varsity basketball players, representing various educational levels, led to the retentionof six factors. The factor of team performance satisfaction accounted for the majority of variance across all levels of competition, ranging from 51% to 65% accountable variance. (Additional information concerning discriminant validity can be found in the reference listed.)

Norms: Not reported. Psychometric data were cited for 92 elementary school basketball players from 8 school teams, 116 junior high school basketball players from 10 school teams, 110 senior high school basketball players from 9 school teams, 115 small college players from 10 teams, and 82 large college basketball players from 7 college teams.

Availability: Contact Joseph Gruber, Department of Health, Physical Education, and Recreation, Seaton Building 216, University of Kentucky, Lexington, KY 40506. (Phone # 606-257-3293)

Reference

*Gruber, J. J., & Gray, G. R. (1982). Responses to forces influencing cohesion as a function of player status and level of male varsity basketball competition. Research Quarterly for Exercise and Sport, 53, 27-36.

Chapter 11

CONFIDENCE

Tests in this chapter assess perceptions of movement competence, confidence in physical fitness, and perceptions of sport competence. The strength of perceived self-efficacy in relation to sport performance and physical ability is also evaluated.

(88)
DIVING EFFICACY SCALE (DES)
Deborah L. Feltz, Daniel M. Landers, and Ursula Raeder

Source: Feltz, D. L., Landers, D. M., & Raeder, U. (1979). Enhancing self-efficacy in high-avoidance motor tasks: A comparison of modeling techniques. Journal of Sport Psychology, 1, 112-122.

Purpose: To assess the strength of self-efficacy among novice divers.

Description: The DES contains eight diving-related items that are presented in increasing order of difficulty. Subjects rate the strength of their expectations for each diving task on a 100-point probability scale, ranging in 10-unit intervals from great uncertainty to complete certainty.

Construction: The design of the scale was modified from Bandura's efficacy scale.

Reliability: Test-retest reliability of the DES was .98 across a one-week interval among seven college students.

Validity: Not discussed.

Norms: Not cited

Availability: Contact Deborah L. Feltz, Department of Physical Education, 138 IM Sports Circle, Michigan State University, East Lansing, MI 48824. (Phone # 517-355-4732)

(89)
GYMNASTIC EFFICACY MEASURE (GEM)
Edward McAuley

Source: McAuley, E. (1985). Modeling and self-efficacy: A test of Bandura's model. Journal of Sport Psychology, 7, 283-295.

Purpose: To assess an individual's belief that he/she can execute successfully a balance beam skill in gymnastics.

Description: Six gymnastic activity items for the balance beam are arranged in hierarchical order of difficulty, with the target task (a dive forward roll mount onto a gymnastic balance beam from a springboard) listed as the final item. For items (tasks) that subjects feel they can perform, they rate on a 100-point probability scale how certain they are about performing them. A rating of 100 points indicates absolute certainty; a rating of 10 points indicates that the subject is highly uncertain about performing the task. Self-efficacy cognitions are assessed by totaling these certainty ratings across across the six items and then dividing by the total number of items.

Construction: Not discussed.

Reliability: Not discussed.

Validity: Path analytic techniques were used to demonstrate that subjects' ($N=39$) self-efficacy cognitions were a significant predictor of their performance of three forward roll mounts onto the balance beam.

Norms: Not indicated. Psychometric data were presented for 39 undergraduate students enrolled in physical education skills classes.

Availability: Contact Edward McAuley, Department of Kinesiology, 906 Louise Freer Hall, University of Illinois, 906 South Goodwin Avenue, Urbana, IL 61801. (Phone # 217-333-6487)

(90)
HIGH-RISK ACTIVITY INVENTORY (HRAI)
Evan B. Brody, Bradley D. Hatfield, and Thomas W. Spalding

Source: Brody, E. B., Hatfield, B. D., & Spalding, T. W. (1988). Generalization of self-efficacy to a continuum of stressors upon mastery of a high-risk sport skill. Journal of Sport & Exercise Psychology, 10, 32-44.

Purpose: To assess an individual's strength of perceived self-efficacy in relation to high-risk physical activities.

Description: The HRAI is a 12-item test that requires the subject to report his/her degree of confidence of ability to perform the following activities: scuba diving, sky diving, hang gliding, mountain climbing, white water rafting, rock climbing, downhill skiing, automobile racing, hot-air ballooning, white water tubing, diving (swimming), and motorcyle racing.

Construction: Not stated.

Reliability: An alpha internal consistency coefficient of .88 was reported.

Validity: Not stated.

Norms: Not available.

Availability*: Contact Bradley D. Hatfield, Department of Physical Education, 2138 PERH Building, University of Maryland, College Park, MD 20742. (Phone # 301-454-2928)

(91)
MOTOR SKILL PERCEIVED COMPETENCE SCALE (MSPCS)
Mary E. Rudisill, Matthew T. Mahar, and Karen S. Meaney

Source: Rudisill, M. E., Mahar, M. T., & Meaney, K. S. (1989). The development of a Motor Skill Perceived Competence Scale for children (abstract). Research abstracts of the annual convention of the American Alliance for Health, Physical Education, Recreation, and Dance (p. 193). Boston, MA.

Purpose: To assess children's (ages 9-12) perceptions of motor skill competence.

Description: The MSPCS is a semantic differential scale containing 18 items. Two parallel forms exist: Form-A and Form-B, each containing 9 items. Each item is designed so that the subject circles the number (5-point scale) between the two opposite statements which best represents his/her feelings about the sentence. For example, the subject is asked to indicate along a 5-point continuum whether he/she cannot or can run fast. Imbedded in both forms is one item based on the subject's general competence.

Construction: A 35-item Likert type scale was originally constructed. Results of the analysis of the original scale indicated that three items were not well understood by the students and were eliminated from the scale. The item analysis identified eleven additional items which could be eliminated without a significant reduction in scale reliability.

To increase the percentage of students responding to each item and to minimize social desirability response distortions, the remaining items were structured in a semantic differential scale format. The revised 21-item semantic differential type scale was administered to 300 children. Item analyses led to the retention of 18 items which were then administered to 929 students. Based on further item analyses, items with similar discrimination indexes were randomly assigned to either Form A or Form B.

Reliability: Internal consistency coefficients ($\underline{n}$=929) were .78, .79, and .88, for Form A, Form B, and both forms combined, respectively. A test-retest reliability coefficient ($\underline{n}$= 322 male and female children, ages 9-12 years) of .88 was reported across a 2-week interval.

Validity: Alpha factor analysis with oblique rotation resulted in the retention of one factor for both Forms A and B. Ratings of perceived motor skill competence correlated .34 to .42 with actual motor skill performance ($\underline{n}$= 929). Also, subjects' responses to the MSPCS correlated .41 with teacher ratings of these subjects' motor skill performance.

Norms: Psychometric data were presented for 929 male and female children, ages 9-12.

Availability: Contact Mary E. Rudisill, Department of Health and Human Performance, University of Houston, Houston, TX 77204-3551 (Phone # 713-749-4386)

Reference

*Rudisill, M. E., Mahar, M. T., & Meaney, K. S. (1989). A comparison of the Motor Skill Perceived Competence Scale and Harter's Physical Domain Perceived Competence Scale for predicting motor skill competence (abstract). Psychology of motor behavior and sport (p. 98). Kent, OH: Proceedings of the North American Society for the Psychology of Sport and Physical Activity annual convention.

(92)
MOVEMENT CONFIDENCE INVENTORY (MCI)
Norma S. Griffin, Jack F. Keogh, and Richard Maybee

Source: Griffin, N. S., Keogh, J. F., & Maybee, R. (1984). Performer perceptions of movement confidence. Journal of Sport Psychology, 6, 395-407.

Purpose: To assess subject perceptions of movement confidence based on competence, potential for enjoying movement sensations, and potential for harm. Movement confidence is defined as how sure a subject is of completing a movement task.

Description: The MCI is organized around 12 movement tasks (such as playing golf or jogging) and requires three different ratings for each movement task situation. Subjects are asked to rate their experience with each task situation (on a 5-point ordinal scale), their level of confidence in performing the task situation (on a 6-point ordinal scale), and to rate the extent to which 22 paired descriptor words contribute to the stated level of confidence in doing the imagined performance of the task.

Construction: Twelve movement tasks were selected in terms of the potential importance of the three confidence components (competence, enjoyment, and harm). Descriptor words (third rating component) were selected from a pool of words obtained by asking children and college students to select words that were important in describing their confidence in movement situations. Overall, the content and format of the MCI were determined by meetings and small-group interactive conferences with consultants.

Reliability: Alpha reliability coefficients obtained among 206 female and 146 male undergraduate students ranged on the subscale tasks from .83 (basketball) to .94 (skiing); an alpha coefficient of .90 was obtained for the composite MCI.

Validity: Partial support for construct validity was obtained through factor analyses (n=352), which indicated that the major contribution to perceived movement confidence is a personal feeling of competence.

Norms. Not reported. Psychometric data were cited for 352 undergraduate students from six colleges in four states.

Availability: Contact Norma S. Griffin, School of HPER, 202 MLH, University of Nebraska, Lincoln, NE 68588-0229. (Phone # 402-472-1701)

(93)
PERCEIVED PHYSICAL COMPETENCE SCALE [PPCS]
Taru Lintunen

Source: Lintunen, T. (1987). Perceived Physical Competence Scale for children. Scandinavian Journal of Sports Sciences, 9, 57-64.

Purpose: To assess cognitive appraisals of physical self among children, including perceptions of both physical performance capacity (physical fitness) and physical appearance.

Description: The child is asked to compare him/herself to children of the same age and sex in terms of physical fitness, motor ability, anthropometric characteristics, and other physical attributes. The child responds to each of the ten items on the PPCS using a 5-point scale in which a discrimination must be made between bipolar adjective descriptors.

Construction: Not discussed.

Reliability: Alpha internal consistency coefficients of .48 and .69 were reported among 45 ten-year-old girls and 73 ten-year-old boys living in Finland for the total test score. Test-retest reliability coefficients were .76 (n=36) across a two-week interval and .63 (n=116) over a 6-month interval.

Validity: Some evidence of convergent validity was shown, particularly among the male children (n=68), when their responses on the PPCS were correlated with their responses to Rosenberg's Self-Esteem Scale (r=.55). In addition, there were positive correlation coefficients among these children's responses to the PPCS and actual estimates of physical fitness and ability.

Norms: Not cited. Psychometric data were presented for 154 Finnish children.

Availability: Contact Taru Lintunen, Department of Physical Education, University of Jyvaskyla, Seminaarinkatu 15, 40100 Jyvaskyla, Finland. (Phone # 358-41-217-711)

Reference
Lintunen, T., Rahkila, P., Leskinen, E., & Salmela, T. (1989). Relationship between physical fitness, perceived physical competence and self-esteem in 11-year-old boys and girls. Abstracts of the 7th World Congress of Sport Psychology (p. 77). Singapore.

(94)
PERCEIVED PHYSICAL COMPETENCE SUBSCALE FOR CHILDREN [PPCSC]
Susan Harter

Source: Harter, S. (1982). The Perceived Competence Scale for Children. Child Development, 53, 87-97.

Purpose: To assess a child's perceptions of his or her physical competence in sports and outdoor games.

Description: The PPCSC is one of four subscales of Harter's Perceived Competence Scale for Children (PCSC). The PCSC assesses a child's sense of competence across the cognitive, social, and physical domains. A fourth subscale is labeled general self-worth. The PPCSC contains seven items. A "structured alternative format" is used. The child is first asked to indicate which kind of kid he or she is most like, based on two alternatives per item. The child is then asked whether the corresponding description selected is sort of true or really true of him or her. Each item is scored from 1 (low perceived physical competence) to 4 (high perceived physical competence).

Construction: A 40-item version of the PCSC was initially constructed. Items were selected based on interviews with children, or were adapted from existing scales. Factor analysis of the responses of 215 third through sixth grade children led to the revision of at least one item per subscale. Subsequent factor analysis of the responses of a new sample of 133 children to the PCSC led to the final 28-item version.

Reliability: A Cronback alpha internal consistency coefficient of .83 was reported for the PPCSC among 341 children, grades 3-6. Across four additional samples, alpha reliabilities ranged from .77 to .86 for this subscale. Test-retest reliability coefficients (corrected for attenuation) across 3 months ($\underline{n}$=208) and 9 months ($\underline{n}$=810) were .87 and .80, respectively.

Validity: Construct validity of the PCSC was supported through factor analysis. Across four independent samples, the hypothesized four-factor model of perceived competence emerged. Concurrent validity of the PPCSC was supported, in that teacher ratings of childrens' actual physical competence in the gymnasium correlated positively with these childrens' corresponding scores on the PPSCS. Discriminant validity was evident in that children ($\underline{n}$=23) selected for sport teams scored higher on the PPCSC than their classmates ($\underline{n}$=57).

Norms: Descriptive and psychometric data were presented for: (a) 341 3-6th graders from California and Connecticut, (b) 714 3-6th graders from New

York, (c) three independent samples of children ($\underline{n}$=470) from Colorado representing the same age range, (d) an additional California sample of 746 children in grades 3-9. Each sample contained an approximately equal number of boys and girls. Samples were drawn from middle- and upper-middle-class populations.

Availability*: Contact Susan Harter, Department of Psychology, University of Denver, University Park, Denver, CO 80208.

References

*Feltz, D. L., & Brown, E. W. (1984). Perceived competence in soccer skills among young soccer players. Journal of Sport Psychology, 6, 385-394.

Feltz, D. L., & Petlichkoff, L. (1983). Perceived competence among inter-scholastic sport participants and dropouts. Canadian Journal of Applied Sport Sciences, 8, 231-235.

Roberts, G. C., Kleiber, D. A., & Duda, J. L. (1981). An analysis of motivation in children's sport: The role of perceived competence in participation. Journal of Sport Psychology, 3, 206-216.

(95)
PERCEIVED PHYSICAL FITNESS SCALE [PPFS]
Ben R. Abadie

Source: Abadie, B. R. (1988). Construction and validation of a perceived physical fitness scale. Perceptual and Motor Skills, 67, 887-892.

Purpose: To assess an individual's perceptions of his/her physical fitness.

Description: The PPFS contains 12 items that assess an individual's perceptions of his/her physical fitness in relation to cardiorespiratory endurance, muscular strength, muscular endurance, flexibility, and body composition. For example, subjects are asked to respond to the item "I possess less muscular strength than most individuals my age." Subjects respond to each item using a 5-point Likert scale.

Construction: A total of 15 items were developed to represent the five above components of physical fitness. Three experts (one physical educator and two exercise physiologists) established the content validity of the items. Based on an item analysis of the responses of 144 men and 166 women to the PPFS, 12 items were retained.

Reliability: An alpha reliability coefficient of .78 was reported ($\underline{n}$=310). A test-retest reliability coefficient of .92 was indicated among 111 of these subjects across a 7-10 day interval.

Validity: A principal component factor analysis (n=310) resulted in the identification of four factors (representing 62.9 percent of the variance) that were labeled physical condition, flexibility, muscular condition, and body composition. Discriminant validity was supported in that high physically fit older adults (n=19) scored higher on the PPFS than low fit older adults (n=22). Furthermore, 49 young adults (M age < 50) who participated in exercise during the last three months scored higher on the PPFS than young adults (n=41) who did not exercise during that time period. In addition, derived factor scores on the PPFS were correlated with actual measures of physical fitness among young (n=28, M age=27.8 years) and older (n=30, M age=68.3 years) adults, except for the muscular strength and flexibility measures obtained among the older adults.

Norms: Not cited. Psychometric data were reported for 144 men and 166 women.

Availability: Contact Ben R. Abadie, Department of HPER, Box 6186, Mississippi State University, Mississippi State, MS 39762. (Phone # 601-325-7235)

Reference

Abadie, B. R. (1988). Relating trait anxiety to perceived physical fitness. Perceptual and Motor Skills, 67, 539-543.

(96)

PERCEIVED SOCCER COMPETENCE SUBSCALE [PSCS]

Deborah L. Feltz and Eugene W. Brown

Source: Feltz, D. L., & Brown, E. W. (1984). Perceived competence in soccer skills among young soccer players. Journal of Sport Psychology, 6, 385-394.

Purpose: To assess childrens' perceptions of their competence in soccer.

Description: The PSCS contains seven items. A structured alternative format is used in which subjects must first decide which kind of person they are most like. Then they decide if the description is "sort of true" or "really true" of themselves. For example, subjects are asked to select between "Some kids do very well at soccer" and "Others don't feel that they are very good when it comes to soccer." Item responses are scored on a 4-point ordinal scale, where a score of 1 is indicative of low perceived soccer competence and a score of 4 is indicative of high perceived soccer competence.

Construction: The PSCS was modified from Harter's (1982) physical subscale of the Perceived Competence Scale for Children. The word "soccer" was substituted for the word "sport" in the original subscale, plus a few minor changes were made in the wording of items to fit the context of soccer.

Reliability: A Cronbach alpha internal reliability coefficient of .75 was reported among 217 youth soccer participants.

Validity: Concurrent validity was supported in that subjects' (n=217) responses to the PSCS were correlated (r=.45) with general self-esteem and also with the physical subscale (r=.66) of Harter's Perceived Competence Scale for Children. Multiple regression analyses indicated that these subjects' responses to the PSCS were more predictive of their soccer abilities than either the physical perceived competence subscale or the general self-esteem scale.

Norms: Descriptive and psychometric data were presented for 205 male and 12 female youth soccer participants ranging in age from 8 to 13 years.

Availability: Contact Deborah L. Feltz, Department of Physical Education, IM Sports Circle, Room 138, Michigan State University, East Lansing, MI 48824. (Phone # 517-355-4732)

Reference

Harter, S. (1982). The Perceived Competence Scale for Children. Child Development, 53, 87-97.

(97)
PHYSICAL ESTIMATION AND ATTRACTION SCALES (PEAS)
Robert J. Sonstroem

Source: Sonstroem, R. J. (1978). Physical Estimation and Attraction Scales: Rationale and research. Medicine and Science in Sports, 10, 97-102.

Purpose: To assess: (1) self-perceptions of physical fitness and athletic ability, hypothesized to be a component of global self-esteem (estimation), and (2) interest in vigorous physical activity (attraction).

Description: The PEAS is an 89 item true-false test containing two subscales - physical estimation (EST) and attraction (ATTR). The test has three versions for different age and sex groups: boys, men, and females.

Construction: Based on an item analysis of male high school students' (n=165) responses to an original pool of 51 EST and 39 ATTR items, a total of 76 items were retained. Borrowing from Kenyon's work on the Attitudes Toward Physical Activity inventory, 54 new items were developed. These items were combined with an enlarged pool of 55 EST items and 46 ATTR items, and the resulting 155 item pool was administered to 710 male students at three high schools. Principal component factor analyses of their responses led to the retention of 89 items representing a 7-factor solution (and accounting for 49.31% of the variance).

Reliability: Kuder-Richardson-20 internal consistency coefficients of .87 (EST) and .89 (ATTR) were reported. Test-retest reliability coefficients of .92 (EST) and .94 (ATTR) were reported for 40 high school males over a two-week interval.

Validity: Using three independent samples of high school males ($n=115$; $n=187$; and $n=109$) and 112 boys in grades 7-8, statistically significant but low correlation coefficients (ranging from .21 to .51) were reported for their EST responses and various global measures of self-esteem and life adjustment (e.g., Tennessee Self Concept Scale), thus supporting the convergent validity of this subscale. EST responses also correlated positively with various measures of physical ability, while global self-esteem did not, thus supporting estimation as a mediating variable in a physical fitness and self-esteem relationship. Subjects' responses on ATTR were related to self-report levels of participation in physical activity. Discriminant validity was evidenced by low correlation coefficients of EST scores with Lie Scale scores and Marlowe-Crowne Social Desirability scale scores, as well as low relationships between ATTR and social desirability.

Norms: Not cited.

Availability: Contact Robert J. Sonstroem, Department of Physical Education, 106 Tootell Center, University of Rhode Island, Kingston, RI 02881-0810 (Phone # 401-792-5434)

References

*Dishman, R. K. (1980). The influence of response distortion in assessing self-perceptions of physical ability and attitude toward physical activity. Research Quarterly for Exercise and Sport, 51, 286-298.

*Fox, K. R., Corbin, C. B., & Couldry, W. H. (1985). Female physical estimation and attraction to physical activity. Journal of Sport Psychology, 7, 125-136.

*Safrit, M. J., Wood, T. M., & Dishman, R. K. (1985). The factorial validity of the Physical Estimation and Attraction Scales for adults. Journal of Sport Psychology, 7, 166-190.

*Sonstroem, R. J. (1974). Attitude testing examining certain psychological correlates of physical activity. Research Quarterly, 45, 93-103.

*Sonstroem, R. J., & Morgan, W. P. (1989). Exercise and self-esteem: Rationale and model. <u>Medicine and Science in Sports and Exercise</u>, <u>21</u>, 329-337.

(98)
PHYSICAL SELF-EFFICACY SCALE (PSE)
Richard M. Ryckman, Michael A. Robbins, Billy Thornton,
and Peggy Cantrell

<u>Source</u>: Ryckman, R. M., Robbins, M. A., Thornton, B., & Cantrell, P. (1982). Development and validation of a Physical Self-Efficacy Scale. <u>Journal of Personality and Social Psychology</u>, <u>42</u>, 891-900.

<u>Purpose</u>: To measure individual differences in perceived physical ability and confidence in physical self-presentation in social situations.

<u>Description</u>: The PSE contains a 10-item Perceived Physical Ability (PPA) subscale and a 12-item Physical Self-Presentation Confidence (PSPC) subscale. An example of an item from the PPA subscale is "I have excellent reflexes." An example of a PSPC subscale item is "People think negative things about me because of my posture." Subjects respond to all items using a 6-point Likert format.

<u>Construction</u>: A pool of 90 items was developed focusing on individuals' generalized expectancies concerning perceived physical skills, and their level of confidence in displaying and being evaluated by others on physical skills. Principal component factor analysis of the responses of 363 undergraduate students resulted in the retention of three factors, one of which was eliminated because it was contaminated by social desirability response distortions. A total of 22 items were retained forming the two subscales noted above.

<u>Reliability</u>: Alpha reliability coefficients ($\underline{n}$=363) for the PSE and the PPA and PSPC subscales were .81, .84, and .74, respectively. Test-retest reliability coefficients ($\underline{n}$=83 undergraduate students) across a 6-week interval were .80 (PSE), .85 (PPA), and .69 (PSPC).

<u>Validity</u>: Convergent validity ($\underline{n}$= 90 undergraduate students) was reported with the Tennessee Physical Self-Concept subscale ($\underline{r}$=.58). Among a sample of 207 undergraduate students, concurrent validity was also demonstrated using locus of control, sensation seeking, and trait anxiety measures. Discriminant validity was evident since the PPA was less related to global self-consciousness than was the PSPC subscale. Predictive validity was also supported among two additional samples of undergraduate students in that subjects with positive perceptions of physical skills outperformed subjects with poorer self-regard on three motor skill tasks.

Norms: Psychometric data were reported for various samples of undergraduate students (above) who were enrolled in introductory classes.

Availability: Contact Richard M. Ryckman, Department of Psychology, University of Maine, Orono, ME 04469. (Phone # 207-581-2046)

References

*Cusumano, J. A., & Robinson, S. E. (1989). Physical self-efficacy levels in Japanese and American university students. Perceptual and Motor Skills, 69, 912-914.

*Gayton, W. F., Matthews, G. R., & Burchstead, G. N. (1986). An investigation of the validity of the Physical Self-efficacy Scale in predicting marathon performance. Perceptual and Motor Skills, 63, 752-754.

*McAuley, E., & Gill, D. (1983). Reliability and validity of the Physical Self-Efficacy Scale in a competitive sport setting. Journal of Sport Psychology, 5, 410-418.

*Salmoni, A. W., & Sidney, K. H. (1989). The effect of exercise on physical self-efficacy in the elderly (abstract). Psychology of motor behavior and sport (p. 151). Kent, OH: Proceedings of the North American Society for the Psychology of Sport and Physical Activity annual convention.

*Thornton. B., Ryckman, R. M., Robbins, M. A., Donolli, J., & Biser, G. (1987). Relationship between perceived physical ability and indices of actual physical fitness. Journal of Sport Psychology, 9, 295-300.

(99)
PHYSICAL SELF-PERCEPTION PROFILE (PSPP)
Kenneth R. Fox and Charles B. Corbin

Source: Fox, K. R., & Corbin, C. B. (1989). The Physical Self-Perception Profile: Development and preliminary validation. Journal of Sport & Exercise Psychology, 11, 408-430.

Purpose: To examine perceptions of the physical self from a multidimensional perspective.

Description: The PSPP consists of five 6-item subscales: Perceived sports competence (Sport), perceived bodily attractiveness (Body), perceived physical strength and muscular development (Strength), perceived level of physical conditioning and exercise (Condition), and physical self-worth (PSW). Subjects respond to each item using a four-choice structured alternative format; scores range from 6-24 on each subscale.

Construction: During Phase I (subdomain identification), a literature review of existing related instrumentation was conducted, subjects' responses (from a previous research study) to two of these instruments were subjected to factor analysis, and the open-ended responses given by 63 college males and 80 college females as to why they felt good about their physical self were evaluated. Based on these criteria, four subdomains were identified: perceived body attractiveness, sports competence, physical strength, and fitness and exercise.

During Phase II (instrument construction), 6-item subscales were constructed for each of the subdomains using a four-choice structured alternative format. In addition, a six-item subscale was developed to assess physical self-worth at the domain level. Based on the responses of 24 female and 28 male students, some items were subsequently revised.

During Phase III, further analyses among 71 male and 80 female college students were made of item characteristics, as well as subscale internal consistency, stability, factor structure, and social desirability response distortions. Exploratory factor analysis with oblique rotation supported a four-factor structure; however, the physical conditioning subscale appeared to have ambiguous items leading to a revision of this subscale.

Upon confirmation of the factorial validity and internal reliability of the revised subscales (n=128 males; n=106 females), the subscale responses of 49 males and 41 college females were evaluated for test-retest stability across 16 or 23 days. In addition, these subjects were administered the Marlowe-Crowne Social Desirability Scale (1982) to examine the extent to which item responses were susceptible to social desirability.

During Phase IV, the responses of 180 male and 175 female undergraduate students were analyzed to confirm the factor structure of the perception profile. In addition, the relationships of subscale responses to measures of global self-esteem and physical activity behavior were examined to establish the preliminary construct validity of the PSPP. Based on these analyses, a 30-item 5-scale PSPP emerged.

Reliability: Cronbach alpha reliability coefficients ranged from .81 to .92 among 128 male and 106 female undergraduates. Test-retest reliability coefficients ranged between .74 and .92 for a 16-day period, and between .81 and .88 across 23 days.

Validity: Exploratory factor analyses supported a four-factor structure explaining 66.2% of the variance. Confirmatory factor analysis (n=375) indicated that subjects' responses to the PSPP were adequately described by four factors. In addition, the PSPP was successful in discriminating between physically active and nonactive undergraduate students, and was predictive of the type of physical activity engaged in by these students.

Norms: Psychometric data for the final version were based on the responses of 589 undergraduate students enrolled at a midwestern university.

<u>Availability</u>: Contact Kenneth R. Fox, Physical Education Association Research Centre, School of Education, University of Exeter, St. Luke's. Heavitree Road, Exeter EX1 2LU, England. (Phone # 0392-264890) Copies of the PSPP manual are available from the Office for Health Promotion, Northern Illinois University, DeKalb, IL 60115 (Phone # 815-753-0112).

(100)
PLAYGROUND MOVEMENT CONFIDENCE INVENTORY [PMCI]
Michael E. Crawford and Norma Sue Griffin

<u>Source</u>: Crawford, M. E., & Griffin, N. S. (1986). Testing the validity of the Griffin/Keogh Model for Movement Confidence by analyzing the self-report playground involvement decisions of elementary school children. <u>Research Quarterly for Exercise and Sport</u>, <u>57</u>, 1, 8-15.

<u>Purpose</u>: To assess a child's sense of adequacy in a movement situation based on the interaction of personal perceptions of competence in performance, the potential for harm, and the potential for enjoyment.

<u>Description</u>: Six playground tasks are pictorially presented to children. The three subscales (competence, harm, and enjoyment) center on questions about the confidence and performance decisions of the children in relation to each playground task shown. Items are assessed using a 4-point ordinal scale.

<u>Construction</u>: A large pool of movement tasks commonly performed on a playground were evaluated by experts and were subjected to a series of field trials. The six tasks selected were judged to be age appropriate, and most representative of the range of playground movement choices/behavior for these children.

<u>Reliability</u>: Alpha reliability coefficients (n=250 fifth grade students), computed by subscale, were .86 (competence), .87 (harm), and .84 (enjoyment). Test-retest reliability coefficients for this sample were .79 (competence), .75 (harm), .78 (enjoyment), and .78 for the combined inventory score.

<u>Validity</u>: The PMCI successfully discriminated between high versus low confidence and high versus low experience children. The index of discriminatory power was 84.65% correct classification accuracy, and the validity coefficient for scale classification power was .98.

   Construct validity was supported through principal component factor analysis. The three hypothesized factors emerged (competence, harm, enjoyment) accounting for 54% of the total variance (with 90% of this variance explained by the competence factor).

Norms: Not reported. Psychometric data were cited for 250 fifth-grade students in the Omaha Public Schools who were selected through cluster sampling; geographical stratification of the school district was utilized to ensure socioeconomic representativeness of the sample. Fifty-one percent of the sample was male and 49% was female.

Availability: Contact Norma Sue Griffin, School of HPER, 202 MLH, University of Nebraska-Lincoln, Lincoln NE 68588-0229. (Phone # 402-472-1701)

(101)
[SELF-CONFIDENCE OF ABILITY QUESTIONNAIRE] [SCAQ]
K. Willimczik, S. Rethorst, and H. J. Riebel

Source: Willimczik, K., Rethorst, S., & Riebel, H. -J. (1986). Cognitions and emotions in sports games--a cross-cultural comparative analysis. International Journal of Physical Education, 23(1), 10-16.

Purpose: To measure self-confidence in one's ability in sport.

Description: The SCAQ contains 5 items that include both volleyball-specific items and items relating to the sport-specific concept of ability. For example, "Before the start of the game, I am confident of giving a good performance." Subjects respond based on a scale of 0 (not at all true) to 6 (completely true).

Construction: Not discussed.

Reliability: Internal consistency coefficients of .66 (n= 137 male and female German volleyball players) and .63 (n=150 male and female Indonesian volleyball players) were reported.

Validity: Not discussed.

Norms: Not cited. Psychometric data were based on the responses of 68 male German volleyball players, 69 female German volleyball players, 90 male Indonesian volleyball players, and 60 female Indonesian volleyball players to the SCAQ.

Availability*: Contact K. Willimczik, Abteilung Sportwissenschaft, Universitat Bielefeld, Universitatsstr., D-4800 Bielefeld 1, Federal Republic of Germany.

(102)
SPORT COMPETENCE INFORMATION SCALE (SCIS)
Thelma Sternberg Horn and Cynthia A. Hasbrook

Source: Horn, T. S., & Hasbrook, C. A. (1987). Psychological characteristics and the criteria children use for self-evaluation. Journal of Sport Psychology, 9, 208-221.

Purpose: To measure children's preferences for particular sources of competence information in a sport setting.

Description: Children are first asked to make judgments regarding their sport competence. They are then asked to rate (using a 5-point Likert scale) how important each of twelve sources is in helping them determine how competent they are in sport. These twelve sources include: coaches' feedback, teammates' feedback, teammates' performance, opponents' performance, personal attraction toward the sport, degree of perceived effort exerted in practice, performance in games, parents' feedback, spectators' feedback, team win-loss record, degree of skill improvement over time, and ease in learning new skills. Four items were written to assess each of the 12 informational sources resulting in a 48-item test.

Construction: The SCIS was modified from the results of interview research conducted by Minton (1979) on types of information children in grades 4-6 use in judging their competence in the cognitive, physical, and social domains. Exploratory factor analysis of the SCIS resulted in six factors labeled Peer comparison, Social evaluation I (Coaches and Peers), Internal standards, Social Evaluation II (Parents and Spectators), Game outcome, and Affect.

Reliability: Not cited.

Validity: Concurrent validity was supported in that young athletes' ($n=175$) with external perceptions of performance control exhibited a greater preference for external information, while those with high perceived competence and an internal perception of control demonstrated greater reliance on self-determined standards of performance. However, among 8-9 year-old soccer athletes ($n=54$), measures of perceived soccer competence and perceived performance control were not related to their scores on the SCIS.

Norms: Not cited. Psychometric data were based on the responses of 90 male and 139 female youth soccer athletes, ages 8-14 years.

Availability: Contact Thelma Horn, Department of PHS, Phillips Hall, Miami University, Oxford, OH 45056. (Phone # 513-529-2723)

Reference

*Horn, T. S., & Hasbrook, C. A. (1986). Information components influencing children's perceptions of their physical competence. In M. Weiss & D. Gould (Eds.), Sport for children and youths: The 1984 Olympic Scientific Congress proceedings (Vol. 10) (pp. 81-88). Champaign, IL: Human Kinetics Publishers.

(103)
STATE SPORT-CONFIDENCE INVENTORY (SSCI)
Robin S. Vealey

Source: Vealey, R. S. (1986). Conceptualization of sport-confidence and competitive orientation: Preliminary investigation and instrument development. Journal of Sport Psychology, 8, 221-246.

Purpose: To assess the belief or degree of certainty individuals possess at one particular moment about their ability to be successful in sport.

Description: The SSCI contains 13 items measured using a 9-point Likert scale. Subjects are asked to indicate how confident they feel right now about competing in an upcoming contest. When responding, subjects are asked to compare their confidence to the most self-confident athlete they know.

Construction: An initial battery of 19 items was evaluated by four experts with extensive background in sport psychology to establish item clarity and face and content validity. Fifteen items were retained and placed in a 5-point Likert scale format. Factor analyses of high school ($\underline{n}$=99) and college ($\underline{n}$=101) students' responses to the SSCI confirmed the unidimensionality of scale items. However, the obtained correlation coefficient ($\underline{r}$=.21) between subjects' responses to the SSCI and the Crowne-Marlowe Social Desirabilty Scale indicated that the SSCI was somewhat contaminated by social desirability response bias.

The SSCI was subsequently modified including conversion of the items to a 9-point Likert scale format. Additional testing utilizing samples of high school ($\underline{n}$=103) and college ($\underline{n}$=96) varsity athletes led to the retention of 13 items that demonstrated adequate variability, internal consistency, item-total score correlation coefficients greater than .50, and acceptable item discrimination coefficients. There was no evidence of social desirability contamination.

Reliability: An alpha reliability coefficient of .95 was obtained ($\underline{n}$=199 high school and college athletes). Test-retest reliability was not evaluated since the SSCI was conceptualized as a state measure.

Validity: Concurrent validity was evident by the positive correlation (.69) of the SSCI with the state self-confidence scale of the CSAI-2. Also, subjects' (n=199 high school and college athletes) responses to the SSCI were inversely related to both their competitive A-trait scores on the SCAT and their responses to the cognitive and somatic state anxiety scales of the CSAI-2. Construct validity of the SSCI was evident by demonstrating that pre- and postcompetitive state sport-confidence was positively correlated to subjects' (n=48 elite gymnasts) initial trait sport-confidence and competitive orientation scores. However, subjects' pre-competitive state sport-confidence scores were not correlated with their subsequent gymnastic performance scores.

Norms: Not available. Psychometric data were reported for 212 high school athletes (n=141 females; n=71 males) and 206 college athletes (n=103 females; n=103 males), and for 48 elite gymnasts.

Availability: Contact Robin S. Vealey, Dept. of PHS, Phillips Hall, Miami University, Oxford, OH 45056. (Phone # 513-529-2700)

References

Feltz, D. L., Corcoran, J. P., & Lirgg, C. D. (1989). Relationship among team confidence, sport confidence and hockey performance (abstract). Psychology of motor behavior and sport (p. 102). Kent, OH: Proceedings of the North American Society for the Psychology of Sport and Physical Activity annual convention.

*Gayton, W. F., & Nickless, C. J. (1987). An investigation of the validity of the Trait and State Sport-Confidence inventories in predicting marathon performance. Perceptual and Motor Skills, 65, 481-482.

*Vealey, R. S., & Campbell, J. L. (1988). Achievement goals of adolescent figure skaters: Impact on self-confidence, anxiety, and performance. Journal of Adolescent Research, 3, 227-243.

(104)
STUNT MOVEMENT CONFIDENCE INVENTORY (SMCI)
Norma S. Griffin and Michael E. Crawford

Source: Griffin, N. S., & Crawford, M. E. (1989). Measurement of movement confidence with a Stunt Movement Confidence Inventory. Journal of Sport & Exercise Psychology, 11, 26-40.

Purpose: To measure self-perceptions of movement confidence among children.

Description: The SMCI contains pictorial representations of six movement tasks such as performing a stunt on a skateboard and jumping while roller skating. The six tasks were selected and designed to present performance demands involving height, speed, strength, balance and/or coordination; stunting was presented as a means of introducing movement challenge. Initial items of the SMCI focus on subject self-ratings of confidence and experience (using a 4-point ordinal scale) in relation to each task. Subjects are then asked to respond to nine items per task (on a 4-point rating scale) based on performance perceptions. These nine items represent the three factors of personal perceptions of competence, perceived potential for enjoying movement, and perceptions of the potentional for physical harm.

Construction: The movement confidence model was selected as a theoretical focus for evaluating children's movement perceptions and decisions. This model guided construction of the two dependent variables measuring perceptions of movement confidence and experience, the six pictorially represented movement tasks, and the three movement confidence factor subscales.

Reliability: Alpha reliability coefficients (n=356 elementary school c h i l d - ren) were .90, .93, and .91 for the subscales of competence, enjoyment, and harm, respectively. Test-retest reliability coefficients across a two-week interval among these subjects were .82 (experience with task), .80 (movement confidence), .88 (competence), .79 (enjoyment), and .85 (harm).

Validity: Multiple discriminant analysis indicated that the SMCI was sufficiently stable to discriminate among high and low confidence/experience groups. This was confirmed by analytical validation of the SMCI indicating minimal R shrinkage. Construct validity was examined through factor analysis which supported the importance of the three model factors of enjoyment, competence, and harm in providing a meaningful analysis of performance decisions.

Norms: Psychometric data were based on a representative sample (n=356), using cluster sampling procedures, of all children in the fourth and fifth grades of the Omaha, Nebraska public school system. No differences were found on the total score of the SMCI when the data were examined as a function of subject gender and ethnic group.

Availability: Contact Norma S. Griffin, School of HPER, 202 MLH, University of Nebraska-Lincoln, Lincoln, NE 68588-0229. (Phone # 402-472-1701)

(105)
SWIM SKILLS EFFICACY SCALE (SSES)
Patricia I. Hogan and James P. Santomier

Source: Hogan, P. I., & Santomier, J. P. (1984). Effect of mastering swim skills on older adults' self-efficacy. Research Quarterly for Exercise and Sport, 55, 294-296.

Purpose: To measure the conviction that one can successfully execute the aquatic behavior required to produce certain outcomes.

Description: The SSES presents 11 swim-skill related items in order of increasing difficulty. The SSES considers the level, confidence, and strength of efficacy expectations.

Construction: Modified from Bandura's efficacy scales.

Reliability: A test-retest reliability coefficient of .99 was obtained across a one-week interval among 15 elderly subjects.

Validity: Not discussed.

Norms: Not cited.

Availability*: Contact James P. Santomier, Program in Physical Education and Sport, New York University, 635 E. Building, New York, NY 10003. (Phone # 212-598-2386)

(106)
TRAIT SPORT-CONFIDENCE INVENTORY (TSCI)
Robin S. Vealey

Source: Vealey, R. S. (1986). Conceptualization of sport-confidence and competitive orientation: Preliminary investigation and instrument development. Journal of Sport Psychology, 8, 221-246.

Purpose: To assess individual differences in the belief or degree of certainty individuals usually possess about their ability to be successful in sport.

Description: The TSCI contains 13 items that were placed in inventory format using a 9-point Likert scale. Subjects are asked to indicate how confident they generally feel when competing in sport. When responding, subjects are asked to compare their confidence to the most confident athlete they know. For example, subjects are asked to "compare your confidence in YOUR ABILITY TO ACHIEVE YOUR COMPETITIVE GOALS to the most confident athlete you know."

Construction: An initial battery of 20 items were evaluated by four experts to establish item clarity and face and content validity. Sixteen items were retained and placed in a 5-point Likert scale format. Factor analyses of high school (n=99) and college (n=101) students' responses to the TSCI confirmed the unidimensionality of scale items. However, the obtained correlation coefficient (r=.23) between subjects' responses to the TSCI and the Crowne-Marlowe Social Desirability Scale indicated that the TSCI was somewhat contaminated by social desirability response bias.

The TSCI was subsequently modified including conversion of the items to a 9-point Likert scale format. Additional testing utilizing samples of high school (n=103) and college (n=96) varsity athletes led to the retention of 13 items that demonstrated adequate variability, internal consistency (r=.93), item-total score correlation coefficients greater than .50, and acceptable item discrimination coefficients. There was no evidence of social desirability contamination.

Reliability: Alpha reliability was reported as .93. Test-retest reliability coefficients among a sample of high school (n=109) and college (n=110) athletes were .86 (1 day interval), .89 (1 week interval), and .83 (1 month interval).

Validity: Concurrent validity coefficients were reported with the Sport Competition Anxiety Test, the Physical Self-Efficacy Scale, Rotter's Internal-External Control Scale, and Rosenberg's Self-Esteem Scale utilizing high school and college athletes (n=199). Construct validity was established by demonstrating among elite gymnasts (n=48) that the TSCI was a significant predictor of pre- and post-competitive state sport-confidence and several subjective outcomes of performance.

<u>Norms</u>: Not available. Psychometric data were reported for 212 high school athletes ($\underline{n}$=141 females; $\underline{n}$=71 males) and 206 college athletes ($\underline{n}$=103 females; $\underline{n}$=103 males) and for 48 elite gymnasts.

<u>Availability</u>: Contact Robin S. Vealey, Dept. of PHS, Phillips Hall, Miami University, Oxford, OH 45056. (Phone # 513-529-2700)

References

Deeter, T. E. (1989). Development of a model of achievement behavior for physical activity. <u>Journal of Sport & Exercise Psychology</u>, <u>11</u>, 13-25.

Dexter, E. K., & Duda, J. L. (1989). Predictors of competitive stress a m o n g female dancers (abstract). <u>Psychology of motor behavior and sport</u> (p. 117). Kent, OH: Proceedings of the North American Society for the Psychology of Sport and Physical Activity annual convention.

*Gayton, W. F., & Nickless, C. J. (1987). An investigation of the validity of the Trait and State Sport-Confidence inventories in predicting marathon performance. <u>Perceptual and Motor Skills</u>, <u>65</u>, 481-482.

*Vealey, R. S. (1988). Sport-confidence and competitive orientation: An addendum on scoring procedures and gender differences. <u>Journal of Sport & Exercise Psychology</u>, <u>10</u>, 471-478.

*Vealey, R. S., & Campbell, J. L. (1988). Achievement goals of adolescent figure skaters: Impact on self-confidence, anxiety, and performance. <u>Journal of Adolescent Research</u>, <u>3</u>, 227-243.

Chapter 12

IMAGERY

Tests in this chapter assess individual differences in visual imagery of movement, the imagery of kinesthetic sensations, and in imagery utilization.

(107)
IMAGERY USE QUESTIONNAIRE (IUQ)
Craig R. Hall, Kathryn A. Barr, and Wendy M. Rodgers

Source: Hall, C. R., Rodgers, W. M., & Barr, K. A. (in press). The use of imagery by athletes in selected sports. The Sport Psychologist.

Purpose: To examine factors related to imagery utilization in sport.

Description: The IUQ contains 37 items. For example, subjects are asked to indicate the extent to which they use imagery before or during practice, or before or during a sport event. Subjects respond to each item using a 7-point Likert scale except for two items that require yes/no responses. The scale anchor points are 1 (never or very difficult) to 7 (always or very easy).

Construction: Items on the IUQ were developed from a review of literature pertaining to imagery in sport, and from consulting experts in the fields of motor learning, sports psychology, and questionnaire development techniques (Hall & Barr, 1989).

Reliability: The authors reported that the average test-retest reliability coefficient across all items on a rowing version of the IUQ was .71.

Validity: The IUQ successfully discriminated between novice and elite rowers. Novices indicated seeing themselves rowing incorrectly more often. Elite rowers reported more frequently using kinesthetic imagery. They also had more structure and regularity to their imagery sessions (Hall & Barr, 1989).

Norms: Not cited. Psychometric data were based on the responses to the IUQ of 348 rowers at high school, college, and national team levels (Hall & Barr, 1989).

Availability: Contact Craig Hall, Faculty of Physical Education, University of Western Ontario, London, Ontario, Canada N6A 3K7. (Phone # 519-661-3076)

Reference
Hall, C., & Barr, K. (1989). Imagery use among rowers (abstract). Proceedings of the 20th annual conference of the Canadian Society for Psychomotor Learning and Sport Psychology (p. 45). Victoria, British Columbia, Canada.

(108)
[MENTAL IMAGERY TESTS] [MIT]
Dorothy L. Moody

Source: Moody, D. L. (1967). Imagery differences among women of varying levels of experience, interests, and abilities in motor skills. Research Quarterly, 38, 441-448.

Purpose: To examine individual differences in motor-skill imagery.

Description: Subjects are presented three filmed subtests, involving observations of objects and/or persons in movement. Imagery subtest I involves recognition of four geometric forms in which subjects respond to 10 test items. Imagery subtest II requires subjects to watch a brief movie of a motor act (such as a golf swing), and then identify that act when it is presented as one of four similar motor acts a few seconds later. Imagery subtest III requires subjects to watch a brief movie of a motor act, and then read and answer a series of five questions on that act. There are ten test films.

Construction: Not indicated.

Reliability: A corrected split-half odd-even internal consistency coefficient of .87 was obtained (composite score) among 77 college women.

Validity: The three subtests were not successful in discriminating between college physical education majors and nonmajors.

Norms: Not reported.

Availability*: Unknown.

(109)
MOVEMENT IMAGERY QUESTIONNAIRE (MIQ)
Craig Hall and John Pongrac

Source: Hall, C., Pongrac, J., & Buckholz, E. (1985). The measurement of imagery ability. Human Movement Science, 4, 107-118.

Purpose: To assess individual differences in visual and kinesthetic imagery of movements.

Description: The MIQ contains 18 items, 9 for the visual subscale and 9 for the kinesthetic subscale. Subjects are asked to use visual or kinesthetic imagery while performing a variety of arm movements, leg movements, and movements involving the entire body. They are asked to rate how difficult it is to use visual or kinesthetic imagery while performing each movement task. Subjects respond to each subscale using a 7-point rating scale. Total scores range from 9 (high score on imagery) to 63.

Construction: An initial pool of 28 items was administered to 74 physical education students. Item analyses led to the retention of 18 items.

Reliability: Cronbach alpha internal consistency coefficients of .87 (visual subscale) and .91 (kinesthetic subscale) were reported based on the responses of another sample of 80 physical education students. A test-retest reliability coefficient of .83 was reported among 32 of these students (no time interval specified).

Validity: Not discussed.

Norms: Not cited. Psychometric data were based on the responses of independent samples of $n=74$ and $n=80$ physical education students.

Availability: Contact Craig Hall, Faculty of Physical Education, University of Western Ontario, London, Ontario, Canada N6A 3K7. (Phone # 519-661-3076)

References
*Goss, S., Hall, C., Buckholz, E., & Fishburne, G. (1986). Imagery ability and the acquisition and retention of movements. Memory and Cognition, 14, 469-477.
*Hall, C., Buckolz, E., & Fishburne, G. (1989). Searching for a relationship between imagery ability and memory of movements. Journal of Human Movement Studies, 17, 89-100.
*Margolies, M. D., Griffey, D. C., & Fahleson, G. A. (1986). Imagery orientation and meta cognitions of athletes during skill acquisition and perform-

ance (abstract). <u>Proceedings of the annual conference of the Association for the Advancement for Applied Sport Psychology</u> (p. 47). GA: Jekyll Island.

*Mumford, B., & Hall, C. (1985). The effects of internal and external imagery on performing figures in figure skating. <u>Canadian Journal of Applied Sport Sciences, 10</u>, 171-177.

*Pargman, D., Juaire, S., & Gill, K. (1987). Comparison of imagery induced arousal effects on performance of a visually distorted, novel ball tossing task in female collegiate athletes of high and low imaging abilities (Abstract). <u>Research Abstracts</u> (p. 210). Reston, VA: Proceedings of the American Alliance for Health, Physical Education, Recreation, and Dance annual convention, Las Vegas, NV.

(110)
VIVIDNESS OF MOVEMENT IMAGERY QUESTIONNAIRE (VMIQ)
Anne Isaac, David F. Marks, and David G. Russell

<u>Source</u>: Issac, A., Marks, D. F., & Russell, D. G. (1986). An instrument for assessing imagery of movement: The Vividness of Movement Imagery Questionnaire (VMIQ). <u>Journal of Mental Imagery, 10</u>(4), 23-30.

<u>Purpose</u>: To assess individual differences in the visual imagery of movement and the imagery of kinesthetic sensations.

<u>Description</u>: The VMIQ contains 24 items. Subjects are asked to rate the vividness of imagery for an item obtained watching somebody else and doing it themselves. Items cover basic body movements to movements requiring precision and control in upright, unbalanced, aerial situations. Examples of items include: "Kicking a ball in the air" and "riding a bike." Subjects respond to each item using a 5-point ordinal scale with the anchorings "perfectly clear and as vivid as normal vision" to "no image at all...."

<u>Construction</u>: Not indicated.

<u>Reliability*</u>: A test-retest reliability coefficient of .76 was reported over a 3-week interval among 220 high school and college undergraduate students.

<u>Validity*</u>: Convergent validity was supported in that subjects' ($\underline{n}$=220) responses to the VMIQ and Marks' Vividness of Visual Imagery Questionnaire were correlated. Furthermore, correlation coefficients ranging from .45 to .75 were reported when comparing the responses of independent samples ($\underline{n}$=25; $\underline{n}$=25; $\underline{n}$=16) of trampolinists on the VMIQ with Marks' imagery questionnaire.

Norms*: Not cited. Psychometric data were presented for 170 undergraduate physical education students, 50 high school students, and 56 trampolinists residing in New Zealand.

Availability: Contact Anne Isaac, School of Physical Education, Box 56, University of Otago, Dunedin, New Zealand. (Phone # 024-798960)

Reference

*Campos, A., & Perez, M. J. (1988). Vividness of Movement Imagery Questionnaire: Relations with other measures of mental imagery. Perceptual and Motor Skills, 67, 607-610.

*Additional data on reliability and validity, and normative data for 1202 subjects are presented in the unpublished doctoral dissertation of the first author (Isaac, personal communication, March 13, 1990).

Chapter 13

LEADERSHIP

The tests in this chapter assess the perceptions/preferences of athletes for specific leader behaviors from the coach, coach's perceptions of his/her own leader behavior, and satisfaction with various aspects of leadership in sport.

(111)
LEADERSHIP SCALE FOR SPORTS (LSS)
Packianathan Chelladurai and S. D. Saleh

Source: Chelladurai, P., & Saleh, S. D. (1980). Dimensions of leader behavior in sports: Development of a leadership scale. Journal of Sport Psychology, 2, 34-45.

Purpose: The LSS can be used to examine: (1) the preferences of athletes for specific leader behavior from the coach, (2) the perceptions of athletes regarding the actual leader behavior of their coach, and (3) the coach's perceptions of his/her own leader behavior.

Description: The LSS is a 40-item questionnaire containing five factors: Training and Instruction, Democratic Behavior, Autocratic Behavior, Social Support, and Positive Feedback. Subjects respond to each item using a five-point Likert scale. Versions include: Athletes' preferred leadership and the athletes' perceived leadership.

Construction: A total of 99 items were chosen and modified from existing leadership scales. Factor analysis of the responses of 80 male and 80 female physical education majors led to the retention of 37 items representing five defined factors. In the second stage of development, seven items were added to tap the instruction behavior of a coach; also, six more social support items were added. The revised questionnaire (containing 50 items) was then administered to 102 physical education students and a male sample of 223 college varsity athletes representing four sports at different Canadian universities. Factor analyses of subjects' responses led to the retention of five factors as previously noted.

Reliability: Alpha reliability coefficients ranged from .66 (Autocratic Behavior) to .79 (Positive Feedback) among 102 physical education majors. Alpha reliability coefficients were also reported for the 223 athletes who were queried regarding both their preferred and perceived leader behaviors. These coefficients ranged from .45 (Autocratic Behavior) to .83 (Training and Instruction) for the preferred version, and from .79 (Autocratic Behavior) to .93 (Training and Instruction) for the perceived version. Test-retest reliability coefficients among 53 of the physical education majors across a 4-week interval ranged from .71 (Social Support) to .82 (Democratic Behavior).

Validity: Construct validity was supported by demonstrating through factor analyses the emergence of five identical factors (noted above) across both the physical education majors ($n=102$) and the varsity athletes ($n=223$). On the average, these five factors accounted for 45.43% of the variance in subjects' responses to the items of the questionnaire.

Norms: Not cited. Descriptive data were reported for 45 male and 57 female physical education majors and 223 varsity athletes representing basketball, track and field, rowing, and wrestling from different Canadian universities. [Also, see Chelladurai, P. (1989). Manual for the Leadership Scale for Sports that is available from the author.]

Availability. Contact Packianathan Chelladurai, Faculty of Physical Education, University of Western Ontario, London, Ontario, Canada N6A 3K7. (Phone # 519-679-2111 [Ext. 8393])

References

*Chelladurai, P. (in press). Leadership in sports: A review. International Journal of Sport Psychology.

*Chelladurai, P., Imamura, H., Yamaguchi, Y., Oinuma, Y., & Miyauchi, T. (1988). Sport leadership in a cross-national setting: The case of Japanese and Canadian university athletes. Journal of Sport & Exercise Psychology, 10, 374-389.

*Dwyer, J. J. M., & Fischer, D. G. (1988). Psychometric properties of the coach's version of Leadership Scale for Sports. Perceptual and Motor Skills, 67, 795-798.

Summers, R. J. (1983). A study of leadership in a sport setting (abstract). In Psychology of motor behavior and sport-1983 (p. 130). Proceedings of the North American Society for the Psychology of Sport and Physical Activity annual convention, East Lansing, MI.

Terry, P. (1984). The coaching preference of elite athletes (abstract). In Proceedings of the 1984 Olympic Scientific Congress (p. 87). Eugene, OR: College of Human Development and Performance Microform Publications.

(112)
[SCALE OF ATHLETE SATISFACTION] [SAS]
Packianathan Chelladurai, Hiroaki Imamura, Yasuo Yamaguchi,
Yoshihiro Oinuma, and Takatomo Miyauchi

Source: Chelladurai, P., Imamura, H., Yamaguchi, Y., Oinuma, Y., & Miyauchi, T. (1988). Sport leadership in a cross-national setting: The case of Japanese and Canadian university athletes. Journal of Sport & Exercise Psychology, 10, 374-389.

Purpose: To assess satisfaction with various aspects of leadership in athletics and the outcomes of athletic participation that can be associated with leadership.

Description: The Scale of Athlete Satisfaction contains 10 items related to leadership in athletics. The respondent is asked to indicate his/her satisfaction with the content of each item using a 7-point Likert scale.

Construction: Items were selected to represent various elements of leadership in athletics. Translations of scale items were made into the Japanese language. Factor analyses of the responses of Canadian ($n=100$) and Japanese ($n=115$) male university athletes to the scale revealed two common factors labeled Leadership (64.9% accountable variance) and Personal Outcome (14.1% accountable variance).

Reliability: Alpha reliability coefficents of the Leadership and Personal Outcome factors were .95 and .86, respectively.

Validity: Not discussed.

Norms: Not cited. Descriptive data were reported for 115 Japanese and 100 Canadian male university athletes.

Availability: Contact Packianathan Chelladurai, Faculty of Physical Education, University of Western Ontario, London, Ontario, Canada N6A 3K7. (Phone # 519-679-2111-Ext. 8393)

Chapter 14

LIFE ADJUSTMENT

Tests in this chapter assess life events, such as injury, that are experienced by athletes, and that necessitate adjustment.

(113)
[ATHLETE ADJUSTMENT PREDICTION SCALE] [AAPS]
Donald I. Templer and Arthur T. Daus

Source: Templer, D. I., & Daus, A. T. (1979). An athlete adjustment prediction scale. The Journal of Sports Medicine and Physical Fitness, 19, 413-416.

Purpose: To evaluate the degree of adjustment/maladjustment among college athletes.

Description: The AAPS contains 43 items including nine items of the MMPI Lie scale. Subjects respond using a 7-point Likert scale.

Construction: The items were developed based on the authors' clinical experiences in working with college athletes.

Reliability: Not reported.

Validity: The majority of items on the AAPS failed to discriminate among 18 "lesser" college football players versus 11 "better" players. Twelve of the lesser players were viewed as problem athletes.

Norms: Not cited. Descriptive statistics and psychometric data were cited for 29 college football players.

Availability*: Contact Donald I. Templer, California School of Professional Psychology, 1350 M Street, Fresno, CA 93721. (Phone # 209-486-8420)

(114)
ATHLETIC LIFE EXPERIENCES SURVEY (ALES)
Michael W. Passer and Marla D. Seese

Source: Passer, M. W., & Seese, M. D. (1983). Life stress and athletic injury: Examination of positive versus negative events and three moderator variables. Journal of Human Stress, 9(4), 11-16.

Purpose: To examine positive and negative life changes among male college athletes.

Description: The ALES contains 70 items (e.g., "conflict with teammates," "troubles with head coach"). Players are asked to report each event they experienced during the last 12 months, whether the event was "good" or "bad" at the time of occurrence, and the impact that the event had on their lives at the time of the occurrence. Scores on the ALES range from +3 (good, great effect) to -3 (bad, great effect).

Construction: The Life Experiences Survey (1977) was modified to be appropriate to assess the events experienced by males participating in college athletics.

Reliability: Not cited.

Validity: NCAA Division II male football players who incurred significant time-loss injuries (n=9) had experienced more negative life changes during the previous 12 months than uninjured players (n=40). However, these findings did not hold up when injured (n=6) versus noninjured (n=49) NCAA Division I football players were compared on the ALES.

Norms: Psychometric data were based on the responses of 104 male collegiate varsity football players representing Division I and Division II teams.

Availability*: Contact Michael W. Passer, Department of Psychology, Ni-25, University of Washington, Seattle, WA 98185.

Reference
Mueller, D. P., Edwards, D. W., & Yarvis, R. M. (1977). Stressful life events and psychiatric symptomology: Change as undesirability. Journal of Health and Social Behavior, 18, 307-317.

(115)
LIFE EVENTS QUESTIONNAIRE (LEQ)
R. Lysens, Y. Vanden Auweele, and M. Ostyn

Source: Lysens, R., Vanden Auweele, Y., & Ostyn, M. (1986). The relationship between psychosocial factors and athletic injuries. Journal of Sports Medicine and Physical Fitness, 26, 77-89.

Purpose: To assess unique life events germane to physical education students that necessitate major life adjustments.

Description: College students are asked to respond to 74 life events, indicating on a 10-point scale the average degree of social readjustment necessary for each event experienced during their first year at the university. Students can include other events not listed.

Construction: Second year college students were administered questionnaires seeking information on life events experienced during their first year at the university that influenced their personal, athletic, and study life, and that resulted in changes in their accustomed living patterns. The LEQ was developed from an evaluation of these responses. The LEQ represents a modification of the Social and Athletic Readjustment Rating Scale (SARRS).

Reliability: Not discussed.

Validity: Concurrent validity was reported by demonstrating positive correlation coefficients ($n=99$) with personality scales measuring neuroticism, hypochondria, state and trait anxiety, and lack of social desirability. However, the LEQ failed to differentiate between students who did or did not experience acute or overuse injuries.

Norms: Not cited. Psychometric data were reported for 66 male and 33 female university freshman physical education students.

Availability*: Contact R. Lysens, Institute of Physical Education, Katholieke Universiteit Leuven, Tervuursevest, 101, Leuven, Belgium.

(116)
SOCIAL AND ATHLETIC READJUSTMENT RATING SCALE
(SARRS)
Steven T. Bramwell, Minoru Masuda, Nathaniel N. Wagner
and Thomas H. Holmes

Source: Bramwell, S. T., Masuda, M., Wagner, N. N., & Holmes, T. (1975). Psychosocial factors in athletic injuries: Development and application of the Social and Athletic Readjustment Rating Scale (SARRS). Journal of Human Stress, 1(2), 6-20.

Purpose: To assess life events that influence sport performance in terms of degree of adjustment made.

Description: The SARRS contains 57 life events likely to be experienced by an athlete that may necessitate major life adjustments. Subjects are instructed to indicate the magnitude of change for each life event item to be scaled.

Construction: A modification of the Social Readjustment Rating Scale was made to include the addition of 20 new life events unique to athletics. These modifications were made based on preliminary questionnaire responses of collegiate and professional athletes. These athletes were asked to identify life events that impacted their career and sport performance. Modifications were also based on the athletic experience of one of the authors.

Reliability: Not cited.

Validity: Comparison of football players' (n=66) responses to the SARRS with an earlier American (nonathlete) sample's responses to the SRRS indicated that the ordering of life events across samples was correlated (r=.84) for both instruments. Furthermore, the SARRS successfully discriminated between injured (n=36) and noninjured (n=46) college football players in terms of stressful life events experienced.

Norms: Not cited. Psychometric data were reported for 66 University of Washington football players.

Availability*: Unknown. Test items are available in the source pending permission to employ.

References
Cryan, P. D., & Alles, W. F. (1983). The relationship between stress and college football injuries. Journal of Sports Medicine and Physical Fitness, 23, 52-58.

May, J. R., Veach, T. L., Reed, M. W., & Griffey, M. S. (1984). A psychological study of health, injury, and performance in athletes on the U.S. Alpine Ski Team. The Physician and Sportsmedicine, 13(10), 111-115.

Chapter 15

LOCUS OF CONTROL

Tests in this chapter assess individuals' perceptions of internal and/or external factors that control their reinforcements in relation to exercise behavior, sport performance, injury rehabilitation, and career choice.

(117)
EXERCISE OBJECTIVES LOCUS OF CONTROL SCALE (EOLOC)
Marina L. McCready and Bonita C. Long

Source: McCready, M. L., & Long, B. C. (1985). Locus of control, attitudes toward physical activity, and exercise adherence. Journal of Sport Psychology, 7, 346=359.

Purpose: To assess individuals' perceptions of what controls their reinforcements in relation to exercise behavior.

Description: The EOLOC consists of three 6-item subscales: Internality, Powerful others, and Chance. For example, subjects respond to the item "I am directly responsible for whether or not I reach my exercise goals" (Internal scale). Subjects respond to each item using a 5-point Likert scale with the anchorings strongly agree to strongly disagree.

Construction: An initial 24-item test pool was developed reflective of the three subdomains (above). Ten graduate students evaluated each item for clarity and content validity. The same 24 items were evaluated through item analysis and internal consistency checks among 60 aerobic fitness class participants (M age=30 years; n=50 females, n=10 males). Six items were eliminated and two new chance subscale items were added. The revised 20-item EOLOC was administered to 87 females (M age= 30 years) involved in fitness programs. Item analysis led to the elimination of two chance subscale items resulting in the 18 item EOLOC. Intercorrelation coefficients among subscales were low, although the Internal and Powerful others subscales were not correlated.

Reliability: Alpha reliability coefficients ($\underline{n}$=87 females) were .79, .69, and .75 for the Internal, Powerful others, and Chance subscales, respectively. Test-retest reliability coefficients for this sample (who were participating in the exercise programs) were .32 (Internal), .72 (Powerful others), and .60 (Chance) across a 3-4 month interval.

Validity: The construct validity of the EOLOC was examined through principal component factor analysis ($\underline{n}$=172 females) in which five factors emerged accounting for 51% of the variance. Factor 5 was not evaluated because it only accounted for 4% of the total variance. Factors 1 & 2 were defined by the all the internal and chance items, while the powerful others items were split between Factors 3 and 4.

Discriminant validity was supported in that subjects' responses to the EOLOC were not related to a measure of social desirability.

Norms: Not reported. Psychometric data were cited for 172 female subjects.

Availability: Contact Bonita C. Long, Department of Counseling Psychology, 210-5780 Toronto Road, University of British Columbia, Vancouver, B. C., Canada V6T 1L2. (Phone # 604-228-4756)

Reference
Long, B. C., & Haney, C. J. (1986). Enhancing physical activity in sedentary women. Information, locus of control, and attitudes. Journal of Sport Psychology, 8, 8-24.

(118)
[FITNESS LOCUS OF CONTROL SCALE] (FITLOC)
James R. Whitehead and Charles B. Corbin

Source: Whitehead, J. R., & Corbin, C. B. (1988). Multidimensional scales for the measurement of locus of control reinforcements for physical fitness behaviors. (1988). Research Quarterly for Exercise and Sport, 59, 108-117.

Purpose: To assess among individuals locus of control of reinforcement beliefs specific to physical fitness behaviors.

Description: The FITLOC is an 11-item test containing three subscales: internality (IFit), powerful others (PFit), and chance (CFit). Subjects respond to each item using a 6-point Likert format.

Construction: After reviewing the literature on social learning and locus of control theory, items were developed reflecting the three dimensions (internality, powerful others, and chance) of physical fitness behavior reinforcement locus of control beliefs. Four exercise psychology experts reduced the battery of items to 18 items. The 18 trial items were evaluated among 119 freshman undergraduate students who were also administered concurrently a shortened version of the Marlowe-Crowne Social Desirability scale, nine ambiguous filler items, Levenson's IPC scales, and the Weight Locus of Control scale. Principal components factor analysis led to the retention of 11 items with moderate alpha reliability. The three subscales correlated positively with the theoretically corresponding IPC and WLOC scales. Correlation coefficients for the IFit, CFit, and PFit subscales with the social desirability scale were statistically significant.

An additional sample of 125 freshman undergraduate students was administered either the 11-item FITLOC or the 11-item FITLOC combined with 6 ambiguous filler items. The addition of these six camouflaging items had minimal effect on the psychometric properties of the FITLOC.

Reliability: Alpha reliability coefficients (n=62 undergraduate students in freshman composition classes) were .62 (IFit), .74 (PFit), and .84 (CFit). For 133 undergraduate students enrolled in physical education, alpha reliability coefficients were .78 (IFit), .74 (PFit). and .82 (CFit). Test-retest reliability coefficients (n=60 freshman composition students) across a two-week interval were .69 (IFit), .59 (PFit), and .67 (Cfit).

Validity: Concurrent validity was evident by the correlation of subjects' (n=115) scores on the FITLOC subscales with the IPC subscales. Weak support for concurrent validity was evident when subjects' (n=133) scores on the FIT-LOC subscales were correlated with self-report estimates of physical activity participation. Construct validity was supported through a series of factor analytic studies that led to the retention of the three subscale factors noted above.

Norms: Not reported. Psychometric data were cited for independent samples (n=115; n=125; n=133) of undergraduate male and female students.

Availability: Contact James Whitehead, Department of HPER, University of North Dakota, Box 8235. Grand Forks, ND 58202. (Phone # 701-777-2992)

Reference

Tappe, M. K., & Duda, J. L. (1988). Personal investment predictors of life satisfaction among physically active middle-aged and older adults. Journal of Psychology, 122, 557-566.

(119)
[LOCUS OF CONTROL IN REHABILITATION SCALE] [LCRS]
Joan L. Duda, Alison E. Smart, and Marlene K. Tappe

Source: Duda, J. L., Smart, A. E., & Tappe, M. K. (1989). Predictors of adherence in the rehabilitation of athletic injuries: An application of personal investment theory. Journal of Sport & Exercise Psychology, 11, 367-381.

Purpose: To examine the degree to which athletes perceive their successful injury rehabilitation to be either under their personal control, or the responsibility of the athletic trainer.

Description: The LCRS contains nine items and includes internal and external locus of control subscales. Subjects respond to each item using a 6-point Likert scale.

Construction: Not discussed.

Reliability: Cronbach alpha reliability coefficients (n=40) for the Internal and External subscales were .77 and .75, respectively.

Validity: Stepwise multiple regression analysis indicated that internal locus of control was a significant predictor of the mean percentage of completed exercises across scheduled rehabiliation sessions.

Norms: Not reported. Psychometric data were cited for 40 male and female intercollegiate athletes who had sustained a sport related injury of at least second-degree severity.

Availability: Contact Joan L. Duda, Department of PEHRS, 113 Lambert Hall, Purdue University, W. Lafayette, IN 47907. (Phone # 317-494-3172)

(120)
[SPORT CAREER LOCUS OF CONTROL TEST] [SCLCT]
M. L. Kamlesh and T. R. Sharma

Source: Kamlesh, M. L. (1989). Internal and external factors affecting sports career. Indian Journal of Sports Science, 1(1), 59-67.

Purpose: To identify the most significant internal and external factors influencing the career of a sportsman.

Description: The SCLCT contains 20 items. The test is designed to assess internal factors (superiority in game skill, practice, and ability) and external factors (financial backing, equipment and coaching, luck, and influence of high-ups) as they affect the sports career of an athlete. Subjects respond to each item (e.g., "To a great extent, my sports career is controlled by accidental happenings"-luck factor) using a 5-point Likert scale.

Construction: Items and factors were identified through an intensive examination of the sociology and psychology of sport literature, and on the basis of experience-oriented observations.

Reliability: A test-retest reliability coefficient (n=23) of .65 was reported.

Validity: Not reported.

Norms: Not cited. Descriptive data were cited for 122 male and 81 female randomly selected athletes (ages 20-33 years) from the National Institute of Sports, Patiala, the Laxmibai College of Physical Education, Gwalior, and the Punjab Goverment College of Physical Education, Patiala, in India.

Availability: Contact M. L. Kamlesh, Lakshmibai National College of Physical Education, Kariavattom P. O., Post Box No. 3, Trivandrum (Kerala) 695 581, India. (Phone # 8712, 8722)

(121)
SPORT LOCUS OF CONTROL SCALE [SLCS]
James Domnick DiFebo   ·

Source: DiFebo, J. D. (1975). Modification of general expectancy and sport expectancy within a sport setting. In D. M. Landers (Ed.), Psychology of sport and motor behavior II (pp. 247-254). State College, PA: Penn State HPER Series No. 10.

Purpose: To assess internal and external dimensions of locus of control as expressed in a sport setting.

Description: The SLCS consists of 20 items measuring internal or external locus of control. Subjects respond to each item using a 4-point Likert scale.

Construction: Not discussed.

Reliability: An alpha reliability coefficient (n=112 college students) of .55 was reported. A test-retest reliability coefficient of .70 was reported across a two-week interval.

Validity: Concurrent validity was supported in that subjects' (n=112) scores on the SLCS were correlated with their responses to the Rotter Internal-External Locus of Control Scale (r=.36). However, construct validity was not supported in that the instrument failed to detect changes in an intervention program designed to modify locus of control in a physical education setting over 16 weeks.

Norms: Not reported. Psychometric data were cited for 112 freshman college students enrolled in a basic instructional Physical Education program at a midwestern university.

Availability*: Contact James D.DiFebo, 419 Salisbury Ave., Meyersdale, PA 15552.

Chapter 16

MISCELLANEOUS

Tests in this chapter examine withdrawal symptoms experienced by runners when a planned run is missed, the job satisfaction of college athletic directors, the emotions of jealousy and envy in a sport context, and behavioral rigidity and superstitious beliefs exhibited among athletes.

(122)
[FRIENDSHIP EXPECTATIONS QUESTIONNAIRE] [FEQ]
Brian J. Bigelow, John H. Lewko, and Linda Salhani

Source: Bigelow, B. J., Lewko, J. H., & Salhani, L. (1989). Sport-involved children's friendship expectations. Journal of Sport & Exercise Psychology, 11, 152-160.

Purpose: To assess the characteristics children conceptualize as important to have in a friendship relationship when involved in sport.

Description: The questionnaire assesses eight friendship expectations (FEs) across five discrete friendship-sport contexts. These FEs include stimulation value, helping, sharing, loyalty and commitment, acceptance, intimacy potential, ego reinforcement, and source of humor. The questionnaire contains a total of 40 items. Subjects respond to each item using a 7-point Likert scale.

Construction: Not discussed.

Reliability: Corrected internal consistency coefficients ($\underline{n}$=40 boys & 40 girls, ages 9-12 years) ranged from .86 to .95 across each of the five sport contexts.

Validity: Not discussed.

Norms: Not presented. Psychometric data were based on the responses of 80 children.

Availability*: Contact John H. Lewko, Centre for Research in Human Development, Laurentian University, Sudbury, Ontario P3E 2C6, Canada.

(123)
[INDEX OF WITHDRAWAL] (WD)
Jeffery J. Summers, Victoria J. Machin, and Gregory I. Sargent

Source: Summers, J. J., Machin, V. J., & Sargent, G. I. (1983). Psychosocial factors related to marathon running. Journal of Sport Psychology, 5, 314-331.

Purpose: To assess the extent to which runners experience psychological symptoms of discomfort when a planned run is missed.

Description: Subjects are asked to indicate on a 3-point scale the extent to which they experience certain feelings of discomfort (e.g., guilt, irritability, depression, frustration) because of running deprivation.

Construction: Items for the WD were drawn from previous studies of withdrawal symptoms following exercise deprivation.

Reliability: An alpha reliability coefficient of .72 was reported.

Validity: Those marathon runners (n=376) who perceived their running as an addiction had a significantly higher composite WD score than marathon runners (n=83) who did not perceive their running as an addiction; this provided support for the construct validity of the WD scale.

Norms: Not reported. Psychometric data were cited for 348 male and 111 female adult (M age= 31.7 years) marathon runners in Australia.

Availability: Contact Jeffery J. Summers, Department of Psychology, University of Melbourne, Parkville, Victoria 3052, Australia. (Phone #03-344-6349)

Reference
*Summers, J. J., & Hinton, E. R. (1986). Development of scales to measure participation in running. In L-E Unestahl (Ed.), Contemporary sport psychology, (pp. 73-84). Orebro, Sweden: VEJE.

(124)
JOB SATISFACTION SCALE [JSS]
Joe P. Ramsey

Source: Evans, E., Ramsey, J. P., Johnson, D., Renwick, D., & Vienneau, J-G (1986). A comparison of job satisfaction, leadership behavior and job perception between male and female athletic directors. The Physical Educator, 43, 39-43.

Purpose: To evaluate the job satisfaction of college athletic directors.

Description: The scale contains 20 items to assess athletic director's satisfaction with the general work situation. Subjects respond to each item using a 5-point ordinal scale.

Construction: Not discussed.

Reliability: An internal consistency coefficient of .81 was reported among 204 college athletic directors.

Validity: Not discussed.

Norms: Psychometric data were cited for 171 male and 33 female college athletic directors representing both Divisions IA ($\underline{n}=79$), II ($\underline{n}=28$), III ($\underline{n}=31$) and 31 Canadian colleges and universities.

Availability*: Contact Joe P. Ramsey, Department of Physical Education, Florida Atlantic University, Boca Raton, FL 33431. (Phone # 305-393-3792)

(125)
POWER VALUE ORIENTATION TEST (PVO)
Brenda J. Bredemeier

Source: Bredemeier, B. J. (1980). An instrument to assess the expressive and instrumental power valued in sport and in everyday life (abstract). Research abstracts-American Alliance for Health, Physical Education, Recreation and Dance (p. 66). Annual convention, Detroit, MI.

Purpose: To assess expressive and instrumental power value orientations in sport and in everyday life.

Description: Not provided.

Construction: Not indicated.

Reliability: Alpha internal consistency coefficients from .86 to .92 were reported among 230 athletes.

Validity: Content validity was established via the use of expert opinion.

Norms: Not cited. Psychometric data were based on 230 male and female athletes representing professional, college varsity, and noncollege varsity levels.

Availability*: Contact Brenda J. Bredemeier, Department of Physical Education, 200 Hearst Gymnasium, University of California, Berkeley, CA 94720.

(126)
SOCIAL COMPARISON JEALOUSY SCALE (SCJ)
Dale G. Pease

Source: Pease, D. G. (1988). Social comparison jealousy and its relationship to group cohesion (abstract). In Psychology of motor behavior and sport (p. 161). Proceedings of the North American Society for the Psychology of Sport and Physical Activity annual convention, Knoxville, TN.

Purpose: To assess the emotions of jealousy and envy in a sport context.

Description: Not indicated.

Construction: The original scale designed to measure jealousy and envy was reduced from 20 to 12 items. This was based on the conceptual framework that jealousy is a triadic relationship, while envy is viewed as a dyadic relationship.

Reliability: An alpha reliability coefficient of .83 was reported for the SCJ among 71 team sport participants.

Validity: The hypothesized inverse relationship between subjects' scores on the SCJ and the social subscales of the Group Environment Questionnaire failed to materialize (n=71).

Norms: Not reported. Psychometric data were cited for 71 team sport participants.

Availability*: Contact Dale G. Pease, Department of Physical Education, 129 Melcher Gym, University of Houston, Houston, TX 77004. (Phone # 713-749-7571)

(127)
SPORT PSYCHOLOGY CONSULTANT EVALUATION FORM (CEF)
John Partington and Terry Orlick

Source: Partington, J., & Orlick, T. (1987). The Sport Psychology Consultant Evaluation Form. The Sport Psychologist, 1, 309-317.

Purpose: To assess the perceptions athletes have of sport psychology consultants, and the amount and type of athlete-consultant contact.

Description: The CEF contains ten consultant characteristic items that athletes rate on a 11-point ordinal scale. Six additional items relate to the duration of several types of contact between athlete and sport psychology consultant. Perceived consultant effectiveness is also assessed by two rating criteria using an 11-point ordinal scale.

Construction: Item selection was based on interview data on consultant effectiveness gathered from 75 Olympic athletes and 17 national team coaches.

Reliability: An alpha internal consistency coefficient of .68 was reported for 104 Canadian Olympic athletes. The test-retest reliability coefficient for the consultant characteristics total scale score ($n=15$ national team athletes) was .81 across a two-day interval.

Validity: Concurrent validity of the consultant characteristics scale was evidenced by demonstrating positive correlation coefficients with perceived consultant effectiveness ($r=.68$, effect on you; $r=.57$, effect on team). Stepwise multiple regression analysis indicated that the scale of consultant characteristics accounted for three times more variance in predicting effectiveness than was possible from knowledge of the amounts and types of consultant contacts.

Norms: Not reported. Psychometric data were cited for 104 Canadian Olympic athletes who evaluated 26 sport psychology consultants.

Availability*: Contact John Partington, Department of Psychology, Carleton University, Ottawa, Canada, K1S 5B6.

(128)
SPORT SELF-IN-ROLE SCALE [SSIRS]
Timothy Jon Curry and Robert Parr

Source: Curry, T. J., & Parr, R. (1988). Comparing commitment to sport and religion at a Christian college. Sociology of Sport Journal, 5, 369-377.

Purpose: To assess a college student's involvement in the sport role, particularly regarding agenda-setting, decision-making, and emotional involvement.

Description: The SSIRS contains thirteen items. Subjects are asked to respond on a 5-point Likert scale to items such as "During the week, I have made several decisions in which my sport involvement has influenced my decision," and "I often dream or daydream about sports."

Construction: Items were selected initially from Jackson's (1981) Social Identity Questionnaire. Five items were eliminated due to extreme response skewness. Three additional items were added that linked thought and identity to the sport role such as "Being an athlete is an important part of who I am."

Reliability: A Cronbach alpha internal consistency coefficent (n=348 male college students) of .92 was reported.

Validity: Concurrent validity was examined in which subjects' (n=220) responses to the SSIRS correlated positively with their commitment to sport (r=.64), their enjoyment of sport role (r=.33), and their time spent in sport role (r=.55) (Curry & Weaner, 1987).

Norms: Not cited. Psychometric data were based on the responses of 348 students attending a small, private, church affiliated institution close to Springfield, Ohio, as well as 220 male college students attending Ohio State University.

Availability: Contact Timothy Jon Curry, Department of Sociology, Ohio State University, 300 Bricker Hall, 190 North Oval Mall, Columbus, OH 43210.

References
*Curry, T. J., & Weaner, J. S. (1987). Sport identity salience, commitment, and the involvement of self in role: Measurement issues. Sociology of Sport Journal, 4, 280-288.

Curry, T. J., & Weiss, D. (1989). Sport identity and motivation for sport participation: A comparison between American college athletes and Austrian student sport club members. Sociology of Sport Journal, 6, 257-268.

Jackson, S. E. (1981). Measurement of commitment to role identities. Journal of Personality and Social Psychology, 40, 138-146.

(129)
SPORT SITUATION RIGIDITY TEST (SSRT)
A. Craig Fisher and Susan K. Borowicz

Source: Fisher, A. C., Borowicz, S. K., & Morris, H. H. (1978). Behavioral rigidity across sport situations. In D. M. Landers and R. W. Christina (Eds.), Psychology of motor behavior and sport-1977 (pp.359-368). Champaign, IL.: Human Kinetics Publishers.

Purpose: To assess an individual's resistance to change across a variety of athletic situations.

Description: The SSRT contains 16 sport situations varying in degree of difficulty of response. Subjects are directed to react to the decision of the coach in the situation (based on their personal coaching philosophy) using a 5-point Likert scale.

Construction: The SSRT was developed with the assistance of several male college coaches and a graduate sport psychology class to ensure that the situations were representative of real-life coaching experiences.

Reliability: Test-retest reliability coefficients (n=56 male undergraduate physical education majors) for the 16 sport situations ranged from .08 to .75.

Validity: Principal component factor analysis resulted in the retention of seven factors. (The reliability of situations loading on these factors ranged from .49 to .75). There was no relationship between subjects' (n=56) scores on the Test of Behavioral Rigidity and the SSRT, thus failing to support the concurrent validity of the SSRT.

Norms: Not cited. Psychometric data were reported for 56 undergraduate students noted above.

Availability: Contact A. Craig Fisher, Department of Exercise and Sport Sciences, Ithaca College, Ithaca, NY 14850. (Phone # 607-274-3112)

(130)
[SPORTSMANSHIP QUESTIONNAIRE] [SQ]
W. Wright and S. Rubin

Source: Wright, W., & Rubin, S. (1989). The development of sportsmanship (abstract). Proceedings of the 7th World Congress in Sport Psychology (# 155). Singapore.

Purpose: To examine sportsmanship attitudes among athletes.

Description: The SQ contains 12 sport situations, each with a moral dilemma. Subjects respond to each situation using a Likert scale.

Construction: Not discussed.

Reliability: Not presented.

Validity: Discriminant validity was supported in that females' sportsmanship was higher than males. Also, sportsmanship was higher among older subjects (21-22 years) than younger subjects (14-15 years old).

Norms: Not cited. Psychometric data were based on the responses of 54 athletes and 56 nonathletes ranging in age from 14 to 22 years.

Availability*: Contact W. Wright, Department of Psychology, Whitman College, Walla Walla, WA.

(131)
STATE OF CONSCIOUSNESS DURING MOVEMENT ACTIVITY
INVENTORY (SCMAI)
Jane Adair

Source: Adair, J. (1987). Development of the State of Consciousness During Movement Activity (SCMAI) and its implications (abstract). Proceedings of the Association for the Advancement of Applied Sport Psychology annual conference (p. 22). CA: Newport Beach.

Purpose: To evaluate the characteristics of states of consciousness that movement performers may experience during participation.

Description: The SCMAI contains two subscales: The Greatest Moment Scale (GMS) measuring a Greatest Moment State of Consciousness, and the Worst Moment Scale (WMS) measuring a Worst Moment State of Consciousness. Subjects are asked to recall a greatest and worst moment from the same movement activity, and respond "to descriptions of phenomena available to consciousness." Subjects respond using a 5-point Likert scale in which they are asked to rate the intensity of the experience.

Construction: Items were developed from a review of psychological and sport consciousness theory, practice, and current method of inquiry. In addition, four pilot studies were completed.

Reliability: Cronbach alpha reliability coefficients of .89 (GMS) and .88 (WMS) were reported; an alpha reliability coefficient of .92 was reported for the SCMAI. A test-retest reliability coefficient of .73 was reported (n=60).

Validity: The SCMAI was successful in discriminating between groups varying in skill level and intrinsic motivation.

Norms: Not cited.

Availability*: Unknown. Test items do no appear in the source.

(132)
[SUPERSTITIOUS BELIEFS AND BEHAVIOR SCALE] [SBBS]
Hans G. Buhrmann, B. Brown, and Maxwell K. Zaugg

Source: Buhrmann, H., Brown, B., & Zaugg, M. (1982). Superstitious beliefs and behavior: A comparison of male and female basketball players. Journal of Sport Behavior, 5, 175-185.

Purpose: To examine superstitious beliefs and practices among athletes.

Description: The scale contains 40 items categorized into seven areas: clothing and appearance, fetish, pre-game, game, team ritual, prayer, and coach. Subjects respond to each item using a 5-point Likert scale.

Construction: Not discussed.

Reliability: A test-retest reliability coefficient of .95 was reported among 24 high school basketball players.

Validity: Not discussed.

Norms: Descriptive data were presented for 272 male and 257 female basketball players, ages 12-22.

Availability*: Contact Hans G. Buhrmann, Department of Physical Education, University of Lethbridge, 4401 University Drive, Lethbridge, Alberta, Canada T1K 3M4.

Reference

*Buhrmann, H. G., & Zaugg, M. K. (1983). Religion and superstitions in the sport of basketball. Journal of Sport Behavior, 6, 146-157.

Chapter 17

MOTIVATION (EXERCISE)

Tests in this chapter assess reasons for adherence to exercise and injury rehabilitaton programs, commitment to running, perceived exertion, perceived barriers to exercise training, and the motives/incentives individuals express for participating in running and other forms of exercise.

(133)
[ADHERENCE TO EXERCISE QUESTIONNAIRE] [AEQ]
Donald Siegel, James Johnson, and Caryl Newhof

Source: Siegel, D., Johnson, J., & Newhof, C. (1987). Adherence to exercise and sport classes by college women (Abstract). Research Abstracts of the American Alliance for Health, Physical Education, Recreation, and Dance annual convention, Las Vegas, NV.

Purpose: To assess reasons for adhering to exercise classes by women.

Description: A 20-item questionnaire.

Construction: Not indicated.

Reliability: A test-retest reliability coefficient of .75 was reported over a one-week period.

Validity: Discriminant validity was supported in that college women ($\underline{n}=135$) who completed exercise classes differed on the questionnaire from those ($\underline{n}=51$) who dropped out in terms of being more positive about developing and utilizing personal skills, using their minds in physical activity, and being involved in social interactions.

Norms: Not cited. Psychometric data were reported for 186 college women.

Availability*: Contact Donald S. Siegel, Exercise and Sport Studies Department, Scott Gymnasium, Smith College, Northampton, MA 01063.

(134)
BARRIERS TO EXERCISE AND SPORT QUESTIONNAIRE (BESQ)
Damon Burton, Tom Raedeke, and Earle Carroll

Source: Burton, D., Raedeke, T., & Carroll, E. (1989). Exercise goals, perceived barriers, and activity patterns of adult exercisers with differential athletic participation backgrounds (abstract). In Psychology of motor behavior and sport (p. 110). Kent, OH: Proceedings of the North American Society for the Psychology of Sport and Physical Activity annual convention.

Purpose: To assess the barriers individuals perceive regarding participating in exercise and sport.

Description: The BESQ (Form D) assesses nine barriers to exercise/sport participation including: program, social support, resource, club, health, other commitments, lethargy, other interests, and program satisfaction. Subjects respond to 32 items using a 4-point Likert scale.

Construction*: An initial pool of 51 items was developed by identifying barriers commonly reported in the exercise adherence literature. Three judges evaluated the items for syntax, clarity, and face validity resulting in the retention of 39 items (Form A). This form was administered to 112 former college athletes and college nonathletes. Item and factor analyses led to the retention of 21 items (Form B) representing five subscales. Then 18 new or reworded items were added to Form B to develop social support, resource, and other commitments barriers subscales as well as improve health/fitness and program satisfaction subscale items. This new 39-item version (Form C) was administered to 292 current and former adult members of faculty/staff wellness programs from three universities and a community college in the Northwest. Item analyses and factor analyses (exploratory and confirmatory) led to the retention of 32 items representing nine subscales and was labeled Form D.

Reliability: Not indicated.

Validity: Confirmatory factor analysis ($n=292$) supported the construct validity of the BESQ. Also, former male collegiate athletes ($n=58$) differed from former high school athletes/nonathletes ($n=54$) in that the former group perceived health and fitness and motivation to be less of a barrier to participating in exercise than the latter group. A median split of both groups based on current levels of physical activity participation revealed that the more active group perceived fewer programming, motivation, and ego barriers than the less physically active group.

*From Burton, Raedeke, and Carroll (1990).

Norms: Not indicated. Psychometric data were presented for 58 male former collegiate athletes and 54 high school athletes/nonathletes, as well as 292 former adult members of faculty/staff wellness programs.

Availability: Contact Damon Burton, Department of Physical Education, 107 PEB, University of Idaho, Moscow, ID 83843. (Phone # 208-885-7921) (The BESQ will only be available once validation has been completed.)

Reference
Burton, D., Raedeke, T., & Carroll, E. (1990). Predicting physical activity patterns of adult males with differential sport participation backgrounds. Manuscript submitted for publication.

(135)
COMMITMENT TO PHYSICAL ACTIVITY SCALE (CPA)
Charles B. Corbin, A. Brian Nielsen, Laura L. Bordsdorf
and David R. Laurie

Source: Corbin, C. B., Nielsen, A. B., Bordsdorf, L. L., & Laurie, D. R. (1987). Commitment to physical activity. International Journal of Sport Psychology, 18, 215-222.

Purpose: To assess an individual's commitment to participating in physical activity.

Description: The CPA is a 12-item questionnaire designed to assess commitment to the broad domain of physical activity.

Construction: The CPA was modified from the Commitment to Running scale by substituting the term physical activity for the term running. Also, slight modifications were made in the wording of some items to make them more readable.

Reliability: Split-half reliabilities were .88 (n=238 males) and .91 (n=212 females). Test-retest reliability coefficients of .76 and .85 were reported for these male and female subjects, respectively, across a one-week interval.

Validity: The CPA was successful in discriminating between subjects (n=450) who differed in self-report levels of involvement in physical activity.

Norms: Not cited. Psychometric data were reported for 450 undergraduate students.

Availability*: Contact Charles B. Corbin, Department of Health and Physical

Education, Arizona State University, Tempe, AZ 85287. (Phone # 602-965-3875)

References
*Deeter, T. E. (1988). Does attitudinal commitment predict physical activity participation? Journal of Sport Behavior, 11, 177-192.
*Nielsen, A. B., Borsdorf, L. L., & Corbin, C. B. (1984). Commitment to general and specific physical activity. Proceedings of the 1984 Olympic Scientific Congress (p. 85). Eugene, OR.: College of Human Development and Performance Microform Publications.
*Nielsen, A. B., Borsdorf, L. L., & Corbin, C. B. (1987). Attitude assessment and term variation in physical education (abstract). Proceedings of the American Alliance for Health, Physical Education, Recreation, and Dance annual convention (p. 86). Las Vegas, NV.

(136)
COMMITMENT TO RUNNING SCALE (CR)
Mary Ann Carmack and Rainer Martens

Source: Carmack, M. A., & Martens, R. (1979). Measuring commitment to running: A survey of runners' attitudes and mental states. Journal of Sport Psychology, 1, 25-42.

Purpose: To assess the feelings individuals have about running.

Description: The Commitment to Running (CR) Scale contains twelve items. Subjects are asked to respond to each item using a 5-point Likert scale indicating the degree to which the item describes their feelings about running.

Construction: An initial pool of 30 items was developed by scanning the popular literature on running and interviewing local runners. Ten runners and five runner-research colleagues evaluated the content validity of each item. Item discrimination coefficients ($n=180$) were computed to evaluate the extent to which each item was sensitive to measuring both extremes of the disposition. The resulting analysis led to the retention of 12 items.

Reliability: A reliability coefficient of .93 was computed using analysis of variance. An internal consistency coefficient of .97 was derived using Kuder-Richardson formula 20. These coefficients were based on the responses of 315 runners. Secondary data are cited indicating a test-retest reliability coefficient ($n=100$ adult males) of .84 across a 2-3 month time interval.

Validity: Concurrent validity was supported by showing an association of subjects' ($\underline{n}$=315) CR scores to length of run, discomfort experienced when a run is missed, and perceived addiction to running. Also, high CR runners were differentiated from low CR runners in terms of the perceived benefits derived from running.

Norms: Descriptive and psychometric data were provided for 315 runners (250 males and 65 females) between the ages of 13 and 60 ($\underline{M}$=28.8 years). The sample included runners from competitive road races, regular mid-day university runners, prospective 1980 Olympic distance and middle-distance runners, runners from a high school track camp, and those participating in community fun runs.

Availability: Contact Rainer Martens, Human Kinetics Publishers, Box 5076, Champaign, IL 61825-5076. (Phone # 217-351-5076)

References

Dyer, J. B., & Crouch, J. G. (1987). Effects of running on moods: A time series study. Perceptual and Motor Skills, 64, 783-789.

Jibaja-Rusth, M. L., Pease, D., & Rudisill, M. (1989). The relationship of goal orientations to running motivation: Commitment and addiction (abstract). Psychology of motor behavior and sport (p. 140). Proceedings of the North American Society for the Psychology of Sport and Physical Activity annual convention, Kent, OH.

*Masters, K. S., & Lambert, M. J. (1989). On gender comparison and construct validity: An examination of the Commitment to Running Scale in a sample of marathon runners. Journal of Sport Behavior, 12, 196-202.

Noble, J. M., Dzewaltowski, D. A., Acevado, E. D., & Gill, D. L. (1989). Sport-specific psychological characteristics and attributions of Leadville Trail 100 ultramarathoners (abstract). Psychology of motor behavior and sport (p. 147). Proceedings of the North American Society for the Psychology of Sport and Physical Activity annual convention, Kent, OH.

Summers, J. J., Machin, V. J., & Sargent, G. I. (1983). Psychosocial factors related to marathon running. Journal of Sport Psychology, 5, 314-331.

(137)
EXERCISE AND SPORT GOAL INVENTORY (ESGI)
Damon Burton, Tom Raedeke, and Earle Carroll

Source: Burton, D., Raedeke, T., & Carroll, E. (1989). Exercise goals, perceived barriers, and activity patterns of adult exercisers with differential athletic participation backgrounds (abstract). In Psychology of motor behavior and sport (p. 110). Kent, OH: Proceedings of the North American Society for the Psychology of Sport and Physical Activity annual convention.

Purpose: To assess the goals individuals express toward the values of exercise and sport.

Description*: The ESGI (Form D) contains 66 items and assesses ten exercise/sport goals including: health/fitness, performance, involvement, outcome, recognition, solitude, social, mental health, muscular fitness, and "feel good." Subjects respond to each item using a 4-point Likert Scale.

Construction*: A battery of 208 items was generated to assess eight exercise and sport incentives. This pool of items was derived by: (a) using selected items from Duda and Tappe's (1989) Personal Incentives for Exercise Questionnaire, (b) modifying items from several goal inventories, and (c) composing items based on current exercise motivation research. Three judges rated the items for syntax, clarity, and face validity, leading to the retention of 156 items (Form A). Form A was administered to 112 former college athletes and 106 university wellness group members and community aerobic dance participants. Item analyses and factor analyses led to the retention of 72 items (Form B) containing six 12-item subscales. A total of 27 new items were added (Form C) to develop further solitude and involvement subscales and strengthen health/fitness and mental health subscales. This 99-item form was administered to 292 current and former adult members of faculty/staff wellness programs from three universities and a community college in the Northwest. Item analyses and factor analyses (exploratory and confirmatory) of these subjects' responses led to the retention of the current 66-item Form D.

Reliability: Not reported.

Validity: Confirmatory factor analysis ($\underline{n}$=292) supported the construct validity of the ESGI. In addition, former collegiate male athletes ($\underline{n}$=58) expressed significantly higher outcome, recognition, and social exercise goals than former high school athletes/nonathletes ($\underline{n}$=54). A median split, based on current physical activity participation, revealed that those individuals still

*From Burton, Raedeke, and Carroll (1990).

highly active had higher performance and social goals and lower outcome goals than those individuals categorized as less physically active.

Norms: Not presented. Psychometric data provided were based on the responses of 58 former male collegiate athletes and 54 former high school athletes/nonathletes, as well as 292 current and former adult members of faculty/staff wellness programs.

Availability: Contact Damon Burton, Department of Physical Education, 107 PEB, University of Idaho, Moscow, ID 83843. (Phone # 208-885-7921) (The ESGI will only be available once validation has been completed.)

Reference
Burton, D., Raedeke, T., & Carroll, E. (1990) Predicting physical activity patterns of adult males with differential sport participation backgrounds. Manuscript submitted for publication.

(138)
[EXERCISE MOTIVATION QUESTIONNAIRE] [EMQ]
David A. Dzewaltowski

Source: Dzewaltowksi, D. A. (1988). Toward a model of exercise motivation Journal of Sport & Exercise Psychology, 11, 251-269.

Purpose: To assess exercise motivation, based on the theory of reasoned action and social cognitive theory.

Description: The questionnaire assesses self-efficacy and outcome expectations in relation to exercise behavior. For example, self-efficacy scores represented an average of subjects' confidence (from 0 to 100) in adhering to an exercise program in spite of their work schedule, when fatigued physically, or when exercise is boring. The questionnaire also assess constructs from the theory of reasoned action, such as behavioral intention and subjective norm.

Construction: Not discussed.

Reliability: Alpha reliability coefficients (n=328 undergraduate students) ranged from .80 to .97 for all constructs.

Validity: Multiple regression analysis indicated that the social cognitive theory constructs accounted for 14 percent of the variance in predicting exercise behavior. Attitude and subjective norm accounted for 20 percent of the variance in behavioral intention using path analysis. Commonality analysis indicated that the theory of reasoned action constructs did not account for any unique variance in exercise behavior over the constructs from social cognitive theory.

Norms: Not reported. Psychometric data were cited for 328 undergraduate students.

Availability: Contact David A. Dzewaltowski, Department of Physical Education, PELS, AHEARN, Kansas State University, Manhattan, KS 66506. (Phone # 913-532-6765)

(139)
FEELING SCALE (FS)
W. Jack Rejeski

Source: Hardy, C. J., & Rejeski, W. J. (1989). Not what, but how one feels: The measurement of affect during exercise. Journal of Sport & Exercise Psychology, 11, 304-317.

Purpose: To measure affective feelings of pleasure/displeasure toward a given exercise workload.

Description: The scale is represented by an 11-point bipolar good-bad format. Scores range from +5 to -5, with verbal anchors provided at the 0 point and at all odd integers. Subjects are asked to indicate how good or bad they feel during various phases of an exercise bout.

Construction: Not discussed.

Reliability: Internal consistency coefficients for this state measure were not reported.

Validity: Concurrent validity was supported in that subjects' ($\underline{n}$=68 undergraduate students) FS scores were inversely related (-.56) to their scores on Borg's Ratings of Perceived Exertion Scale, although the authors concluded that the scores were not isomorphic constructs, particularly at high intensity work. Furthermore, the authors reported that "... FS ratings were directly related to past and present level of involvement in physical exercise/activity, the number of miles spent in aerobic activity, and the belief that excercise is an important component of one's lifestyle" (p. 310).

Norms: Not cited. Psychometric data were reported for 33 females and 35 males enrolled in health and fitness courses at a southeastern university.

Availability: Contact W. Jack Rejeski, Department of Health and Sport

Sciences, Wake Forest University, Box 7234, Winston-Salem, NC 27109.
(Phone # 919-759-5837)

References
Hardy, C. J., Kirschenbaum, D. S., Heaney, T., & Imhoff, L. R. (1989). Affect as an antecedent variable in exercise behavior: The consequences of pre-exercise affective states (abstract). In Psychology of motor behavior and sport (p. 87). Kent, OH: Proceedings of the North American Society for the Psychology of Sport and Physical Activity annual convention.

*Kenney, E. A., Rejeski, W. J., & Messier, S. P. (1987). Managing exercise distress: The effect of broad spectrum intervention on affect, RPE, and running efficiency. Canadian Journal of Sport Sciences, 12, 97-105.

Rejeski, W. J. (1989). The measurement of in-task affect during exercise related tasks (abstract). In Psychology of motor behavior and sport (p. 86). Kent, OH: Proceedings of the North American Society for the Psychology of Sport and Physical Activity annual convention.

*Rejeski, W. J., Best, D., Griffith, P., & Kenney, E. (1987). Sex-role orientation and the responses of men to exercise stress. Research Quarterly, 58, 260-264.

(140)
GENERAL AFFECT SCALE [GAS]
Shirley A. Hochstetler, W. Jack Rejeski, and Deborah L. Best

Source: Hochstetler, S. A., Rejeski, W. J., & Best, D. L. (1985). The influence of sex-role orientation on ratings of perceived exertion. Sex Roles, 12, 825-835.

Purpose: To assess feelings of comfort and confidence prior to treadmill exercise.

Description: The GAS consists of 13 bipolar adjectives arranged on a 7-point Likert scale (e.g., tense-relaxed, positive-negative, good-bad, etc.).

Construction: Not discussed.

Reliability: A Cronbach alpha internal consistency coefficient of .96 was reported among 33 females.

Validity: Not discussed.

Norms: Not cited. Psychometric data were based on the responses of 33 female undergraduate students from Wake Forest University, Winston-Salem, North Carolina.

Availability: Contact W. Jack Rejeski, Department of Health and Sport Science, Box 7234, Wake Forest University, Winston-Salem, NC 27109. (Phone # 919-759-5837)

(141)
MASTERS-OGLES MARATHON SCALE (MOMS)
Kevin S. Masters and Benjamin M. Ogles

Source: Masters, K. S., & Ogles, B. M. (1990, August). Development and validation of the Masters-Ogles Marathon Scale. Paper presented at the 98th annual convention of the American Psychological Association, Boston, MA.

Purpose: To identify and measure motivations for running a marathon.

Description: The MOMS contains 56 items. Subscales include: Life meaning, Psychological coping, Self-esteem, Health Orientation, Weight Concern, Personal Striving, Competition, Social Recognition, and Socialization. Subjects are asked to respond to each item in terms of how important it is as a reason for why they trained for and ran a marathon (e.g., "To improve my self-esteem"). Subjects respond to each item on a 7-point ordinal scale.

Construction: One-hundred twenty reasons for running a marathon were derived from a review of the literature. These reasons were submitted to 12 local marathon runners. They were asked to add reasons that were not included and to otherwise evaluate the instrument. As a result of their comments, the instrument was reduced to 93 questions by deleting items very similar in content.

The responses to this version by 387 male and 97 female participants at three midwestern marathons were evaluated. Items with corrected item-to-total score correlations above .50 on each scale were selected to constitute the final version of the instrument.

Reliability: Coefficient alphas for each scale (n=482) are as follows: Life Meaning (.88); Psychological Coping (.91); Self-Esteem (.89); Health Orientation (.86); Weight Concern (.87); Personal Striving (.80); Competition (.83); Social Recognition (.92); and Socialization (.89). Test-retest reliability data are currently being collected.

Validity: Construct validity of the MOMS was examined through principal components factor analysis with a varimax rotation. Five factors accounting for 84.9% of the variance emerged. These factors were labeled: 1) psychological (life meaning, psychological coping, and self-esteem scales); 2) competition (competition and personal striving scales; 3) physical (health orientation and weight concern scales); 4) social recognition (social recognition scale) and 5) socialization (socialization scale).

Norms: Not presented. Psychometric data were based on the responses of 387 male and 97 female marathon runners.

Availability: Contact Kevin S. Masters, Department of Psychological Science, College of Sciences and Humanities, Ball State University, Muncie, IN 47306-0520. (Phone # 317-285-1707)

Reference

Masters, K. S., & Lambert, M. J. (1989). The relations between cognitive coping strategies, reasons for running, injury, and performance of marathon runners. Journal of Sport & Exercise Psychology, 11, 161-170.

(142)
[MOTIVATION FOR PARTICIPATION IN PHYSICAL ACTIVITY QUESTIONNAIRE] [MPPAQ]
B. C. Watkin

Source: Watkin, B. C. (1978). Measurement of motivation for participation in physical activity. In U. Simri (Ed.), Proceedings of the International Symposium on Psychological Assessment in Sport (pp. 188-194). Netanya, Israel: Wingate Institute for Physical Education and Sport.

Purpose: To assess the motives individuals express for participating in physical activity.

Description: The questionnaire contains 19 motivators for participation in physical activity. Subjects respond to each motivator using a 4-point Likert scale.

Construction: Previous attitudinal inventories (such as the Attitudes Toward Physical Activity Inventory), together with discussion with students and colleagues, led to the selection of 14 motivator items. Based on the responses of 181 male and female Grade 10 students in Brisbane, Australia, seven motivator items were retained. Consequently, a revised questionnaire containing a more extensive list of 19 motivators was developed and tested.

Reliability: Test-retest reliability coefficients for a derived composite motivation score were .74 ($n=30$ male undergraduate students) and .80 ($n=30$ female undergraduate students) across a seven-week interval.

Validity: The total number of hours spent participating in physical activity the previous week was correlated with the composite motivation score, .50 (n=80 male undergraduate students) and .63 (n=158 female undergraduate students). Furthermore, scores on this questionnaire successfully discriminated between undergraduate students electing or not electing to participate in physical education classes.

Norms: Not cited. Psychometric data were provided for 80 male and 158 female freshman students enrolled åt Wollongong Institute of Education in Australia.

Availability*: Contact B. C. Watkin, Department of Human Movement and Sport Science, Institute of Education, University of Wollongong, Wollongong NSW, Australia 2500.

(143)
MOTIVATION FOR PHYSICAL ACTIVITY QUESTIONNAIRE
[MPAQ]
Risto Telama and Martti Silvennoinen

Source: Telama, R., & Silvennoinen, M. (1979). Structure and development of 11- to 19- year-olds' motivation for physical activity. Scandinavian Journal of Sports Science, 1, 23-31.

Purpose: To assess the reasons young adults participate in physical exercise and leisure-time physical activity.

Description: The MPAQ contains 33 items focusing on the conscious reflection of physical activity interests, the advance planning of physical activities, and the influence of weather and friends on one's own physical activities. Subjects respond using a 3-point ordinal scale.

Construction: Previous empirical research on motivation for physical activity was drawn upon in constructing the items and measurement methods.

Reliability: Not discussed.

Validity: Principal component factor analysis (n=3106) followed by varimax rotation supported an eight-factor solution accounting for 23.0% of the variance. The factors were labeled as fitness related to self-image, relaxation, sociability, preference for outdoor activities, normative health, competition and achievement, improving one's physique, and functional health.

Norms: Not cited. Psychometric data were reported for 3106 students residing in Finland. These students were selected through stratifed random cluster sampling, and represented grades 2-3, 5-6 and 8-9.

Availability*: Contact Risto Telama, Department of Physical Education, University of Jyvaskyla, SF 40100 Jyvaskyla 10, Finland.

(144)
PERSONAL INCENTIVES FOR EXERCISE QUESTIONNAIRE
(PIEQ)
Joan L. Duda and Marlene K. Tappe

Source: Duda, J. L., & Tappe, M. K. (1989). The Personal Incentives for Exercise Questionnaire: Preliminary development. Perceptual and Motor Skills, 68, 1122.

Purpose: To evaluate the personal incentives individuals express for participating in exercise.

Description: The PIEQ (4th version) assesses 10 categories of personal incentives related to the exercise context: flexibility/agility, appearance, competition, weight management, mastery, affiliation, social recognition, health benefits, mental benefits, and fitness (strength/endurance). Subjects respond to 48 items using a 5-point Likert scale.

Construction: Based on the Theory of Personal Investment, the open-ended responses of 165 adult exercise participants, and a review of the exercise psychology literature, 85 items were developed and administered to 212 male and 313 female undergraduates from a large midwestern university. Principal component factor analyses (oblique and orthogonal rotations) led to the retention of nine factors. Based on additional analyses, 48 items were retained and administered to samples of 135 male and 217 female college students. Factor analyses supported a stable factor structure across the two samples.

Reliability: Cronbach alpha reliability coefficients ranged from .74 to .94 (n=135 college males) and from .77 to .92 (n=217 female college students). Test-retest reliability coefficients ranged from .58 to .86 across a two-week interval (n=106).

Validity: Construct validity was supported through factor analyses as noted above.

Norms: Not presented. Psychometric data were reported for 135 male and 217 college females.

Availability: Contact Joan L. Duda, Department of PEHRS, 113 Lambert Hall, Purdue University, West Lafayette, IN 47907. (Phone # 317-494-3172)

References

Duda, J. L., & Tappe, M. K. (1989). Personal investment in exercise among adults: The examination of age and gender-related differences in motivational orientation. In A. C. Ostrow (Ed.), Aging and motor behavior (pp. 239-256), Indianapolis, IN: Benchmark Press.

Stainback, R., Ondrea, P., & Hunter, G. (1989). Development and evaluation of an exercise program for outpatient alcoholics (abstract). Proceedings of the Association for the Advancment for Applied Sport Psychology annual convention (p. 100). Seattle, WA.

*Tappe, M. K., & Duda, J. L. (1988). Personal investment predictors of life satisfaction among physically active middle-aged and older adults. Journal of Psychology, 122, 557-566.

Tappe, M. K., Duda, J. L., & Menges-Ehrnwald, P. (in press). Personal investment predictors of adolescent motivational orientation toward exercise. Canadian Journal of Sport Sciences.

(145)
RATINGS OF PERCEIVED EXERTION SCALE (RPE)
Gunnar A. V. Borg

Source: Borg, G. A., & Noble, B. J. (1974). Perceived exertion. In J. H. Wilmore (Ed.), Exercise and sport sciences reviews (pp. 131-153). New York: Academic Press.

Purpose: To evaluate subject perceptions of effort and exertion during exercise.

Description: The RPE scale consists of 15 grades from 6 (very, very light) to 20 (very, very hard). These gradiations correspond roughly to 1/10 the heart variation from 60 to 200 in healthy, middle-aged individuals. The subject is asked to estimate the degree of exertion he/she feels, and select the appropriate number on the scale correponding to this perception of exertion.

Construction: The RPE scale was constructed to follow heart rate for work on the bicycle ergometer among healthy, middle-aged men performing moderate-to-hard exercise. Thus, heart rate should be about ten times the RPE value.

*Reliability: Test-retest reliability coefficients of .80 to .98 were reported over a 2-4 week period among 21 male and 15 female subjects.

*Validity: Correlation coefficients of .65 and .68 were reported with heart rate.

Norms: Not cited.

Availabililty*: A copy of the scale appears in the source identified above.

References

*Borg, G. A. V. (1982). Psychophysical bases of perceived exertion. Medicine and Science in Sports and Exercise, 14, 377-381.

*Borg, G. (1985). An introduction to Borg's RPE scale. Ithaca, NY: Mouvement Publications.

*Carton, R. L., & Rhodes, E. C. (1985). A critical review of the literature on ratings scales for perceived exertion. Sports Medicine, 2, 198-222.

*Morgan, W. P. (1981). Psychophysiology of self-awareness during vigorous physical activity. Research Quarterly for Exercise and Sport, 52, 385-427.

*Morgan, W. P., & Borg, G. A. V. (1976). Perception of effort in the prescription of physical activity. In T. T. Craig, (Ed.), The humanistic and mental health aspects of sports, exercise and recreation (pp. 126-129). Chicago, IL: American Medical Association.

(146)
REASONS FOR RUNNING SCALE (RFR)
James M. Robbins and Paul Joseph

Source: Robbins, J. M., & Joseph, P. (1985). Experiencing exercise withdrawal: Possible consequences of therapeutic and mastery running. Journal of Sport Psychology, 7, 23-39.

Purpose: A self-report measure of why runners continue to run regularly.

Description: Subjects are asked to respond to 21 items using a 7-point ordinal scale with the anchorings very important (7 points) to not at all important (1 point). Examples of items include "opportunities to relax" and "chance for association and friendship."

Construction: Not discussed.

Reliability: Not cited.

---

*See Carton and Rhodes (1985) for a more current update on the psychometric properties of RPE scales.

Validity: Construct validity was examined through principal component factor analysis. Five factors emerged accounting for 63.20% of the variance: Mastery, Recognition, Escape, Novelty, and Health.

Norms: Not cited.

Availability: Contact James M. Robbins, Department of Psychiatry, Jewish General Hospital, 4333 Chemin de la Cote Ste-Catherine, Montreal, Quebec, Canada H3T 1E4. (Phone # 514-340-8210)

(147)
REHABILITATION ADHERENCE QUESTIONNAIRE [RAQ]
A. Craig Fisher and Mary A. Domm

Source: Fisher, A. C., Domm, M. A., & Wuest, D. A. (1988). Adherence to sports-injury rehabilitation programs. The Physician and Sportsmedicine, 16(6), 47-54.

Purpose: To identify the personal and situational factors related to rehabilitation adherence among athletes.

Description: The RAQ contains six scales: perceived exertion, pain tolerance, apathy, support from significant others, scheduling of rehabilitation, and environmental conditions. For example, subjects are asked to respond to the item "I worked out until I felt pain and then stopped" (pain tolerance). Subjects respond to the 40-item questionnaire using a 4-point Likert scale, with the anchors strongly agree to strongly disagree.

Construction: Items were derived from an analysis of the content of the adherence literature.

Reliability: Not reported.

Validity: Discriminant validity was supported in that the RAQ differentiated between college athlete adherents ($n=21$) and nonadherents ($n=20$), with the adherents perceiving they worked harder at rehabilitation, were more self-motivated, and made a greater effort to fit rehabilitation into their schedules.

Norms: Not reported. Psychometric data were cited for 41 college athletes ($n=21$ males; $n=20$ females) who had been injured in sports.

Availability: Contact A. Craig Fisher, Department of Exercise and Sport Sciences, Ithaca College, Ithaca, NY 14850. (Phone # 607-274-3112)

(148)
SELF-MOTIVATION INVENTORY (SMo)
Rod K. Dishman, William Ickes, and William P. Morgan

Source: Dishman, R. K., Ickes, W., & Morgan, W. P. (1980). Self-motivation and adherence to habitual physical activity. Journal of Applied Social Psychology, 10, 115-132.

Purpose: To assess the tendency to engage in vigorous physical activity regardless of extrinsic reinforcement.

Description: The SMo consists of 40 items. Subjects are asked to respond to each item using a 5-point Likert format.

Construction: An original pool of 60 items (developed by one author) was administered to 399 undergraduate students. Examination of item-total score correlation coefficients led to the retention of 48 items. Factor analysis of subjects' responses resulted in the retention of 40 items loading on 11 factors and accounting for 40.5% of the total variance.

Reliability: An alpha reliability coefficient of .91 (standard error = 5.84) was reported for the 399 undergraduate students. A second independent sample of undergraduate students produced an alpha coefficient of .86, and a test-retest reliability coefficient of .92 over a 1-month interval.

Validity: Concurrent validity was evidenced by the correlation of the SMo with a self-report assessment of exercise frequency ($r=.23$; $n=399$). Also, subjects' scores on the SMo correlated ($r=.63$) with their responses to the Thomas-Zander Ego-Strength Scale. However, subjects' responses to the SMo also correlated with the Marlowe-Crowne Social Desirability Scale.
       Support for the construct validity of the scale was demonstrated in two field studies that indicated subjects' responses to the SMo were significantly associated with adherence to programs of physical exercise. Subjects were middle-aged adult males involved in a health-oriented exercise program and college females participating in a crew training program.

Norms: Psychometric data were reported for 399 male and female undergraduate students enrolled in introductory psychology classes, 64 female intercollegiate athletes, and 66 middle-aged adult males.

Availability*: Contact Rod Dishman, Department of Physical Education,

University of Georgia, Athens, GA 30602.

References

*Heiby, E. M., Onorato, V. A., & Sato, R. A. (1987). Cross-validation of the self-motivation inventory. Journal of Sport Psychology, 9, 394-399.

*Knapp, D., Gutmann, M., Foster, C., & Pollock, M. (1984). Self-motivation among 1984 Olympic speed skating hopefuls and emotional response and adherence to training (abstract). Proceedings of the 1984 Olympic Scientific Congress. Eugene, OR: College of Human Development and Performance Microform Publications.

*Pain, M. D., & Sharpley, C. F. (1986). Some psychometric data on predictive validity of self-motivation inventory. Perceptual and Motor Skills, 63, 294.

Tappe, M. K., & Duda, J. L. (1988). Personal investment predictors of life satisfaction among physically active middle-aged and older adults. Journal of Psychology, 122, 557-566.

*Wankel, L. M., Yardley, J. K., & Graham, J. (1985). The effects of motivational interventions upon the exercise adherence of high and low self-motivated adults. Canadian Journal of Applied Sport Sciences, 10, 147-156.

(149)
TEST OF ENDURANCE ATHLETE MOTIVES (TEAM)
Keith Johnsgard

Source: Johnsgard, K. (1985). The motivation of the long distance runner: II. Journal of Sports Medicine and Physical Fitness, 25, 140-143.

Purpose: To assess the relative strength of ten motives which appear to encompass the major reasons for endurance training.

Description: The TEAM involves a paired-comparison procedure with subjects required to make 45 forced choices between motives paired randomly. These motives include addictions, afterglow, centering, challenge, compete, feels good, fitness, identity, slim, and social. The test is scored by adding up the number of times each motive is selected. No motive can have a score greater than nine, and the total of the ten scores must be 45.

Construction: Not discussed.

Reliability: Test-retest reliabilty coefficients (149 male and 31 female members of the Fifty-Plus Runners' Association) across a one-week interval were .74 (retrospective) and .78 (current). Retrospective referred to the initial motives for entering endurance training, whereas current referred to the motives for currently being involved in endurance training.

<u>Validity</u>: Not discussed.

<u>Norms</u>: Not cited. Psychometric data were presented for 149 male runners ($\underline{M}$ age= 56.3 years) and 31 female runners ($\underline{M}$ age= 52.5 years).

<u>Availability</u>: Contact Keith Johnsgard, Department of Psychology, San Jose State University, One Washington Square, San Jose, CA 95192-0120. (Phone # 408-924-5641)

Chapter 18

MOTIVATION (SPORT)

Tests in this chapter assess the motives individuals express for participating in sport, the degree of satisfaction derived from sport participation, and the reasons that inhibit people from engaging in sport.

(150)
COACHING ORIENTATION INVENTORY (COI)
Rainer Martens and Daniel Gould

<u>Source</u>: Martens, R., & Gould, D. (1979). Why do adults volunteer to coach children's sports? In G. C. Roberts and K. M. Newell (Eds.), <u>Psychology of motor behavior and sports-1978</u> (pp. 79-89). Champaign, Il.: Human Kinetics Publishers.

<u>Purpose</u>: To assess the general orientations or motives adults express for coaching youth sport teams.

<u>Description</u>: The COI contains 7 items, with each item having three response alternatives (i.e., the three orientations). The subject is asked to indicate the most and least preferred alternative for each item.

<u>Construction</u>: The COI was modified from Bass' Orientation Inventory. The content validity of the COI was verified by 12 prominent sport psychologists with 98% confirmation that the alternatives for each item correctly assessed the intended orientation.

<u>Reliability</u>: Test-retest reliability coefficients across a one-week interval were .86 (self orientation), .77 (affiliation orientation), and .84 (task orientation).

<u>Validity</u>: Not presented.

<u>Norms</u>: Not cited. Descriptive data were presented for 423 youth sport coaches representing eight sports in communities of three different sizes in Illinois and Missouri.

Availability: Contact Rainer Martens, Human Kinetics Publishers, Box 5076, Champaign, IL 61825-5076. (Phone # 217-351-5076)

(151)
[INCENTIVE MOTIVATION INVENTORY] [IMI]
Richard B. Alderman and Nancy L. Wood

Source: Alderman, R. B., & Wood, N. L. (1976). An analysis of incentive motivation in young Canadian athletes. Canadian Journal of Applied Sport Sciences, 1, 169-176.

Purpose: To evaluate the incentives perceived by young athletes as being available and attractive to them through competitive sport participation.

Description: The inventory contains 70 items and assesses seven major incentive systems including independence, power, affiliation, arousal, esteem, excellence, and aggression. Subjects respond using a 4-point ordinal scale.

Construction: Based on Birch and Veroff's (1966) classification of incentive systems and items from several well-known personality assessment instruments, a pool of 500 items were developed. Face validity was determined by the investigators, several graduate students, and interested coaches. Item analyses led to the retention of 70 items.

Reliability: Kuder-Richardson formula 20 internal consistency coefficients ranged from .27 (arousal) to .67 (aggression) when evaluated among 425 youth ice hockey players, ages 11-14 years.

Validity: Not discussed.

Norms: Not available. Psychometric data were based on 425 youth ice hockey players, ages 11-14 years.

Availability*: Contact Richard B. Alderman, Department of Physical Education, University of Alberta, Edmonton, Alta., Canada T6G 2H9.

References
Birch, D., & Veroff, J. (1966). Motivation-A study of action. Belmont, CA: Brooks/Cole.

Pongrac, J. (1984). Sports participation incentives, locus of control and competitive trait anxiety (abstract). Proceedings of the annual conference of the Canadian Society of Psychomotor Learning and Sport Psychology (p. 9). Kingston, Ontario, Canada.

(152)
INTRINSIC/EXTRINSIC SPORT MOTIVATION SCALE [IESMS]
Maureen R. Weiss, Brenda Jo Bredemeier, and Richard M. Shewchuk

Source: Weiss, M. R., Bredemeier, B. J., & Shewchuk, R. M. (1985). An intrinsic/extrinsic sport motivation scale for the youth sport setting: A confirmatory factor analysis. Journal of Sport Psychology, 7, 75-91.

Purpose: To assess the motivational orientations of children within a physical education or sport environment.

Description: Subjects respond to five motivational orientation subscales containing six items each. They are first asked to decide for each item whether the statement on the left or the right side was most descriptive, and then to indicate whether the statement selected was really true or just sort of true for him or her. Items are scored on a four-point ordinal scale according to the degree of intrinsic orientation expressed.

Construction: The IESMS represents a modification of Harter's (1981) Motivational Orientation in the Classroom scale in which items were reworded to be compatible with a physical education or sport setting. Exploratory factor analyses (n=155) resulted in the retention of six preliminary subscales accounting for 83.3% of the variance.

Reliability: Cronbach alpha internal reliability coefficients for the six subscales (n=155) were .81 (challenge), .61 (curiosity/interest), .64 (mastery), .64 (judgment), .75 (criteria), and .65 (curiosity/improve skills).

Validity: Not discussed.

Norms: Not cited. Psychometric data were presented for 86 male and 69 female youth sport participants, ranging in age from 8 to 12 years.

Availability*: Contact Maureen R. Weiss, Department of PEHMS, 131 Esslinger Hall, University of Oregon, Eugene, OR 97403. (Phone # 503-686-4108)

Reference
Harter, S. (1981). A new self-report scale of intrinsic versus extrinsic orientation in the classroom: Motivational and informational components. Developmental Psychology, 17, 300-312.

(153)
MINOR SPORT ENJOYMENT INVENTORY (MSEI)
Leonard M. Wankel and Philip S. J. Kreisel

Source: Wankel, L. M., & Kreisel, P. S. J. (1982). Factors underlying enjoyment and lack of enjoyment in minor sport: Sport and age group comparisons. In L. M. Wankel and R. B. Wilberg (Eds.), Psychology of sport and motor behavior: Research and practice (pp. 19-43). Edmonton, Alberta: University of Alberta.

Purpose: To assess the reasons underlying sport enjoyment among youth sport participants.

Description: The MSEI contains 10 items such as being with friends or pleasing others. Using a Thurstonian paired comparison approach to scaling, subjects are asked to select the preferred enjoyment factor from each of the 45 possible pairs of items.

Construction: Items for the inventory were derived from an extensive review of the literature on intrinsic motivation and on youth sport motivation, and from open-ended interviews of 50 youth sport participants. The items generated were reviewed by five experts. Pilot testing ($n=20$) of the ten retained items was conducted to ensure item clarity and the suitability of the items for the targeted age groups. One item was subsequently discarded and one item was separated into two items. (Wankel & Kreisel, 1985a)

Reliability: Item-to-item test-retest reliability over a 1-week interval was 73% among 7- to 12-year-old boys ($n=23$). Item-to-item test-retest reliability over a 2-day interval was 86% among an older sample ($n=25$; M age = 16.0 years). (Wankel & Kreisel, 1985a)

Validity: Not discussed.

Norms: Psychometric data were reported for 822 male youth sport participants, ages 7-14 years, representing soccer ($n=310$), hockey ($n=338$), and baseball ($n=174$). A representative sample was obtained from 20 schools in a large western Canadian city. In addition, Wankel (1983a) provided comparative data for 949 female youth sport participants representing softball ($n=260$), soccer ($n=223$), volleyball ($n=92$), basketball ($n=94$), gymnastics ($n=227$), and other activities (e.g., ringette, track and field; $n=53$).

Availability: Contact Leonard M. Wankel, Department of Recreation and Leisure Studies, University of Alberta, Edmonton, Alta., Canada T6G 2E1. (Phone # 403-492-5171)

References

*Wankel, L. M. (1983a). Factors influencing girls' enjoyment of sport. Report submitted to Fitness and Amateur Sports Canada (Project No. 217, 1982-1983). Ottawa: Fitness and Amateur Sport. 64p.

*Wankel, L. M. (1983b). Girls enjoyment of sport: Age and sport group differences (abstract). In Psychology of motor behavior and sport-1983 (p. 135). Proceedings of the North American Society for the Psychology of Sport and Physical Activity annual convention, Michigan State University, East Lansing.

*Wankel, L. M., & Kreisel, P. S. J. (1985a). Factors underlying enjoyment of youth sports: Sport and age group comparisons. Journal of Sport Psychology, 7, 51-64.

Wankel, L. M., & Kreisel, P. S. J. (1985b). Methodological considerations in youth sport motivation research: A comparison of open-ended and paired comparison approaches. Journal of Sport Psychology, 7, 65-74.

(154)
[MOTIVES FOR COMPETITION SCALE] [MCS]
David Youngblood and Richard M. Suinn

Source: Youngblood, D., & Suinn, R. M. (1980). A behavior assessment of motivation. In R. M. Suinn (Ed.), Psychology in sports (pp. 73-77). Minneapolis, MN: Burgess Publishing Company.

Purpose: To identify the motivational characteristics of athletes.

Description: The scale contains 95 items and 19 categories such as social approval, competition, self-mastery, fear of failure, status, heterosexuality, and emotional release. Items within each category can be answered using a yes-no format or a 5-point rating scale format.

Construction: The authors developed a list of needs that might influence the personal choice to be involved in athletics. The list was reviewed by 17 psychology faculty, 22 coaches (college level), and 16 members of the physical education faculty who had prior participation or experience in coaching. A final list of 19 categories resulted.

Reliability: A test-retest reliability coefficient for the total score was .93, with the median test-retest reliability for the subscales of .76, on data from 25 female college swimmers and divers.

Validity: There was a significant correlation coefficient between these ($n=25$) female athletes' total scores on the scale and their coaches' ratings of their level of motivation at four different times during the season.

Norms: Not cited.

Availability: Contact Richard M. Suinn, Department of Psychology, Colorado State University, Fort Collins, CO 80523. (Phone # 303-491-6364)

References

*Raugh, D., & Wall, R. (1987). Measuring sports participation motivation. International Journal of Sport Psychology, 18, 112-119.
*Straub, W. (1984). The motives of athletes (abstract). In Proceedings of the 1984 Olympic Scientific Congress (p. 106). Eugene, OR: College of Human Development and Performance Microform Publications.

(155)
[MOTIVES FOR PARTICIPATING IN GYMNASTICS] [MPG]
Kimberley A. Klint and Maureen R. Weiss

Source: Klint, K. A. , & Weiss, M. R. (1987). Perceived competence and motives for participating in youth sports: A test of Harter's competence motivation theory. Journal of Sport Psychology, 9, 55-65.

Purpose: A self-report questionnaire used to determine motives for participating in gymnastics.

Description: This test contains 32 items; each item is rated on a 5-point Likert scale.

Construction: The test is a modification of instruments developed by Gill, Gross, and Huddleston (1983) and Gould, Feltz, and Weiss (1985). It was adopted specifically to evaluate the reasons children participate in gymnastics.

Reliability: Alpha reliabilities were reported for seven derived subscales. Coefficients ranged from .53 to .86 among a sample of 27 boys and 40 girls ($\underline{M}$ age = 11.4 years, $\underline{SD}$ = 2.3 years).

Validity: Content validity was established by asking seven experts (coaches, teachers, researchers) to evaluate each item based on their understanding of children's experiences and motives in sport.

Norms: Not available. Item descriptive statistics were reported for the 67 children.

Availability*: Contact Maureen R. Weiss, Department of PEHMS, 131 Esslinger Hall, University of Oregon, Eugene, OR 97403. (Phone # 503-686-4108)

References

Gill, D. L., Gross, J. B., & Huddleston, S. (1983). Participation motivation in youth sports. International Journal of Sport Psychology, 14, 1-14.

Gould, D., Feltz, D., & Weiss, M. (1985). Motives for participating in competitive youth swimming. International Journal of Sport Psychology, 16, 126-140.

(156)
PARTICIPATION MOTIVATION QUESTIONNAIRE [PMQ]
Diane L. Gill, John B. Gross, and Sharon Huddleston

Source: Gill, D. L., Gross, J. B., & Huddleston, S. (1983). Participation motivation in youth sports. International Journal of Sport Psychology, 14, 1-14.

Purpose: To assess the motives children express for participating in youth sport.

Description: Subjects are asked to respond to 30 reasons for participating in sports including "I like to win," and "I like to meet new friends." Subjects respond to each item using a 3-point ordinal scale (with anchorings of Very important, Somewhat important, and Not at all important).

Construction: The original 37-item questionnaire was developed based on a review of the youth sport literature and from the results of two pilot projects administered to participants at a summer sports school. General categories or dimensions of participation motivation were derived through factor analysis, and resulted in the 30-item questionnaire.

Reliability: Cronbach alpha internal consistency coefficients ($\underline{n}$=1138) for the eight derived factors (see Validity section) accounting for participation motivation ranged from .30 (Friends) to .78 (Team).

Validity: Factor analyses of the responses of 720 boys and 418 girls to the PMQ suggested that the reasons these children participated in youth sport centered on basic orientations such as achievement, team, friendship, fitness, energy release, skill development, and fun. Success orientation accounted for the largest percent of the variance (19.4%), with all eight factors accounting for 100% of the variance in the factor analytic model utilized. The authors noted, however, that "... considerable psychometric work is needed before the items or factors can be accepted as reliable, valid and comprehensive measures of participation motivation in youth sports " (p. 12).

Norms: Not indicated. Psychometric data were cited for 720 boys (ages 9-18 years) and 418 girls (ages 8-18 years) attending the University of Iowa Summer Sports School.

Availability: Contact Diane L. Gill, Exercise and Sport Science Department, University of North Carolina, Greensboro, NC 27412. (Phone # 919-334-3033)

References

*Gill, D. L., Gross, J. B., & Huddleston, S. (1980). Participation motivation in youth sports (abstract). In G. C. Roberts and D. M. Landers (Eds.), Psychology of motor behavior and sport-1980 (p. 111). Champaign, IL.: Human Kinetics Pubishers.

*Gould, D., Feltz, D., & Weiss, M. (1985). Motives for participating in competitive youth swimming. International Journal of Sport Psychology, 16, 126-140.

*Passer, M. W. (1982). Participation motives of young athletes as a function of competitive trait anxiety, self-esteem, ability, and age (abstract). In Psychology of motor behavior and sport-1982 (p. 103). Proceedings of the annual convention of the North American Society for the Psychology of Sport and Physical Activity, University of Maryland, College Park.

(157)
SPORT NON-PARTICIPATION QUESTIONNAIRE (SNQ)
Jane McNally and Terry Orlick

Source: McNally, J., & Orlick, T. (1977). The Sport Non-Participation Questionnaire: An exploratory analysis. In Human performance and behavior (pp. 111-117). Proceedings of the 9th Canadian Psycho-motor Learning and Sport Psychology Symposium, Banff, Alberta, Canada.

Purpose: To assess the relative importance of various reasons that inhibit sport participation.

Description: The SNQ contains 55 items. Subjects respond to each item using a 10-point ordinal scale.

Construction: A review of the literature, discussions with teachers, coaches, and several sport psychologists, and a pilot study of 144 females who responded to open ended questions about their perceived reasons for not playing more sports led to the formation of 18 categories depicting reasons that inhibit sport participation. These categories included Significant Others, Ability, Facilities, Health, Sexuality, Self-concept, Competition, Cosmetic, Physique, Injury, Time, Coaching, Self-consciousness, Models, Socialization, Organization, Learning, and Aggression. Fifty-five items were developed depicting these 18 areas of concern.

Reliability: Not reported.

Validity: Exploratory factor analysis was conducted among 310 female and 407 male high school students to examine construct validity. Two factors emerged, labeled Self Esteem/Competitive Threat and Socio-Cosmetic.

Norms: Not cited. Descriptive and psychometric data were presented for 717 high school students.

Availability: Contact Terry Orlick, Department of Kinanthropology, University of Ottawa, Ottawa, Canada, K1N 6N5.

(158)
SPORT SATISFACTION INVENTORY (SSI)
N. R. Whittall and Terry D. Orlick

Source: Whittall, N. R., & Orlick, T. D. (1979). The Sport Satisfaction Inventory. In G. C. Roberts and K. M. Newell (Eds.), Psychology of motor behavior and sport-1978 (pp. 144-155). Champaign, IL: Human Kinetics Publishers.

Purpose: To assess the degree of satisfaction an individual derives from participating in sport.

Description: The SSI assesses six dimensions of sport satisfaction: the Sport or game itself, Practice, Coach, Teammates, Opposition, and Personal ability and performance. Subjects respond to this 84-item inventory using a 5-point Likert scale.

Construction: Initial categories of sport satisfaction were developed after an extensive review of the sport and industrial psychology literature. An evaluation of the open-ended responses of 44 athletes by four judges led to the creation of seven categories of sport satisfaction. An additional 91 sport participants assisted in the creation of items reflective of each category. Item analyses of the responses of 80 additional athletes representing eight teams led to the retention of 84 items.

Reliability: Internal consistency coefficients ($n=120$ males and 32 females from 14 teams) ranged from .81 to .93 using the corrected split-half method, and averaged .85 across the six dimensions. Test-retest reliability coefficients ($n=23$ males and 10 females from 3 teams) ranged from .42 to .91 across a one-week interval; the average test-retest reliability coefficient was .81 when the lowest test-retest reliability coefficient (for the Opposition dimension) was not considered.

Validity: Not discussed.

Norms: Psychometric data were presented for 400 male and female sport participants, ages 10 to 39 years, representing a wide range of athletic abilities (excluding the professional level). These athletes represented 13 different sports.

Availability: Contact Terry D. Orlick, Department of Kinanthropology, University of Ottawa, Ottawa, Canada, K1N 6N5.

(159)
[WOMEN'S SPORTS ORIENTATION SCALES] [WSOS]
Donald Siegel and Caryl Newhof

Source: Siegel, D., & Newhof, C. (1984). The sport orientation of female collegiate basketball players participating at different competitive levels. Perceptual and Motor Skills, 59, 79-87.

Purpose: To evaluate the reasons given for athletic participation among female athletes.

Description: Sixteen concepts related to the reasons generally given for athletic participation (e.g., self-improvement, excitement) were presented in a semantic differential format using 15 bipolar adjective scales. Scale responses ranged from 1 (extremely negative feelings) to 4 (neutral feelings) to 7 (extremely positive feelings). The semantic differential factors of evaluation, potency, and activity were represented by five adjective pairs each.

Construction: Concepts related to the reasons generally given for athletic participation were derived from a review of literature. A total of 25 coaches and physical education graduate students eliminated or revised concepts thought to be ambiguous.

Reliability: Alpha internal consistency coefficients (n=258 female basketball players) were only acceptable for the evaluative factor (and not for the potency and activity factors). The coefficients ranged from .64 (physical fitness) to .94 (power) with a mean alpha coefficient of .88 reported across the 16 concepts.

Validity: Exploratory factor analysis (n=258) of the evaluative component produced three factors accounting for 48.3% of the variance. Factor 1 (27.9%

accountable variance) represented the more personal, non-competitive types of rewards related to sport participation. Factor 2 (10.9% accountable variance) related to competitive achievement, while Factor 3 (9.5% accountable variance) appeared to represent pressure from family and friends to participate in athletics.

Norms: Not cited. Psychometric data were reported for female varsity basketball players participating in AIAW programs in Divisions I ($n=76$), II ($n=90$), and III ($n=92$).

Availability*: Contact Donald Siegel, Exercise and Sport Studies Department, Scott Gymnasium, Smith College, Northampton, MA 01063.

Chapter 19

MULTIDIMENSIONAL

Tests in this chapter assess multiple personality traits, attitudes, motives, or beliefs among individuals participating in sport or exercise.

(160)
ATHLETIC MOTIVATION INVENTORY (AMI)
Bruce Ogilvie, Leland Lyon, and Thomas Tutko

Source: Hammer, W. M., & Tutko, T. A. (1974). Validation of the Athletic Motivation Inventory. International Journal of Sport Psychology, 5, 3-12.

Purpose: To assess personality traits relevant to athletic performance.

Description: The AMI contains subscales designed to assess Drive, Aggression, Determination, Guilt-proneness, Leadership, Self-confidence, Emotional control, Mental toughness, Conscientiousness, Coachability, and Trust, plus accuracy and honesty scales.

Construction: Not discussed.

Reliability: Reliability coefficients ranged from .78 (Determination) to .93 (Mental toughness)-- based on secondary reporting of data.

Validity: Correlation coefficients with relevant scales of Cattell's 16 PF among 112 collegiate football players indicated a number of significant but low relationships. However, there was evidence that many of the AMI scales also correlated with the honesty scale.

Norms: Not reported. Psychometric data were cited for 112 collegiate football players.

Availability*: Contact Thomas Tutko, Department of Psychology, San Jose State University, San Jose, CA 95114. (Phone # 408-277-2786)

References

Jones, H. B. (1975). Athletic Motivation Inventory of sport women and non-athletes. In D. M. Landers (Ed.), Psychology of sport and motor behavior II (pp. 153-164). State College, PA: Penn State HPER Series No. 10.

*Lyon, L. P. (1971). A method for assessing personality characteristics in athletics: The Athletic Motivation Inventory. Unpublished master's thesis, San Jose State College, San Jose, CA. (This thesis was used to summarize existing psychometric data on the AMI.)

*Morris, L. D. (1975). A socio-psychological study of highly skilled women field hockey players. International Journal of Sport Psychology, 6, 134-147.

Thomas, G. C., & Sinclair, G. D. (1977). The relationship between personality and performance of Canadian women intercollegiate basketball players. In Human performance and behavior (pp. 205-214), Proceedings of the 9th Canadian Psycho-motor Learning and Sport Psychology Symposium, Banff, Alberta, CA.

*Tutko, T. A. (October, 1969). A method of assessing athletic motivation: The Athletic Motivation Inventory. Presentation made at the First Canadian Psycho-motor Learning and Sport Psychology symposium, University of Alberta, Edmonton, Alberta, Canada.

(161)

BELASTUNGS-SYMPTOM-TEST (BST)
R. Frester

Source: Cited by H. Rieder (1979). Measurement of precompetitive conditions with different sport groups. In G. C. Roberts and K. M. Newell (Eds.), Psychology of motor behavior and sport-1978 (pp. 90-97). Champaign, IL: Human Kinetics Publishers.

Purpose: To determine precompetitive psychological conditions that the athlete views as activating or inhibiting to his/her performance.

Description: The BST contains 21 items that describe conditions the athlete must overcome in a competitive situation. The athlete responds to these items using a 9-point ordinal scale. Each point on the scale denotes how the athlete would respond to that particular condition.

Construction: Not discussed.

Reliability: A reliability coefficient of .88 was reported.

Validity: A factor analysis of the responses of 200 athletes resulted in three factors: psychological consistency, social/personal stability, and state anxiety.

Norms: Not cited.

Availability*: Contact Hermann Rieder, Institut fur Sport U. Sportwissenschaft, Universitat Heidelberg, Germany.

(162)
DAILY ANALYSES OF LIFE DEMANDS FOR ATHLETES (DALDA)
Brent S. Rushall

Source: Rushall, B. S. (1990). A tool for measuring stress tolerance in elite athletes. Journal of Applied Sport Psychology, 2, 51-66.

Purpose: To asssess sources of stress in sport, as well as external to sport, that affect the training and/or competitive performances of elite athletes.

Description: The first part of the DALDA asks the athlete to respond to general stress sources that occur in everyday life including diet, home-life, school/work, friends, training, climate, sleep, recreation, and health. The second part of the DALDA asks the athlete to respond to a list of 25 stress-reaction symptoms that he/she may be experiencing, such as muscle pains, tiredness, irritability, skin rashes, running nose, and boredom. Subjects respond to each item using one of three categories- "worse than normal," "normal," and "better than normal."

Construction: The author identified 12 areas of life-stress and 42 symptoms of stress reaction, which were then subject to content validation using nine experts familiar with stress evaluation and high-level sports. On the basis of these experts' analyses, one further life-stress and two symptoms were added. "It was deemed that this accumulation of factors represented the scope of sources of stress and symptoms of stress reactions that were associated with sporting environments" (p. 53).
     A readability check was made using pupils in a sixth-grade elementary school. They were asked to read the test booklet and indicate words they could not understand. As a result, seven definitions and four labels were changed.

Reliability: The DALDA was administered five times, fourteen days apart to 22 swimmers of the Nova Scotia Scientific Training Squad (ranging in age from 11 to 19 years). The criterion for reliability was that a stress source or symptom had to be responded to in exactly the same manner across 80% of the testing sessions by 80% of the subjects. This analysis led to the retention of 9 sources of life-stress and 25 symptoms.

Validity: See discussion of content validity above.

Norms: Not indicated.

Availability*: Contact Brent S. Rushall, Department of Physical Education, San Diego State University, San Diego, CA 92182-0171. (Phone # 619-594-4094)

(163)
[ENVIRONMENT SPECIFIC BEHAVIOR INVENTORIES] [ESBI]
Brent S. Rushall

Source: Rushall, B. S. (1978). Environment specific behavior inventories: Developmental procedures. International Journal of Sport Psychology, 9, 97-110.

Purpose: To assess behavior unique to and consistent within a given sport.

Description: These sport-specific behavioral inventories contain items focusing on social, attitudinal, training, pre/post competitive behaviors, reactions to difficulties, rewards and goals, and reactions to pre-competitive stress. Behavioral inventories have been developed for such sports as swimming, soccer, rowing, and basketball. The majority of items on each inventory contain three response alternatives.

Construction: Item pools for each sport were generated from open-ended interviews with coaches, observations of coach and athlete behaviors in competitive and training situations, reviews of existing psychological tests, and reviews of sport science textbooks. Content validity of items was established by a panel of experts including national and provincial coaches.

Reliability: All items had a minimum percent of agreement value of 64 percent between test and retest.

Validity: Not discussed.

Norms: Not cited. Sampling procedures for deriving reliability data were not discussed.

Availability*: Contact Brent S. Rushall, Department of Physical Education, San Diego State University, San Diego, CA 92182. (Phone # 619-594-4094)

References
*Rushall, B. S., & Frey, D. C. (1980). Behaviour variables in superior swimmers. Canadian Journal of Applied Sport Sciences, 5, 177-182.

*Rushall, B. S., & Jamieson, J. (1979). The prediction of swimming performance from behavioral information: A further note. Canadian Journal of Applied Sport Sciences, 4, 154-157.

(164)
FAMILY SPORTS ENVIRONMENT INTERVIEW SCHEDULE (FSE)
Terry D. Orlick

Source: Orlick, T. D. (1974). An interview schedule designed to assess family sports environment. International Journal of Sport Psychology, 5, 13-27.

Purpose: To assess factors related to the family sports environment such as parental expectancies and encouragement of the child's participation.

Description: The FSE contains 27 questions used in interview format that describe five parts of the family sports environment including primary and secondary sports involvement of family, parental expectancies and athletic aspirations for child, encouragement for participation by parents, and general sports information. A 5-point ordinal scale is used to respond to the majority of items.

Construction: Items were derived from theoretical and empirical work on socialization, child development, psychology, and physical education. The items were reviewed by a psychologist and a sport psychologist. A pilot study contributed to the final refinement of the items.

Reliability: Interrater reliability coefficients ranged from .82 to .97 between a male physical education graduate student and a female teacher based on an analysis of taped interviews of four subjects.

Validity: The FSE discriminated between 8-9 year-old boys ($\underline{n}$=16) in organized sports from those boys ($\underline{n}$=16) who were not participants, based on interviews conducted with the boys' mothers.

Norms: Not cited.

Availability: Contact Terry Orlick, Department of Kinanthropology, University of Ottawa, Ottawa, Canada K1N 6N5.

(165)
[HEALTH BELIEF QUESTIONNAIRE FOR JOGGERS] [HBQJ]
Suzanne E. Slenker, James H. Price, Stephen M. Roberts,
and Stephen G. Jurs

Source: Slenker, S. E., Price, J. H., Roberts, S. M., & Jurs, S. G. (1984). Joggers versus nonexercisers: An analysis of knowledge, attitudes and beliefs about jogging. Research Quarterly for Exercise and Sport, 55, 371-378.

Purpose: To assess the knowledge, attitudes, and beliefs individuals have about jogging based on the Health Belief Model.

Description: The questionnaire contains 49 items designed to measure the Health Belief dimensions including Barriers, Motivation, Benefits, Complexity, Severity, Susceptibility, and Cues. Subjects respond to each item using a 5-point Likert scale.

Construction: An open-ended questionnaire based on the Health Belief Model was developed to elicit beliefs about jogging from a group of 40 joggers and 39 nonexercisers. All responses were accepted for the questionnaire until a cutoff point of 75% of total responses was reached.

Reliability: Kuder-Richardson Formula 20 internal consistency coefficients ($\underline{n}$=124 joggers and 96 nonexercisers) were, for the majority of subscales, above .75.

Validity: Factor analysis supported, for the most part, the hypothesized constructs of perceived susceptibility, severity, benefits, barriers, health motivation, support, complexity, and cues. Barriers to action, such as lack of time, job, or family was the most potent predictor of nonexercising versus jogging behavior, accounting for approximately 40% of the variance.

Norms: Not cited. Psychometric data were cited for 124 joggers present at an organized race and 96 nonexercisers employed at a major corporation.

Availability*: Contact James H. Price, Department of Human Performance, University of Toledo, 2801 W. Bancroft, Toledo, OH 43606.

(166)
[JACKSON PERSONALITY INVENTORY-WRESTLING] (JPI-W)
John J. Dwyer and Albert V. Carron

Source: Dwyer, J. J., & Carron, A. V. (1986). Personality status of wrestlers of varying abilities as measured by a sport specific version of a personality inventory. Canadian Journal of Applied Sport Sciences, 11, 19-30.

Purpose: To examine personality traits considered to be desirable or undesirable in wrestling.

Description: The JPI-W contains the following personality scales with items worded specifically for wrestling: anxiety, energy level, interpersonal affect, organization, risk taking, self-esteem, social participation, tolerance, and infrequency (validity). The inventory contains 20 items per scale. Subjects respond true or false to each item.

Construction: Six experts (1 psychologist, 2 sport psychologists, 2 wrestling coaches, and 1 wrestler) converted the Jackson Personality Inventory items to JPI-W items. Three of the scales were conceptually altered: the risk taking scale emphasized physical risks, the self-esteem scale focused on performance self-esteem, and the tolerance scale emphasized openness to ideas and behaviors pertaining to wrestling. Item analyses (n=98 freestyle wrestlers) indicated that the items within a scale correlated favorably with the derived total score of that scale.

Reliability: Kuder-Richardson formula 20 internal consistency coefficients(n=87 freestyle wrestlers) ranged from .43 (tolerance) to .81 (energy level). Test-retest reliability coefficients (n=21 freestyle wrestlers) ranged from .65 (organization) to .93 (interpersonal affect) across an average time interval of 43 days.

Validity: Intercorrelation coefficients with corresponding JPI scales (n=87 freestyle wrestlers) were statistically significant supporting convergent validity. Discriminant function analyses yielded JPI-W self-esteem differences between wrestlers categorized as qualifiers (n=40) or nonqualifiers (n=47), based on whether these individuals were represented or had placed at specified wrestling tournaments.

Norms: Not cited. Descriptive and psychometric data were based on the responses of 98 freestyle wrestlers, ages 17-21+, who had competed in Ontario, Canada in 1982-83.

Availability: Contact John Dwyer, School of Recreation, Physical and Health Education, Dalhousie University, Halifax, Nova Scotia, Canada B3H 3J5. (Phone # 902-424-1157)

(167)
MOTIVATIONAL RATING SCALE (MRS)
Thomas A. Tutko and Jack W. Richards

Source: Reviewed by Corbin, C. B. (1977). The reliability and internal consistency of the Motivational Rating Scale and the General Trait Rating Scale. Medicine and Science in Sports, 9, 208-211.

Purpose: To identify personality traits appropriate for success at high levels of athletic competition.

Description: The MRS is a 55-item test containing 11 subscales (and five items per subscale). Subscales include Aggression, Coachability, Emotional control, Mental toughness, Drive, Self-confidence, Determination, Leadership, Responsibility, Trust, and Conscience development. Subjects respond to each subscale on a 5-point Likert scale.

Construction: Not discussed. These traits are the same as evaluated on the original Athletic Motivation Inventory (AMI).

Reliability: Alpha internal consistency coefficients (n=74 male high school basketball players) ranged from .05 (Trust) to .76 (Leadership). Among 75 female high school basketball players, alpha internal consistency coefficients ranged from -.02 (Trust) to .67 (Coachability).
       Test-retest reliability coefficients among these male subjects across a 7-10 day interval ranged from .49 (Emotional control) to .80 (Leadership). For the female sample, test-retest reliabilities (7-10 day interval) ranged from .55 (Conscience development) to .83 (Drive).

Validity: Concurrent validity was examined by correlating these subjects' scores on the MRS with their respective coaches' ratings of these athletes on these traits. The correlation coefficients ranged from -.01 (Mental toughness) to .36 (Self-confidence).

Norms: Not reported.

Availability*: Contact Thomas A. Tutko, Department of Psychology, San Jose State University, San Jose, CA 95114. (Phone # 408-277-2786)

Reference
Dennis, P. W. (1978). Mental toughness and performance success and failure. Perceptual and Motor Skills, 46, 385-386.

(168)
PROJECTIVE SPORT TEST (PST)
Michel A. Bouet

Source: Bouet, M. A. (1970). A projective test for sport participants. In G. S. Kenyon (Ed.), Contemporary psychology of sport (pp. 747-752). Chicago: Athletic Institute.

Purpose: To describe the motivation of sport participants in terms of the importance attributed to competition, reactions to success and failure, aggressiveness, personal conflicts, emotional maturity, and other factors.

Description: The PST is a sport-specific version of the projective technique titled the Thematic Apperception Test. The PST contains 16 photographs of action scenes from events in different sports. Subjects are asked to examine each photo and respond by creating a story to what they see occurring in the photo. Responses are evaluated clinically in terms of the subject's depiction of the main character and his/her motivation, the subject's description of the obstacles the main character overcomes, etc.

Construction: Not discussed.

Reliability: Not presented.

Validity: Convergent validity was supported in that subjects' (n=40 approx.) responses to the PST were related to their responses to the Rorschach Ink Blot Test, and two projective techniques (Machover and Koch) which involve drawing.

Norms: Not presented.

Availability*: Contact Michel A. Bouet, Section de Psychologie et Sciences Sociales, Universite de Rennes, Avenue Gaston-Berger, 35 Rennes, France.

(169)
[RUNNING ADDICTION SCALES] [RAD]
Jeffrey J. Summers and Elizabeth R. Hinton

Source: Summers, J. J., & Hinton, E. R. (1986). Development of scales to measure participation in running. In L-E Unestahl (Ed.), Contemporary sport psychology (pp. 73-84). Oreboro, Sweden: VEJE.

Purpose: To assess (1) addiction and commitment to running, (2) withdrawal symptoms associated with non-running periods, and (3) mood states during a run.

Description: The RAD contains eight scales: (1) addiction to running, (2) commitment to running, (3) exercise running, (4) runner's high, (5) psychophysiological well-being during running, (6)psychophysiological uneasiness during running, (7) withdrawal effects for addicted runners, and (8) withdrawal effects for exercise runners. Subjects respond to all items using a 5-point Likert scale.

Construction: Items were either empirically or rationally generated.

Reliability*: Cronbach alpha internal consistency coefficients (n=220 runners) ranged from .77 (withdrawal effects for exercise runners) to .95 (withdrawal effects for addicted runners). Test-retest reliability coefficients (n=49 runners) ranged from .48 (withdrawal effects for exercise runners) to .89 (addiction to running; commitment to running).

Validity: Principal components factor analysis with iteration and varimax rotations (n=179 runners) supported the construct validity of the RAD. Multiple regression analyses indicated that the scales were useful in predicting addiction to running. Multivariate analyses of variance indicated that runners high on addiction and low on commitment could be differentiated on the basis of frequency of running, number of breaks from running taken, and number of fun races run.

Norms: Not cited. Psychometric data were reported for 154 male and 24 female runners recruited in Australia from the University of Melbourne and Lincoln Institute of Technology, from three fun/run races, and from two private companies. Subjects ranged in age from 18-60 years.

Availability: Contact Jeffery J. Summers, Department of Psychology, University of Melbourne, Parkville, Victoria 3052, Australia. (Phone # 03-344-6349)

*Personal correspondence with principal author on March 9, 1990.

Reference
*Summers, J. J., Machin, V. J., & Sargent, G. I. (1983). Psychosocial factors
related to marathon running. Journal of Sport Psychology, 5, 314-331.

(170)
SPORT MOTIVATION SCALES [SMS]
D. Susan Butt

Source: Butt, D. S. (1979). Short scales for the measurement of sport motivations.
International Journal of Sport Psychology, 10, 203-216.

Purpose: To assess various motivational and personality dispositions in sport.

Description: The SMS assesses aggression, conflict, competence, competition, and cooperation in athletics. Each construct is measured by ten item
self-report scales. Subjects respond to each item in a true/false format.

Construction: Ten items were written to assess each of the five constructs
resulting in a pool of 50 items. Item analyses led to the retention of a total of
25 items. Subsequent revisions led to the current 50 items.

Reliability*: Split-half internal consistency coefficients ($\underline{n}$=67 male u n d e r -
graduate students) ranged from .51 (aggression) to .72 (competition). Test-
retest reliability coefficients ($\underline{n}$=35 male and female undergraduate students)
ranged from .50 (competence) to .80 (conflict) across a two-week interval.

Validity*: Convergent and discriminant validity were demonstrated when
correlating subjects' ($\underline{n}$=67 males; $\underline{n}$=121 females) responses to the subscales
to a battery of self-report psychological tests such as the Affect Scales, the
Femininity and Socialization Scales, and the California Psychological Inventory.

Norms: Not cited. Psychometric data were based on the responses of 73
competitive swimmers ($\underline{M}$ age=12 years) and 115 undergraduate students.

Availability: Contact Susan Butt, Department of Psychology, University of
British Columbia, 2136 West Mall, Vancouver, British Columbia, Canada
V6T 1W5. (Phone # 604-228-3269)

*The author noted (personal correspondence on March 16, 1990) that addi-
tional psychometric data are available in Butt (1987).

References

*Butt, D. S. (1985). Psychological motivation and sports performance in world class women field hockey players. International Journal of Women's Studies, 8, 328-337.

*Butt, D. S. (1987). Psychology of sport: The behavior, motivation, personality and performance of athletes. New York: Van Nostrand Reinhold.

*Wrisberg, C. A., Donovan, T. J., Birtton, S. E., & Ewing, S. J. (1984). Assessing the motivations of athletes: Further tests of Butt's theory. Proceedings of the 1984 Olympic Scientific Congress (p. 90). Eugene, OR: College of Human Development and Performance Microform Publications.

Chapter 20

SEX ROLES

Tests in this chapter assess role expectancies for female versus male participation in sport. Attitudes toward female involvement in sport, and perceived and experienced role conflict among female athletes are also evaluated.

(171)
[ATHLETE SEX ROLE CONFLICT INVENTORY] [ASRCI]
George H. Sage and Sheryl Loudermilk

Source: Sage, G. H., & Loudermilk, S. (1979). The female athlete and role conflict. Research Quarterly, 50, 88-96.

Purpose: To assess perceived and experienced role conflict among female athletes in enacting the roles of both female and female athlete.

Description: The 20-item inventory contains two parts, with the same 10 items used in both parts. The first part measures role conflict perception (RCP) and the second part measures role conflict experience (RCE). Content areas relate to attitudes of society toward females and athletic participation, physical appearance and motor skills that may be incompatible with femininity, and incompatibility of expectations of parents, friends, and others regarding sex roles and athlete roles. Subjects respond to each item on the inventory using a 5-point ordinal scale.

Construction: Item content was partially derived from the literature on sex role stereotypes and the literature describing athletic role expectations. Other sources included interviews with female athletes and coaches. The content validity of the items was evaluated by professionals in sociology, psychology, and physical education.

Reliability: Test-retest reliability (n=24 female athletes) coefficients over a 2-3 week period were .72 for RCP and .76 for RCE.

Validity: Female athletes ($\underline{n}$=30) differing on the Spence-Helmreich Attitudes Toward Women Scale also differed on RCP in that athletes with a traditional orientation toward women's role in society perceived greater role conflict in terms of their involvement in athletics.

Norms: Psychometric data were presented for 268 collegiate female athletes from 9 sports, representing 13 colleges.

Availability: Contact George H. Sage, Department of Kinesiology, University of Northern Colorado, Greeley, CO 80639. (Phone # 303-351-1737)

(172)
[ATTITUDES OF ATHLETES TOWARD MALE VERSUS FEMALE COACHES] [AAMFC]
Robert Weinberg and Margie Reveles

Source: Weinberg, R., Reveles, M., and Jackson, A. (1984). Attitudes of male and female athletes toward male and female coaches. Journal of Sport Psychology, 6, 448-453.

Purpose: To assess the attitudes and feelings of male and female athletes toward having a female coach versus a male coach.

Description: The subject was presented a paragraph describing a male or female coach who (hypothetically) was to be the subject's coach the following year. The subject was asked to respond to 11 items using an 11-point Likert scale (with the anchorings Not at all to Very much). Examples of items include "I would like her as a coach" and "I could not take orders from him easily."

Construction: Not discussed.

Reliability: Test-retest reliability coefficients ($\underline{n}$=60) were reported as .80 and .77 for the male and female questionnaires across a 2-week interval.

Validity: Construct validity was supported by demonstrating among 34 junior high, 27 high school, and 24 college basketball athletes that males displayed more negative attitudes toward female coaches than did females; however, male and female athletes did not differ in their view of male coaches.

Norms: Not cited. Test-retest reliability data were reported for an independent sample of 60 subjects.

Availability: Contact Robert Weinberg, Department of Kinesiology, University of North Texas, Box 13857, Denton, TX 76203-3857. (Phone # 817-565-3430)

(173)
[ATTITUDES TO MALE AND FEMALE ATHLETES QUESTIONNAIRE] [AMFAQ]
Joan Vickers, Michael Lashuk, and Terry Taerum

Source: Vickers, J., Lashuk, M., & Taerum, T. (1980). Differences in attitude toward the concepts "male," "female," "male athlete," and "female athlete." Research Quarterly for Exercise and Sport, 51, 407-416.

Purpose: To assess attitudes toward the concepts "male," "female," "male athlete," and "female athlete."

Description: Subjects respond to each of the four concepts (e.g., male athlete) using the semantic differential technique. A total of 14 bipolar adjective pairs are presented requiring a 7-point ordinal scale response for each pair.

Construction: The adjective pairs were selected based on a review of factor analytic studies of the dimensions of the semantic differential technique.

Reliability: Kuder Richardson-21 internal consistency coefficients (n=132 male and 132 female athletes) ranged from .75 for the term female to .82 for the term female athlete.

Validity: Analyses of variance supported differences between male and female subjects on the evaluative and activity-potency dimensions identified through factor analyses. For example, female subjects (but not male subjects) perceive the concepts female athlete and male to be similar in the activity-potency dimension.

Norms: Not reported. Psychometric data were cited for 132 male and 132 female athletes representing independent samples of grades 7, 10, and university students.

Availability: Contact Joan Vickers, Faculty of Physical Education, University of Calgary, Calgary, Alta., Canada, T2N 1N4. (Phone # 402-220-3420)

(174)
[ATTITUDES TOWARD WOMEN'S ATHLETIC COMPETITION SCALE] [AWACS]
Bea Harres

Source: Harres, B. (1968). Attitudes of students toward women's athletic competition. Research Quarterly, 39, 278-284.

Purpose: To examine the attitudes of male and female undergraduate students toward the desirability of intensive athletic competition for girls and women.

Description: The attitude inventory contains 38 items subdivided into the areas of socio-cultural, mental-emotional, physical, and personality. Subjects respond to each item using a five-point Likert scale.

Construction: Previous attitude scales were the basis for the initial development of 62 items which were pilot tested using 113 undergraduate students. Using Flanagan's index of discrimination, 38 items were retained.

Reliability: A corrected split-half odd-even internal consistency coefficient of .92 was reported among 100 undergraduate students.

Validity: Not discussed.

Norms: Not reported. Descriptive and psychometric data were cited for 284 undergraduate students (n=131 males and n=153 females) attending the University of California at Santa Barbara.

Availability*: Unknown. Test items are not identified in the source.

(175)
CHILDREN'S ATTITUDES TOWARD FEMALE INVOLVEMENT IN SPORT QUESTIONNAIRE (CATFIS)
Rosemary Selby and John H. Lewko

Source: Selby, R., & Lewko, J. H. (1976). Children's attitudes toward females in sports: Their relationship with sex, grade, and sports participation. Research Quarterly, 47, 455-463.

Purpose: To measure grade school childrens' attitudes toward female involvement in sports.

Description: The CATFIS is a 20-item questionnaire. Subjects respond using a 5-point Likert scale.

Construction: Based on an item analysis of the responses of 40 third grade children to 60 items, the item pool was reduced to 20 items.

Reliability: A test-retest reliability coefficient of .81 was reported for 33 boys and girls in grades 3-6.

Validity: Construct validity of the CATFIS was supported in that 185 boys and 84 girls (grades 3-6) who participated in a YMCA-sponsored sports program for five months became more positive in their attitudes toward female involvement in sport than those boys ($\underline{n}$=126) and girls ($\underline{n}$=168) who did not participate in the program.

Norms: Psychometric data were cited for 709 children in grades 3-9.

Availability*: Contact John H. Lewko, Centre for Research in Human Development, Laurentian University, Sudbury, Ontario, Canada P3E 2C6.

ADDITIONAL SPORT- OR EXERCISE-SPECIFIC PSYCHOLOGICAL TESTS

The following references contain information about additional sport- or exercise- specific psychological tests. Descriptions of these tests were not included in the Directory because of insufficient information (in the refereed literature), or because a test author (designated by an asterisk) indicated that he/she did not wish to have available information about the test summarized in the Directory.

Achievement Orientation
176. Ewing, M. (1988). Psychometric properties of the Achievement Orientation Questionnaire and associated methodological issues (abstract). Psychology of motor behavior and sport (p. 91). Proceedings of the North American Society for the Psychology of Sport and Physical Activity annual convention. Scottsdale, AZ. [Achievement Orientation Questionnaire]
177. Kamlesh, M. L. (in press). Construction and standardisation of a Sports Achievement Motivation Test. National Institute of Sports Scientific Journal (India). [Sports Achievement Motivation Test]
178. Yin, Z., Callaghan, J., & Simons, J. (1989). An examination of the reformulated attributional model of learned helplessness and depression in an athletic population (abstract). Proceedings of the Association for the Advancement for Applied Sport Psychology annual convention. Seattle, WA. [Swimming Achievement Motivation Scale]

Aggression
179. Kumar, A., & Shukla, P. S. (1989). Development and validation of the Sport Aggression Inventory. Proceedings of the 7th World Congress in Sport Psychology (# 150). Singapore.
180. Radford, P. F., & Gowan, G. R. (1970). Sex differences in self-reported feelings about activities at the extremes of the Aggressiveness/Competitiveness Scale. Presentation made at the 2nd Canadian Psychomotor Learning and Sports Psychology Symposium, Windsor, Ontario, Canada.

Anxiety

181. Allyson, B., & Murray, J. H. (February, 1990). An investigation of competitive anxiety as a positive effect. Presentation made at the Southeastern Sport and Exercise Psychology Symposium, Greensboro, NC. [Competitive Anxiety Perception Scale]

182. Neely, R. K., & Ewing, M. E. (1989). Precompetitive anxiousness: Is it apprehensive anticipation, eager anticipation, or a combination of both? (abstract). Psychology of motor behavior and sport (p. 128). Proceedings of the North American Society for the Psychology of Sport and Physical Activity annual convention (p. 128). Kent, OH. [Precompetitive "Butterflies" Questionnaire]

183. Wang, Y., & *Morgan, W. P. (1987) Convergent validity of a Body Awareness Scale (abstract). Proceedings of the annual convention of the American College of Sports Medicine. Las Vegas, NV. [Body Awareness Scale]

Attention

184. Summers, J. J., & Ford, S. (1989). The TAIS as a research instrument: Time for a change? (abstract). Proceedings of the 7th World Congress in Sport Psychology (# 216), Singapore. [Basketball Test of Attentional and Interpersonal Style]

Attitudes

185. Jones, J. M., & Williamson, S. A. (1973). Personality correlates of athletes' attitudes toward performance (abstract). Proceedings of the First Canadian Congress for the Multi-Disciplinary Study of Sport and Physical Activity (p. 17). Montreal, Quebec, Canada. [Athletic Profile Inventory]

186. King, N., Tricker, R., & Cook, D. (1988). Athletes and drug abuse: A comparison of differences in attitudes between college athletes. Proceedings of the Association for the Advancement for Applied Sport Psychology annual convention, Nashua, NH. [Athletes' Attitude Toward Drug Abuse Questionnaire]

Confidence

187. Burton, D. (1989). Winning isn't everything: Examining the impact of performance goals on collegiate swimmers' cognitions and performance. The Sport Psychologist, 3, 105-132. [Sport Confidence Inventory]

188. Fox, K. R., & Corbin, C. B. (1989). The Physical Self-Perception Profile: Development and preliminary validiation. Journal of Sport & Exercise Psychology, 11, 408-430. [Perceived Importance Profile]

189. Mumford, B. (1989). The development and assessment of a sport psychology mental training program with young figure skaters (abstract). Proceedings of the Association for the Advancement for Applied Sport Psychology annual convention (p. 80). Seattle, WA. [Self-

control scale]
190. Yin, Z., Callaghan, J., & Simons, J. (1989). An examination of the reformulated attributional model of learned helplessness and depression in an athletic population (abstract). Proceedings of the Association for the Advancement for Applied Sport Psychology annual convention, Seattle, WA. [Perceived Swimming Success Scale and Expecting for Future Swimming Success Scale]

Leadership
191. Glenn, S. D., Horn, T. S., Dewar, A., & Vealey, R. S. (1989). Psychological predictors of leadership behavior in female soccer athletes (abstract). Psychology of motor behavior and sport (p. 122). Kent, OH: Proceedings of the North American Society for the Psychology of Sport and Physical Activity annual convention. [Sport Leadership Behavior Inventory]

Miscellaneous
192. Ho, K., & Gordon, S. Leadership behaviour and the satisfaction of athletes (abstract). Proceedings of the 7th World Congress in Sport Psychology (# 162), Singapore. [Athlete Satisfaction Inventory]
193. Orlick, T. (1986). Psyching for sport (pp. 22; 181-182). Champaign, Il: Human Kinetics Publishers. [Competition Reflections form]

Motivation
194. Berlin, P. (1971, October). A theoretical explanation of the motives of college women to engage in competitive sport (abstract). Paper presented at the Canadian Psycho-motor Learning and Sports Psychology Symposium, Vancouver, British Columbia, Canada. [Motives of College Female Athlete Toward Sport Competition; Q-sort]
195. *Duda, J. L., Smart, A. E., & Tappe, M. K. (1989). Predictors of adherence in the rehabiliation of athletic injuries: An application of Personal Investment theory. Journal of Sport & Exercise Psychology, 11, 367-381. [Personal Incentives for Sport Participation Questionnaire]
196. Mumford, B. (1989). The development and assessment of a sport psychology mental training program with young figure skaters (abstract). Proceedings of the Association for the Advancement for Applied Sport Psychology annual convention (p. 80), Seattle, WA. [Commitment to Sport Scale]
197. Watson, G. G., Blanksky, B. A., & Bloomfield, J. (1985). Competing to swim or swimming to compete. Some motivational problems in junior swimming The Australian Journal of Science and Medicine in Sport, 17, 24-26. [Swimming Motivational Inventory]

Multidimensional

198. Lonetto, R., & Marshall, J. D. (1973). Personality, perception, and performance of hockey players: Assessment and prediction (abstract). Proceedings of the First Canadian Congress for the Multi-Disciplinary Study of Sport and Physical Activity (p. 17). Montreal, Quebec, Canada. [Athlete Apperception Test]

Subject Index

Note: Numbers refer to test numbers and not page numbers in book.

Subject Index (Cont'd)

Note: Numbers refer to test numbers and not page numbers in book.

Subject Index (Cont'd)

Note: Numbers refer to test numbers and not page numbers in book.

Subject Index (Cont'd)

Note: Numbers refer to test numbers and not page numbers in book.

Note: Numbers refer to test numbers and not page numbers in book.

Subject Index (Cont'd)

Note: Numbers refer to test numbers and not page numbers in book.

Subject Index (Cont'd)

Note: Numbers refer to test numbers and not page numbers in book.

Subject Index (Cont'd)

Note: Numbers refer to test numbers and not page numbers in book.

Test Author Index

Note: Numbers refer to test numbers and not page numbers in book.

Test Author Index (Cont'd)

Note: Numbers refer to test numbers and not page numbers in book.

Note: Numbers refer to test numbers and not page numbers in book.

Test Author Index (Cont'd)

Note: Numbers refer to test numbers and <u>not</u> page numbers in book.

Test Title Index

Note: Numbers refer to test numbers and not page numbers in book.

Test Title Index (Cont'd)

Note: Numbers refer to test numbers and not page numbers in book.

Test Title Index (Cont'd)

Note: Numbers refer to test numbers and not page numbers in book.

Test Title Index (Cont'd)

Note: Numbers refer to test numbers and not page numbers in book.

Note: Numbers refer to test numbers and <u>not</u> page numbers in book.

Test Acronym Index

Note: Numbers refer to test numbers and not page numbers in book.

Test Acronym Index (Cont'd)

Note: Numbers refer to test numbers and not page numbers in book.

Test Acronym Index (Cont'd)

Note: Numbers refer to test numbers and <u>not</u> page numbers in book.

CODE OF FAIR TESTING PRACTICES IN EDUCATION

Prepared by the Joint Committee on Testing Practices

The Code of Fair Testing Practices in Education states the major obligations to test takers of professionals who develop or use educational tests. The Code is meant to apply broadly to the use of tests in education (admissions, educational assessment, educational diagnosis, and student placement). The Code is not designed to cover employment testing, licensure or certification testing, or other types of testing. Although the Code has relevance to many types of educational tests, it is directed primarily at professionally developed tests such as those sold by commercial test publishers or used in formally administered testing programs. The Code is not intended to cover tests made by individual teachers for use in their own classrooms.

The Code addresses the role of test developers and test users separately. Test users are people who select tests, commission test development services, or make decisions on the basis of test scores. Test developers are people who actually construct tests as well as those who set policies for particular testing programs. The roles may, of course, overlap as when a state education agency commissions test development services, sets policies that control the test development process, and makes decisions on the basis of the test scores.

The Code presents standards for educational test developers and user in four areas:
A. Developing/Selecting Tests
B. Interpreting Scores
C. Striving for Fairness
D. Informing Test Takers

Organizations, institutions, and individual professionals who endorse the Code commit themselves to safeguarding the rights of test takers by following the principles listed. The Code is intended to be consistent with the relevant parts of the Standards for Educational and Psychological Testing (AERA, APA, NCME, 1985). However, the Code differs from the Standards in both audience and purpose. The Code is meant to be understood by the general public, it is limited to educational tests; and the primary focus is on those issues that affect the proper use of tests. The Code is not meant to add new principles over and above those in the Standards or to change the meaning of the Standards. The goal is rather to represent the spirit of a selected portion of the Standards in a way that is meaningful to test takers and/or their parents or guardians. It is the hope of the Joint Committee that the Code will also be judged to be consistent with existing codes of conduct and standards of other professional groups who use educational tests.

The Code has been developed by the Joint Committee on Testing Practices, a cooperative effort of several professional organizations, that has as its aim the advancement, in the public interest, of the quality of testing practices. The Joint Committee was initiated by the American Educational Research Association, the American Psychological Association, and the National Council on Measurement in Education. In addition to these three groups, the American Association for Counseling and Development/Association for Measurement and Evaluation in Counseling and Development, and the American Speech-Language-Hearing Association are now also sponsors of the Joint Committee.

This is not copyrighted material. Reproduction and dissemination are encouraged. Please cite this document as follows:

Code of Fair Testing Practices in Education. (1988). Washington, D.C.: Joint Committee on Testing Practices. (Mailing Address: Joint Committee on Testing Practices, American Psychological Association, 1200 17th Street, NW, Washington, D.C. 20036).

A. Developing/Selecting Appropriate Tests*

Test developers should provide the information that test users need to select appropriate tests.

Test Developers Should:

1. Define what each test measures and what the test should be used for. Describe the population(s) for which the test is appropriate.
2. Accurately represent the characteristics, usefulness, and limitations of tests for their intended purposes.
3. Explain relevant measurement concepts as necessary for clarity at the level of detail that is appropriate for the intended audience(s).
4. Describe the process of test development. Explain how the content and skills to be tested were selected.
5. Provide evidence that the test meets its intended purpose(s).
6. Provide either representative samples or complete copies of test questions, directions, answer sheets, manuals, and score reports to qualified users.
7. Indicate the nature of the evidence obtained concerning the appropriateness of each test for groups of different racial, ethnic, or linguistic backgrounds who are likely to be tested.
8. Identify and publish any specialized skills needed to administer each test and to interpret scores correctly.

Test users should select tests that meet the purpose for which they are to be used and that are appropriate for the intended test-testing populations.

Test Users Should:

1. First define the purpose for testing and the population to be tested. Then, select a test for that purpose and that population based on a thorough review of the available information.
2. Investigate potentially useful sources of information, in addition to test scores, to corroborate the information provided by tests.
3. Read the materials provided by test developers and avoid using tests for which unclear or incomplete information is provided.
4. Become familiar with how and when the test was developed and tried out.
5. Read independent evaluations of a test and of possible alternative measures. Look for evidence required to support the claims of test developers.
6. Examine specimen sets, disclosed tests or samples of questions, directions, answer sheets, manuals, and score reports before selecting a test.
7. Ascertain whether the test content and norms group(s) or comparison group(s) are appropriate for the intended test takers.
8. Select and use only those tests for which the skills needed to administer the test and interpret scores correctly are available.

B. Interpreting Scores

Test developers should help users interpret scores correctly.

Test Developers Should:

9. Provide timely and easily understood score reports that describe test performance clearly and accurately. Also explain the meaning and limitations of reported scores.
10. Describe the population(s) represented by any norms or comparison group(s), the dates the data were gathered, and the process used to select the samples of test takers.
11. Warn users to avoid specific, reasonably anticipated misuses of test scores.
12. Provide information that will help users follow reasonable procedures for setting passing scores when it is appropriate to use such scores with the test.
13. Provide information that will help users gather evidence to show that the test is meeting its intended purpose(s).

Test users should interpret scores correctly.

Test Users Should:

9. Obtain information about the scale used for reporting scores, the characteristics of any norms or comparison group(s), and the limitations of the scores.
10. Interpret scores taking into account any major differences between the norms or comparison groups and the actual test takers. Also take into account any differences in test administration practices or familiarity with the specific questions in the test.
11. Avoid using tests for purposes not specifically recommended by the test developer unless evidence is obtained to support the intended use.
12. Explain how any passing scores were set and gather evidence to support the appropriateness of the scores.
13. Obtain evidence to help show that the test is meeting its intended purpose(s).

---

*Many of the statements in the Code refer to the selection of existing tests. However, in customized testing programs test developers are engaged to construct new tests. In those situations, the test development process should be designed to help ensure that the completed tests will be in compliance with the Code.

C. Striving for Fairness

Test developers should strive to make tests that are as fair as possible for test takers of different races, gender, ethnic back-grounds, or handicapping conditions.

Test users should select tests that have been developed in ways that attempt to make them as fair as possible for test takers of different races, gender, ethnic backgrounds, or handicapping conditions.

Test Developers Should:

14. Review and revise test questions and related materials to avoid potentially insensitive content or language.
15. Investigate the performance of test takers of different races, gender, and ethnic backgrounds when samples of sufficient size are available. Enact procedures that help to ensure that differences in performance are related primarily to the skills under assessment rather than to irrelevant factors.
16. When feasible, make appropriately modified forms of tests or administration procedures available for test takers with handicapping conditions. Warn test users of potential problems in using standard norms with modified tests or administration procedures that result in non-comparable scores.

Test Users Should:

14. Evaluate the procedures used by test developers to avoid potentially insensitive content or language.
15. Review the performance of test takers of different races, gender, and ethnic backgrounds when samples of sufficient size are available. Evaluate the extent to which performance differences may have been caused by inappropriate characteristics of the test.
16. When necessary and feasible, use appropriately modified forms of tests or administration procedures for test takers with handicapping conditions. Interpret standard norms with care in the light of the modifications that were made.

D. Informing Test Takers

Under some circumstances, test developers have direct communication with test takers. Under other circumstances, test users communicate directly with test takers. Whichever group communicates directly with test takers should provide the information described below.

Test Developers or Test Users Should:

17. When a test is optional, provide test takers or their parents/guardians with information to help them judge whether the test should be taken or if an available alternative to the test should be used.
18. Provide test takers the information they need to be familiar with the coverage of the test, the types of question formats, the directions, and appropriate test-taking strategies. Strive to make such information equally available to all test takers.

Under some circumstances, test developers have direct control of tests and test scores. Under other circumstances, test users have such control. Whichever group has direct control of tests and test scores should take the steps described below.

Test Developers or Test Users Should:

19. Provide test takers or their parents/guardians with information about rights test takers may have to obtain copies of tests and completed answer sheets, retake tests, have tests rescored, or cancel scores.
20. Tell test takers or their parents/guardians how long scores will be kept on file and indicate to whom and under what circumstances test scores will or will not be released.
21. Describe the procedures that test takers or their parents/guardians may use to register complaints and have problems resolved.

Note: The membership of the Working Group that developed the Code of Fair Testing Practices in Education and of the Joint Committee on Testing Practices that guided the Working Group was as follows:

Theodore P. Bartell	Edmund W. Gordon	John T. Stewart
John R. Bergan	Jo-Ida C. Hansen	Carol Kehr Tittle (Co-Chair, JCTP)
Esther E. Diamond	James B. Lingwall	
Richard P. Duran	George F. Madaus (Co-Chair, JCTP)	Nicholas A. Vacc
Lorraine D. Eyde		Michael J. Zieky
Raymond D. Fowler	Kevin L. Moreland	Debra Boltas and Wayne Camara of the American Psychological Association served as staff liaisons
John J. Fremer (Co-Chair, JCTP and Chair, Code Working Group)	Jo-Ellen V. Perez	
	Robert J. Solomon	

Additional copies of the Code may be obtained from the National Council on Measurement in Education, 1230 Seventeenth Street, NW, Washington, D.C. 20036. Single copies are free.

About the Editor

Andrew C. Ostrow completed the Ph.D. degree at the University of California, Berkeley. Currently, he is a professor in the Department of Sport and Exercise Studies, and an adjunct professor in the Department of Psychology at West Virginia University. Dr. Ostrow has taught undergraduate and graduate courses in the psychology of sport for the last 17 years, including a graduate course ("Sport Psychometrics") on psychological assessment in sport. He has directed a number of theses and dissertations focusing on the development of sport-specific psychological tests, including two published tests that appear in this directory.

Dr. Ostrow is the author and editor of two textbooks related to the psychological aspects of aging and physical activity. He is a member of the American Psychological Association, Association for the Advancement for Applied Sport Psychology, and the North American Society for the Psychology of Sport and Physical Activity.

Dr. Ostrow is married and has two teenage daughters. He competes in racquet sports, and scored his first hole-in-one in golf the day before he wrote this biographic synopsis.